Life Is For The Living

Life Is For The Living

Kathryn Graham

Published by CreateSpace

ISBN 978-1-5234125-3-2

Book formatted by www.bookformatting.co.uk.

Introduction

I love writing and am an avid reader and book lover who has always wanted to write a book one day. For years that day was somewhere in the far distant future as my life was busy and full. It was perhaps a goal for retirement when there was time to slow down and do some of those things of which I'd always dreamt. Then life took a twist that brought me to that day in the most unexpected way.

I'd had many ideas for stories to write over the years but, not for one minute, did I ever imagine I'd write this story – one about myself, a memoir of an experience so dramatic that it would change my life forever.

When I began putting pen to paper, I started looking for hints and advice on writing. After reading several publications, blogs and articles, I began to feel overwhelmed about what I should, or shouldn't, be writing – there seemed to be so many rules and regulations. That's when I decided to drop the research, stop over-facing myself and simply write – write frankly and truthfully about events from my perspective. Write straight from the heart – my heart, my donor's heart.

As I began the story, it transformed into a kind of therapy, an outlet to express all those emotions, thoughts and feelings that had amassed inside me over the years as I encountered one trial after another, and then another. I realised then that my story might resonate with, and possibly even be helpful to, people who experience challenges with their health and especially those families who are living and coping daily with Pulmonary Hypertension ('PH') or the world of Transplantation.

This is a very personal story and in no way purports that all individuals suffering with PH or going through Transplantation react to diagnoses, medications or surgery as I did. It is a true story, though – time, people, places, nature, events, warts and all – so I have given an honest account of what happened from my own viewpoint and, at times, have deliberately decided not to hold back on some of the more difficult aspects of my journey.

The book also gives my own version and understanding of PH and, as I'm not a qualified medical practitioner, I apologise for any misunderstandings or inaccurate information I may have inadvertently conveyed. Any statistics quoted in this book were given to me by my consultants at the time the events took place and so these may no longer be current at the time of publication or on reading.

I sincerely hope that my book will help to raise awareness of both PH and organ donation to those who have little understanding of the issues involved and that it will demonstrate what an enormous difference organ donation can make to someone's life and the lives of their family and friends. More than anything, I truly hope it may encourage people to sign up to the NHSBT Organ Donor register.

Now my book is complete, it may, with luck, reach and appeal to a wide and varied audience. The long writing process, although very painful at times, has proved cathartic and helped to soothe me, but if it can help someone else, then that will make it all the more worthwhile.

For anyone reading and facing similar health problems, I want my book to inspire rather than cause alarm, and show that you aren't alone and isolated in feeling, experiencing and dealing with a range of mixed, and often conflicting, emotions. Also, I think it demonstrates that there are ways and possibilities to adjust to a life that becomes extremely different and more arduous than the one that had been expected, so giving some optimism and faith.

In an attempt to give something back to the causes and organisations which have supported me and are close to my heart, I intend to donate and distribute any profits from this book amongst PHAUK, the Transplant and PH units at Papworth Hospital and their respective patient support groups.

Finally, this is simply a story about an ordinary family, united together in facing and overcoming adversity – a story of human kindness and miracles. One that I hope will appeal to anyone who just loves a good story with a happy ending and a dose of human warmth and love.

Kathryn

Links

My website:
http://kaggraham.wix.com/kathryngrahamauthor

NHSBT Organ donation website:
https://www.organdonation.nhs.uk

Papworth Hospital Charity website:
http://papworthhospitalcharity.org.uk

PHAUK website:
http://www.phassociation.uk.com

For my donor,
with love and heartfelt thanks

Prologue

I feel as though I've stepped into an illusion – hemmed in on all sides by vibrant colours, which reach far ahead and leave a trail behind me. A tangle of fragrant scent wafts from the flowers as I weave my way through the narrow pathways, brushing against other tourists.

I'm full of excitement. This is what I love about travelling – just stumbling on an unexpected pleasure. A new discovery that takes your breath away. There's going to be so much more time for these new adventures.

My mind flits backwards to the last few months – the hesitancy, the doubts and the decisions. I'm free of them all now, in this moment. I'm able to glimpse an exciting future to embrace. I browse array upon array of flower stalls, enclosures of vivid shapes and sizes, soaking up the ambience as I go.

Rows of terracotta pots and galvanised steel urns are brimming with an eclectic assortment of plants. They pave the way as I wander along the quirky pathways, pondering the next new phase of my life, leaving the last one behind, now just a pleasant memory. A contented time, yet still a significant phase of my life to relinquish. Life changes though, and it's time for me to make that change with it, to keep abreast of my own shifting situation.

The paths lead on to intriguing stalls, spilling with trinkets and gifts, a feast and delight for the tourist in pursuit of unusual souvenirs. I wish I could have an empty case to fill with many of the eccentric and whimsical pieces I've spotted to bring them back home with me.

I carry on through the floral pavilions and tumble back out onto the busy street into the glow of the spring sunshine. I feel inspired and uplifted. The future looks bright and exciting and I've a swirl of emotions deep inside – anticipation, expectation and eagerness.

Ambling on, I turn the next corner and, in that moment, the cathedral stands tall and proud in all its grandeur right in front of me, flanked by pink cherry blossom in full bloom. A perfect picture.

Forgetting my thoughts, I sit on a bench in the gardens and admire the spring flowers. A choir of daffodils, tulips and primroses, purposefully crowding each border, is joined in song. I'm carefree and so looking forward to life being much easier and more relaxed from here on.

I sit and wait patiently in the sunshine, while Rob takes photographs, listening to the birds chattering to the promise of summer, people-watching – wondering as strangers go by, just what their story might be?

PART ONE

New Beginnings

'What we call the beginning is often the end
And to make an end is to make a beginning.
The end is where we start from.'
TS Eliot

One

Harefield

(1999 – 2002)

I'm waking up. I can hear voices shouting and sounding panicked, high-pitched and chattering – the voices of children. There's the noise of traffic too – a loud throbbing as cars speed along, reducing to an easy drone as they come to a slow for something I can't quite fathom.

Rousing myself I can hear a child screaming, 'That's my mummy.' It slowly dawns on me that I'm not in bed. I'm lying in a busy road and it's my own daughter I can hear screaming.

I can see everyone now. Two people helping me to regain consciousness; a man, a total stranger, coming out of a nearby house with a cushion in his hands; the teacher leading all the children away from us; my daughter in tears; one lady is phoning for an ambulance.

Gradually, I begin to remember … I was helping with Sarah's class. We were on a school geography outing and I was supposed to be looking after a small group of infant children. We'd been ambling along towards a farm, following the group in front of us, chatting and laughing as we went. We were having fun and enjoying ourselves – a bit lost in our own little group chatter when I realised that we were lagging behind a little. I remember shouting, 'Come on kids, we need to catch up the others!' We'd stepped up our pace abruptly and then everything went blank.

I'm moved onto the pavement and laid down with a cushion for my head. 'Can you please cancel the ambulance? I really don't think it's necessary and I'll be wasting their time.' I feel silly lying on the pavement and manage to get up. I don't like all the commotion I'm causing and feel embarrassed being the centre of all this attention. I just want to dust myself down and carry on with what we're doing and stop all this fussing.

I thank the kind stranger, who leaves reluctantly with his cushion. I think to myself, 'What if his cushion's got dirty on the road?' It is funny some of the things that pop in your head in times of crisis.

***

I wasn't used to hospitals as I'd only ever been admitted when I gave birth to our daughters, Sarah and Rose. I'd never even had to go to A&E and I could count on one hand how many times I'd been to a GP. I was in my late thirties and hospitals, doctors or illness hadn't figured very much in my own life.

The fainting episodes started shortly after Rose, our younger daughter, was born. She was a toddler of about eighteen months when I ran upstairs too quickly and blacked out on the bathroom floor. I think it happened more than once or twice, so I'd been to my GP.

My blood pressure was quite low. The fainting episode tied in with this diagnosis. I was told it was healthy to have low blood pressure: there was less risk of strokes, heart attacks and general heart problems. I was advised I needed to stop and think before I ran upstairs too quickly, or if I stood up when I'd been sitting for a long time.

The advice seemed good to me: I was delighted my GP told me it was because of low blood pressure and that this was a healthy place to be. I started adhering to the advice. I stopped rushing up stairs; I would sit for a minute or two and take my time standing up or getting out of bed. It seemed to work, and the routines became embedded in my daily life without me thinking too much about it.

The incident on the school trip changed all that.

***

I'm sitting with a different GP, nearly in tears, my voice wobbling as she listens intently. 'I'm really worried this has happened while I was looking after children. It bothers me I landed in a busy main road. It worries me it might happen again when I'm on my own with my two small children. I'm frightened of seriously injuring myself.'

Our girls are only seven and five. I've dreams of becoming a teacher one day and know these will be quashed if I have serious health problems. We've just bought new bikes but I feel frightened of using mine, especially on my own with the kids. I keep visualising myself falling in roads, my children helpless.

It's frightening to faint. You don't know what's happening, you're out of control and then there are the consequences of how and where you fall.

The GP checks me over and asserts that my blood pressure isn't so low that it should be causing these problems, and she decides to play safe and refer me to a cardiologist. She acknowledges that I'm anxious and need my mind putting at rest.

I see a cardiologist at the Lister Hospital in Stevenage and undergo a whole series of tests. An ECG, to monitor my heart rhythms – normal; an echocardiogram to estimate my heart pressures and look for any abnormalities – normal; a stress test to see how my heart responds to exercise – again normal.

The consultant advises I undertake a couple of further investigations. He suggests either a tilt test, where you are laid flat for a length of time, then abruptly tilted upright to see whether this induces a faint, or I could have a type of heart monitor fitted which might establish what's happening.

Everything takes time to unfold while you have hospital tests: waiting for appointments; waiting for the actual test once you obtain the appointment; waiting for test results. The circle continues endlessly as each result either eliminates something or poses a new question. A tilt test can't be done at my local hospital, so I have to wait for an appointment from Harefield, a specialist heart and lung hospital.

Waiting, waiting, waiting…

A few months pass and we're on our way, Rob negotiating the M25 with his usual lack of patience. The hospital is unfamiliar, big and bustling. I'm pretty clueless about the routines and what the test will entail. Hospitals can be a little overwhelming if you aren't used to them and especially if it's your very first visit. It's a bit scary thinking I've come here to faint.

Drilling, banging, drilling, banging – on it goes as we wander through a maze of boarded tunnels and scaffolding to the main central reception area. The building work adds to our confusion and bewilderment as we follow the flow of others.

We report in and are directed to some seats while I wait for an ECG. Everyone else looks like they know what they're doing. I don't. I'm ushered to a changing cubicle – there's a long busy row of them. I enter one door, change into a hospital gown then fumble my way through an opposite door for my ECG. It feels a little daunting for a first timer. ECG all done, it's back through one door, a quick change, then out of the other, returning to wait once more.

Leaving Rob behind and following a nurse through more un-known corridors, I'm ushered into another unfamiliar room. It's cluttered with equipment, a cross between a hospital bedroom, storeroom and consulting room. Desks, sink units, machinery, beds… A doctor joins us. Another new face. More wiring up. An-kles. Chest. Abdomen. Wrists. I'm placed on a heart-tracing ma-chine while lying on a bed. I'm being strapped in as though I'm off for a ride at the fairground. It all feels very bizarre.

The lights are dimmed and I'm supposed to relax. It's a tall or-der with two people observing me while being strapped on a bed and unable to move.

After fifteen minutes the bed is tilted upright abruptly. The situation is becoming more surreal by the minute. I have to remain upright strapped to the bed for three quarters of an hour keeping absolutely still. The trouble with not being allowed to move is that I suddenly become desperate to fidget. It feels endless.

An image of Hannibal Lecter from the film *Silence of the Lambs* pops into my thoughts. I'm imagining the part where he is strapped up against a board outside his cage, planning his next move. I want to start giggling. I begin plotting how I might escape.

The test reveals nothing, doesn't make me faint and the outcome is normal. I'm pleased – it's the result I want to hear.

Sitting back with the cardiologist he explains. 'As your faints are infrequent, a possible step is to consider having a small implant placed on an artery leading into your heart, so if you have any more episodes you can press a button on a separate device and record what's just happened.'

We aren't sure whether my case merits such intervention, but after some discussion we decide we will pursue this option, as we want to get to the bottom of things.

He warns me, 'This is an operation – you'll be left with a small scar and the recording device could stay implanted for up to two years.'

I'm advised it may take six months or more for an appointment for the operation. Although this seems a long time, I'm not unduly concerned, as all the tests so far have found nothing. In myself I'm feeling perfectly healthy and living quite normally as a busy mum and working in my children's school.

***

I arrive on the day ward early in the morning as instructed. It happens to be my children's school sports day. I'm waiting with Rob in a cosy lounge area until they have a bed ready.

'You aren't here for an angiogram like the others, are you?' states the nurse checking me in. 'It's unusual to have one of these devices implanted – we don't do many. You'll probably be first on.'

I can overhear a doctor explaining the ins and outs of angiograms to another patient. I don't like the sound of that procedure – it makes me feel squeamish.

We continue our conversation. 'Do you think I will done by lunchtime?'

The nurse laughs at me, rolling her eyes. 'We'll see.'

The same nurse gives me directions to my hospital bed. I'm given a gown to change into and sent off to the usual central area to have an ECG. As Rob and I find our way through the hospital, other patients are being wheeled around on trolleys or in wheelchairs; some are wired up to machines; some appear to be quite poorly; some unconscious.

I can see there is some very serious stuff happening in this hospital and wonder if I should be here. I begin to feel like a complete fraud and question what I'm doing. I've been living a normal and busy life and the fainting incidents are few and far between. I feel fit and well. Am I one of those timewasters you hear about? Am I clogging up valuable time that could be spent caring for people who are truly sick?

Back on the ward a priest is visiting, talking to patients and giving an occasional blessing. I suppress a giggle as he comes over to chat. He blesses me. I didn't really think I merited being blessed!

Rob jokes as the priest moves on. 'Bloody hell, they don't think you're going to get out of here alive!'

We can barely control ourselves as the nurse arrives to bring me a wheelchair. 'I don't need it. I'm fine to walk to the theatre.'

I've never been in an operating theatre before. Everyone is smiling, friendly and trying to put me at ease, but I feel uncomfortable with my chest exposed. Vulnerable.

I'm given a local anaesthetic and the surgeon gently talks me through the procedure, while a nurse holds my hand. 'We're manipulating it in now, it may feel uncomfortable. Just trying to fix it in position. We're nearly finished, just a few stitches.' It keeps me calm hearing his voice, and knowing where they are up to throughout. I refuse the wheelchair again and walk back to the ward. I don't want to be treated as though I'm ill.

'Is it okay to go now, as I don't want to miss my girls' sports day?' I ask the nurse as soon as I get back to the ward. Naively, I've no idea of what formalities follow a hospital procedure.

The nurse explains I'm not fit enough to go anywhere just yet, as I need to rest and see a doctor before I'm discharged. She seems quite amused by me.

I'm eventually discharged and even make it to the sports day. The traffic has been kind and Rob has put his foot down to get us here on time. It isn't long into the events when the anaesthetic wears off and I begin to realise why the hospital staff had looked at me strangely when I said I wanted to rush to attend a sports day. Exhaustion waves over me and I feel battered and bruised. The recorder is inside me at least, so I just need to have another faint and we can get to the bottom of things.

***

Life is never that straightforward. The recorder had a battery life of two years. Two weeks before I had to go back in hospital to have it removed at the end of its shelf life, remarkably I hadn't had a single faint. In one way this was good news, in another I felt I'd been through an operation unnecessarily, and still needed another operation to have it removed. All this and for nothing, again I felt like I'd been a fraud, going to great lengths to be checked out when I was perfectly fine.

I dash up the stairs, forgetting myself. I feel it coming. Rushing from my feet. Enveloping me. I make it to our bed and thud down. Damage limitation. I'd learned over the years to try and get in a safe position if there was time.

I'm not unconscious for long and luckily Rob is in the house, so he rushes to me when I call him after I regain my senses. He hasn't witnessed this faint, although the episodes he has seen have been particularly frightening for him and the girls. Every last drop of colour drains from my face; my lips turn blue; my eyes stare blankly into space; my jaw becomes rigid. I'm only out for about thirty to sixty seconds, but I know it's an unpleasant and stressful sight for them to see, especially on the occasions I've injured myself when I've fallen.

Rob tries to look on the bright side. 'At least we have a recording now.'

***

It feels more familiar this time. Although I haven't been here for two years, I know where to go and what to expect. I'm in the operating theatre again. This time I'm more relaxed and there's a light-hearted banter as I'm prepped. I'm under a cover so I don't have to see what they are doing to my chest, and a nurse is holding my hand once more. The team respectfully talks me through each step of the operation. Even though I've been given a local anaesthetic, the procedure is much more uncomfortable than before, as the event-recording device has been in place for a few years and needs some pressure to be removed.

I'm more than happy this time to accept the wheelchair to be taken back to the day ward. I'm given time to rest, then later in the day I see a doctor.

'Sorry you've waited so long, we've had a problem finding the correct machine to play back the reading. It's been a few years and the recording device is out of date now.'

'Typical,' I think to myself. 'This would happen to me. We aren't ever going to find what's causing it.'

'Don't worry, after some rummaging about we've managed to find one gathering dust in the back of a cupboard.'

Rob and I think he is only half joking.

Thankfully the results show nothing remarkable has happened to my heart during the faint, and the doctor is to discuss the results with a consultant. I will have a follow up appointment in due course. I'm discharged.

* * *

It's autumn 2002 and the weather is turning. It's going to be a long afternoon. I've worked all morning at school and we're driving back to Harefield for the formal results. We need to go to Luton afterwards to my after-school university session. I'm studying for an education degree as part of my training to become a teacher, as well as working as a teacher assistant.

The M25 is snarled up, but we make it in the nick of time. The clinic's busy and packed with people waiting. We wait ages, and at last my turn arrives to see the consultant.

He's looking at my notes for the very first time. He describes my faint as, 'Simply looking like vasovagal syncope,' which he explains is 'a temporary decline in blood flow to the brain.' This can be caused by an abnormal heart rhythm – which from my tests is looking extremely unlikely – or it can be neurological.

When the cause is neurological, a faint is triggered by inappropriate relaxation of the blood vessels, which leads to low blood pressure at a time when the body actually needs constriction of the blood vessels and a slightly higher heart rate.

Most people can control these symptoms with simple measures such as keeping hydrated, recognising the signs of a pre-syncope – light headedness and dizziness – and taking preventative strategies such as lying down with your legs raised or pausing to catch your breath while climbing stairs. I'd already become well versed in these actions.

We're pleased with these results and relieved there are no indications of heart problems. We discuss with the cardiologist what else could be done if the situation becomes worse. He mentions an angiogram for further investigations, or beta-blockers or possibly a pacemaker. We agree that these measures don't seem appropriate for now, taking into account all the test results so far and the relative infrequency of my fainting episodes. I had been controlling the symptoms very well and knew the triggers. I certainly wasn't keen on being on medication for life or having a pacemaker fitted.

Nonetheless, it's decided I should stay on Harefield's patient register and I will return annually, or I can phone them if things worsen. We leave feeling satisfied. I can get on with my life again and keep up my teacher training without having to worry about my health.

***

And so it went on … a few incidents; sometimes a few close together; sometimes a year or two with nothing at all. I became busier and busier with studies and work. Things didn't deteriorate. I was living my life normally.

Harefield was quite difficult to travel to with the M25 sandwiched in between us and, although I was only going once a year, I began to feel like I was wasting my time and effort and theirs too, when there was nothing new to report. Eventually, after a few years I made the decision to stop going back, thinking it more appropriate to return to my GP for a referral if matters escalated. In any event, Rob and I had felt very reassured by the extensive tests I'd undergone at Harefield and that nothing had changed since then.

Busy family life just carried on.

Two

Choices

(April 2010)

We arrive excitedly at Gare du Nord, clamber off the Eurostar with our baggage and follow the stream of travellers off the platform towards the taxis. It's the school Easter holidays and the station is bustling with tourists and families wandering, stopping hesitantly to search their maps. Everyday commuters are purposefully working their way through all the mayhem.

There's a long queue for taxis. Rob looks disgruntled and I gently try to appease him. 'We'll just have to be patient. It's going to be a long wait, but we'll get there.' Travelling from one place to another usually requires some level of waiting and patience. On this occasion I don't mind waiting. I'm feeling so upbeat and excited.

It's my birthday and I've never been to Paris before. Rob booked it as a last minute surprise. We've recently been enjoying travelling and discovering new foreign cities and culture, and I was thrilled when he told me we were going to Paris. I am going to have more time for this.

We arrive at our rather chic Parisian hotel room with a distant view of the Eiffel Tower. Rob has planned everything to the last detail. He's trying hard to show me a taste of our new future: more travelling together and more time together. I know the future in front of me looks promising and that's why I've chosen this new path, but I still feel sad about what I've left behind. There's no way he's going to let me look back, only forwards to a new and more relaxed phase in our lives. He's pulled out all the stops.

We wrestle and wrench about decisions in life, chopping and changing our minds, thinking carefully about all the 'what ifs'. Sometimes they are big decisions – or we think they are at the time – sometimes they are only small, but whatever their size, they can shape the destiny of our future.

We enjoy the day visiting some of those 'must see' places. We slowly wander on foot until we reach the Eiffel Tower, where we absorb the panorama high up from the viewing gallery. Later we enjoy a romantic cruise along the Seine, drinking in the sights from the river and the twinkling lights of the city.

***

Today we have a whole day in Paris. We take the Metro crossing the Seine and stroll along to visit Saint Chapelle and stare in awe at the beauty of the streaming light cast through its stained glass windows. We weave our way through the intricate streets and magnificent buildings towards Notre Dame chatting and admiring the architecture.

I'm relieved to be away from it all now, my decision made to take a new path in life. I've left my full time position as a primary teacher, and decided to give up on ambition and heavy responsibilities for now and only work part-time. I've secured a new part-time teaching post in a different school. Although this may appear trivial, in all our own little worlds decisions and actions like these can be significant. We fear making a mistake and making the wrong choice. We fear failure and we fear regret. Sometimes it's about taking a leap of faith and knowing instinctively which choice is the right one to make.

I visited my new school earlier in the Easter break and met some of my colleagues. Everyone had been welcoming and friendly. I'd organised my first lessons for the summer term already. I was feeling quite settled and I hadn't even officially started. That was a clear sign to me that I'd made the right choice.

As we continue to explore and enjoy the sanctuary of the Ile de la Cité, we spot by chance a mismatch of old pavilions full of colour – the 'Marché aux fleurs'. There is always something new to see, something new to experience. Travelling, just like life, can be full of surprises.

I instantly fall in love with this little flower market, full of plants and bric-a-brac. It feels like an oasis of calm after the turbulence of the last few months.

**

Breathing in the heavy scents my mind darts back to different phases in my life – different pathways, which led me from one place to another.

I hadn't always been a primary teacher. I worked for a high street bank for many years until I had our two girls. After they were born I gave up my banking career to become a full-time mum. I'd left school at eighteen after taking my A levels. All the way through school from being a little girl I wanted to be a teacher. The seed was sown then. I'd obtained a place at teacher training college, but somehow during my last year at school I began to get cold feet.

I remember back to how my teaching career had started, what an impact it had had on my life, which is why I'd found it so hard to switch to a slower pace in my career. I skip quickly from one part of my life to another while I browse amongst the plants and squeeze past other tourists.

I'd fallen into a banking career without too much deliberation. I believed that if I went on to be a teacher, I would effectively be at school all my life. I couldn't really envisage this for myself, so I started looking at other opportunities. Yet I always knew I would go to university one day and obtain a degree and go on to teach. I just knew deep down I would always do it. It was always there inside me – the desire to teach.

I joined a busy high street bank near to where I was born and brought up in Lancashire. I worked in the same branch for ten years and when I met Rob, who worked for the same organisation, we moved to Hertfordshire and were married. I cast my mind back to this chapter in my life when I joined the daily hub of commuters and took the train and tube every day to work in the bank's head office in London, where I worked in both personnel and strategy departments.

Banking had certainly given me a varied and largely fulfilling career, but when I had our girls I gave it up, as I didn't think working and commuting every day would combine with being a 'hands-on' mum. It was being a mum that brought me into the world of children, and back to those dreams of completing a degree and wanting to be a teacher.

Years followed – our girls both in school full-time, me following them closely behind. Initially I worked as a volunteer in class, helping with reading and supporting groups of children. Then I started working for just a few hours a week one-to-one with a child who needed extra support. I loved this work and it led to more hours supporting groups of children.

I enjoyed this period as a teaching assistant, but I had a strong fire inside me to become a fully-fledged teacher and have my own class. It wasn't an easy road to become qualified. I needed a degree, for one thing. I managed to find a teaching degree course that was held in the evenings and at weekends. This fitted in with working part-time in school, looking after the girls and helping to look after my in-laws, who were both becoming elderly and increasingly infirm. It was a lot to juggle, but when you really want something badly enough, you find a way to do it.

I found some issues challenging during this period: I had to go back to some of my least favourite subjects – maths, physics and chemistry – and I had to become computer literate.

I smile when I think back to this manic phase. When I began I didn't even know whether I would be able, or have the confidence, to complete the course. I wanted to finish it and prove myself so much, but it was still a surprise when I completed it with flying colours, gaining a first class honours degree.

My studies were not without their drawbacks. There was an impact on our family weekends when I had to complete my coursework, and Rob had the added burden of caring as much as he could for his parents. By now his mother had severe dementia and his father was becoming even more fragile.

My own family lived miles away in Lancashire, so Rob and I were used to coping under our own steam. We became a close-knit family unit of four. I had some wonderful friends who helped me out, and I was always grateful for their support.

I choose some flowers and pay absented-mindedly, distracted by the memories of completing my teacher training at the girls' school, Holy Family in Welwyn Garden City. I'd been working there for six years and was awarded a work-based graduate programme to qualify as a teacher. I was thrilled that I'd managed to achieve my dreams and at the same time fit everything around my family needs.

I studied at university for a year to be a 'Specialist Teaching Assistant', then it took four years of studying and training to complete my degree and placement year. I then completed an 'induction' year to become a fully trained teacher, and that brought to mind a very happy and contented phase of my life at Templewood School, also in Welwyn Garden City. Here I'd spent the last few years as a full-time teacher and also embarked on a Master's degree.

But now I've decided to leave Templewood, work just part-time and step off my Master's course, achieving a post-graduate advanced diploma instead, because of family circumstances and other pressing needs of my own.

When I think of these phases, standing here in this floral market, it seems a hard decision to have made after all the training and dedication. I've made a complete u-turn in my career aspirations, but as we step back out onto the streets and into the warm light, I know it's the right decision.

***

Finally we arrive at Notre Dame. It is a magnificent building. The sight of it washes away these past thoughts and I relax into the day. There are long queues to look inside, but as the day is so beautiful we decide to simply saunter outside in the gardens and enjoy the spring sunshine.

A man dressed as Quasimodo runs up behind me and makes me jump out of my skin. Everyone laughs and Rob and I join in. A little random moment. My family always laughs at me – wherever we go I seem to attract some kind of strangers.

We have a lovely lunch in a tiny French restaurant, which Rob had planned and booked in advance, before heading off for a cultural whistle stop tour of the Louvre.

***

It's our final day in Paris and we aren't due back on the Eurostar until mid afternoon, so we carry on exploring, this time nearer to where we are staying. We visit the Arc de Triomphe, but I'm unable to climb the steps to the top of the building as I'm beginning to flag. I admire the view down the Champs-Elysées from street level instead.

I'm always feeling so tired at the moment. I assume the frantic rush to leave my old school and have everything properly organised and prepared for the staff taking over from me is taking its toll: that and the organising I've already started for my new school. It's always of paramount importance to me that everything goes as smoothly as possible for my pupils, old and new, so I've invested a huge amount of extra time on this.

We wander up and down the Champs-Elysées, doing a bit of daydreaming again, window-shopping in all the designer shops, stopping for a lingering look in Cartier. I think 'When I win the lottery one day, I might go back there with a supermarket trolley!' A ridiculous thought, as I don't even play the lottery. 'What chance do you have of winning anyway?' I reason. 'Winning any lottery in life?'

We finish our exploring. I'm filled with enthusiasm, as Rob's new job is taking him travelling to various European cities. We plan that I can accompany him now I will have more time. We are at that age: me not far from fifty, Rob just over, our girls growing up – certainly old enough to leave them to fend for themselves for a while. We are enjoying new things together as a couple again: a new freedom.

***

If it was busy when we arrived, it's positively frantic now. My high spirits suddenly dampen and recede. I have this strong sense that things are about to go awry.

We can barely get into the station, let alone near the check-in for Eurostar. We soon learn that we've just walked straight into the middle of the volcanic ash chaos, as Iceland's volcano Eyjafjalla-jökull has erupted. It is something of an extraordinary phenomenum, no one in Northern Europe can fly, or so it seems, and it feels like everyone has decided to flock to the Gare du Nord instead.

We queue and queue – not that there really is a proper queue – not one for specific trains or for people who actually have their tickets and seats booked. It's a complete free-for-all with people scrambling and clamouring to capture the few remaining seats and tickets. We chat to others while we wait. Some people have been trying to get home for a few days. Once again I encourage Rob to be patient, but this time I'm not really sure our patience will be rewarded.

We're waiting behind a pleasant young couple. They've two little girls. We smile at them as they remind us of Sarah and Rose when they were small.

'We've been trying to get home from Disneyland Paris for the last two days now,' the young mum explains wearily. 'Getting tickets for the Eurostar is our last ditch attempt, otherwise I think we may be stranded here.'

We sympathise with them, move on and a while later find ourselves in another queue, once again side by side with the same family. By now they've managed to obtain tickets for a later train. 'Do you know whether food and drink is served on the train and whether or not you have to pay? We've no euros left.' says the mother anxiously.

Rob and I both have the idea at the same time. We have plenty of euros left. Rob pulls some notes from his wallet and suggests, 'Look, take this cash then you know you'll be able to get something to eat and drink.' They don't like to accept the money, but we insist.

We had simultaneously been thrown back to our honeymoon, years earlier in Kenya. At the end of our holiday, the tour operator had neglected to arrange our transfer to the airport. We had to organise our own transport urgently, and spent our every last Kenyan shilling in the process. At the airport, the plane was delayed and the heat was sweltering. An older couple took pity on us and gave us some money to buy refreshments. Acts of spontaneous kindness are always welcome, but generosity from strangers can be overwhelming.

We explain our little story to the couple and are adamant they take the money. 'One day when you meet someone else like yourselves in a similar situation, you can offer the same help,' says Rob. It strikes me how much I like this concept of unsolicited generosity being passed amongst complete strangers.

We manage to race through customs with our bags. I'm feeling truly exhausted – we really need to run to the platform, but I'm so tired from all the sightseeing and stress of the last few hours that I just can't. Rob has to drag both our bags to the train. I'm anxious the dizziness and faint feeling will play its tricks on me once more – rearing its head when I least want it – like it keeps on doing every once in a while.

By the skin of our teeth we reach the train on time as the whistle blows. Other people are frantically dashing, just jumping on wherever they can. We make our way to our seats and breathe a massive sigh of relief. It's been nerve-wracking, but we are on our way.

Three

Alarm Bells

(Spring 2010)

I arrive at Howe Dell in Hatfield, my new school. I feel as if I've crash-landed after all the fury and disquiet of yesterday's extraordinary events at Gare du Nord. But here I am at Hertfordshire's flagship 'eco' child centre and primary school, with its very own wind turbine, sedum roof areas, pioneering water and heating systems and, not least of all, thriving pupils.

Although I'm feeling apprehensive about my new role and meeting new people, the ethos and atmosphere of the school feels lovely and the staff, most of whom I don't know, are warm and welcoming.

In a school you are thrust straight into the throes of everything with the children, and my new role will give me the opportunity to teach four separate classes over the week, which will be very different to having my own class as in my previous job. Immediately I'm enjoying new and challenging experiences, which was something I feared I might lose in taking a part-time role. By the end of the week I feel as though I am slipping easily into the hub of my new school's life.

I smile to myself, after all those months of angst and dithering about what to do and making the right decision – all my anxieties have just melted away into insignificance. I only have two regrets – that I'd not made the changes much earlier, and that I'd wasted too much time worrying about making the wrong decision. If only we could see into the future, we could save ourselves so much stress.

***

I'd been wrestling so hard with myself beforehand. I felt a real pressing need to change things in my life, and this built up more and more since the start of the school year. I wrestled this way and wrangled that way, backwards and forwards, up and down and round again.

Rob had changed his job the summer beforehand, and had taken on a finance role that involved travelling abroad to Europe and further afield. It often meant that he was away, so I was carrying all the family and home responsibilities during the week, as well as working a sixty-five hour week as a full time teacher. It was just about manageable, but while Rob was away little incidents would throw things out of balance and make me think it was time to change.

I was driving home tired and late after a parents' evening at school when a stone hit my car. Then there was a loud crack, and I was left with a fragmented windscreen. Do I stay stranded in the dark? Do I walk the next three or four miles? Do I try and carry on driving? I opted to drive cautiously home, as I needed to get back to my girls and there were things to be done before the day ended. There wasn't any leeway in my day for messing about. I managed to get home – now I had to think about the morning and getting to school. I organised a plan and collapsed into bed. I was exhausted. My tiredness was becoming overwhelming at times.

Beep, beep, beep... I roused myself, it was the fire alarm signalling – its battery was dying. I grabbed a chair and went to remove the battery from the unit in the ceiling. It wouldn't come out. The alarm was fixed to the mains electric, I couldn't unscrew it. Sarah and Rose sleepily joined me – we all took turns at climbing on the chair in the middle of the night, screwdrivers in hand trying to dismantle it with no success. Beep, beep, beep... It continued all night.

The next day we started early – well we had never really

stopped. Sarah dropped me in her car to my school before going back home to collect Rose so they could go to their own school together. Sarah was in her final year of sixth form and Rose was revising for her GCSEs. I managed a lift home late after another parents' evening with a friend.

Back to the beeping – luckily Rob was home by now, but he hadn't managed to stop the noise. I was glad in a perverse way, as it didn't make me feel as useless. He ended up wrenching the damn thing out of the ceiling. Plaster was everywhere, but it went on beeping. Impatiently Rob threw it into the outside shed and slammed the door shut – still it beeped. The girls found this amusing. It reminded them of an episode of *Friends*, where Phoebe had the same problem. I wasn't laughing though. I was exhausted. An alarm in my own head sounded. 'I need to change things.'

I always worked some of the weekend to ensure my lessons were prepared for the following week, or if not that, I'd be working on pupil assessments, reports and other various paperwork. Rob and I found we weren't having the time together that we would have liked. We managed to snatch some time out on the garden on the weekend – we could still hear that bloody thing sounding off in the shed. The tension broke and allowed us to laugh and relax. It had just been a bad and heavy week.

The car was fixed and another week or two passed relatively smoothly. Our family balance remained intact. I felt happy again – no need to change anything. It was just the ups and downs of daily life that everyone has.

It was time for another orthodontist appointment for Rose – not an easy arrangement as the orthodontist wasn't that local. The same week, Sarah had a university open day. It was term time, so it was out of the question for me to do either. Rob eroded his precious holiday allocation so we could manage it all. He didn't mind, but as he was away from home more often than not, I felt it was unfair on him. He was carrying us at the weekends too and the burden on us both seemed to be getting heavier and heavier. My own alarm beeped again. 'I need to change things.'

Increasingly I felt like I was missing out on activities I should have been doing as a mum. I wanted to go with my girls to look at universities. I wanted to be part of the important decisions they were making. I began to feel like I was devoting my whole life to other people's children, while my own children were having to cope with little or no help from me. I'm sure all mothers feel guilty like this at times, but it had set me off once more, thinking that I needed to readdress the balance in my life.

During this period, we lost Rob's father while my own dad, who was in his seventies at the time, suffered a heart attack. He had already been diagnosed with COPD, a chronic lung disease, and was waiting for a heart bypass operation. I knew my dad was becoming more frail and that, as things stood, I would be struggling to visit him in Lancashire, let alone offer any practical support unless it was the school holidays.

I knew from our experience with Rob's parents how difficult it can be when your parents are unwell. We had lived nearby them and had done our best to try and give them the support they needed. It never felt enough, it never does, but we did what we could. There was the alarm in my mind signalling once more, 'Change things.' Then I would grapple with this thought and decide, 'We are coping quite well at the moment, do I really need to make changes?'

So it went on.

It was the tiredness that kept on defeating me – the simple, overwhelming tiredness – I always felt so tired – an extreme kind of tired. I put it down to my age as I was nearing fifty, and believed I was terribly unfit and had been neglecting myself on the exercise front. I kept feeling like I was about to start with a virus or come down with a bug, and couldn't quite get on top of things. Some nights I would come home and do what was necessary and then fall into bed at eight o'clock, then other nights I would be burning the candle at both ends and getting myself even more tired. It was becoming a vicious circle.

I wasn't particularly worried about my health – ask any teacher and they will tell you that the job is exhausting – but even so, I knew that my work-life balance was becoming more and more out of kilter and it was time to make adjustments.

Giving up on my full time teaching career was a thought I hated, but I realised I was putting my head in the sand by continuing as I was. My mind kept telling me to keep on going and it would just work out somehow – most families have to juggle to get by and we weren't any different. I loved teaching with a passion, and had always been dedicated to it and determined to progress my career. Teaching is one of the most rewarding and varied jobs ever. I'd invested so much time and effort to accumulate my experience, training and qualifications, that to give it all up would be a tragedy.

I wanted both – my career as it was and the time and space to cope with everything properly – but I knew something had to give, and I knew it shouldn't be my family. The alarm kept nagging at me, and however hard I tried to ignore it, it would persist. I could ignore it no longer.

Finally and reluctantly, I decided to step out of teaching for the summer term and then look for a part-time post for September. Just as I'd decided, I saw the ideal part time job advertised, which would mean I would have to start straight after Easter without my intended break.

The job was in a flagship, purpose built eco school. I had been the science and sustainability coordinator in my previous school and had led several eco based projects to teach the children about recycling and sustainability. We had worked determinedly hard to attain the coveted eco-school Green Flag award.

My new job would be working with infant pupils, where I'd already had several years experience. It would enable me to build on my knowledge and interests even though it was part time hours, so it seemed perfect. I would have plenty of that much needed time for my family and my weekends free to do what I wanted. I would be living my new dream.

***

It's only my second week and I wake with a terrible headache, my vision blurring badly for a while. I'd had rare episodes of blurred vision since having our girls – they usually lasted just a few minutes and I'd stop and rest and then they'd go. I'd put it down to hormonal changes. They never bothered me unduly because of their infrequency, and there were never any ill effects afterwards.

This time my vision blurs for longer, and when it returns the headache is intense. I'm reluctant to stay off sick – I've barely even started my new job. I'd taken minimal time off sick in all the years I'd been teaching.

I go into work and carry on, but I don't feel myself. The symptoms have passed, but I'm feeling overwhelmingly tired – fatigued. I'm feeling annoyed more than anything and thinking it's just my luck that I'm coming down with a virus or something.

Over the next couple of days the tiredness eases and by my third week, thankfully, I'm feeling refreshed and back to normal again. I'm really enjoying the job and my new work-life balance.

I have it in the back of my mind that I'm unfit. In fact I feel so unfit – exercise wise – that I'm embarrassed to enroll with a gym. Here I am, nearly fifty and I've never even stepped inside a gym. I'm determined to get myself fitter, so I buy a Wii Fit. I think if I can exercise at home first, become a little fitter, then I might enroll at a gym in a few months. With my new extra time, I should be able to concentrate on myself at last.

The Wii Fit is set and ready to go. I play around with the controls and find my way through the programs – some yoga – deep breathing. Yes, I can manage that I hope! I twiddle around with the controls a little and click on 'step basics' next. Just a three-minute step routine. Suddenly I'm breathless and dizzy, and have to clamber my way to the nearest chair. I think I might faint. I'm shocked. I'm much worse than I imagined. I'm so shocked that I've let myself go to this extent. 'I'm only nine stone in weight, I can't be that bad!' I say to myself. 'But you are,' I reply.

I decide to start small and build up gradually – one step at a time – I need to repair the damage I've done to myself for not exercising regularly. I'm glad I've reduced my hours, so I can devote some time to this. I keep on trying out the exercises, but keep on being defeated. It keeps making me breathless. I'm appalled at myself for letting it come to this. I only seem to be able to cope with the breathing and the gentle stretching exercises. 'It's a start,' I say to myself, 'better than nothing.' It bothers me though. That alarm again. I'm not sure if I'm alarmed I'm so unfit or if I'm alarmed because it isn't normal to be this unfit.

'I don't think you're unfit,' says Rob. 'You're active enough and you're certainly not overweight – something's not right, perhaps it's time you went back to see a doctor.'

I argue back. 'A doctor will just tell me I'm getting breathless because I'm not used to exercising, you are supposed to build your exercise tolerance up first, that's what I'm trying to do!'

It's clear Rob doesn't agree with me, but I'm sure I'm right.

***

The voices coming from the table with the large party are loud and raucous with laughter. There's quite a queue, but somehow we manage to squeeze ourselves onto a table. It's the weekend. We've popped down to our local Indian restaurant, just a couple of hundred yards from our house. I enjoy a glass of wine or two. The atmosphere is lively and buzzing with fun and enjoyment. Rob, Rose and I relax into the vibes of the evening. Then it happens. It's as if an off switch has been thrown inside my body – in an instant I've turned from chattering, laughing and joking to yawning, trying to stay awake and 'with it' the next.

'You've gone white,' says Rob. 'It looks like you've hit a brick wall.'

We leave sharply. It's pouring with rain – sweeping, heavy, drizzling rain. Rob and Rose take me by each arm and guide me up the street. The slight incline on the short walk home feels like a mountain. I'm climbing a mountain. We're all soaked. Brollies are abandoned as they almost carry me. Cars splash past with their blinding headlights, their occupants probably thinking I'm a Saturday night drunk.

I'm dreaming. I'm soaked wet through. Sodden. Voices. Where are they coming from? Why am I so wet? Then the ringing – becoming louder in my ears. The sound that gives it all away and answers my thoughts. I'm devastated. It's happened again. I'm drenched, laid out on the deep, wet gravel of our drive amongst the puddles. It's pouring. Pouring. We're all soaked in the gloom of the night.

Rob and Rose manhandle me inside and straight into bed. Something feels different about this one. I'd begun to feel strange at the restaurant before I'd even stood up. I hadn't been running upstairs or jumping up from sitting down too quickly. I don't feel right. I fall off to sleep wondering if we should have gone to A&E for help.

***

'One problem, one appointment' it states on signs everywhere around the doctors' surgery. I feel bewildered. Where on earth do I start? I feel like I'm falling to bits! What with my fainting, my dizziness, my fatigue, my headaches and bleary eyes. What a mess I am! It doesn't occur to me that this growing set of symptoms may be connected.

I go in to see the GP. I've already decided that most of my symptoms are quite vague, but my biggest concern is definitely the worsening fainting. He gives me a good check up and all seems and sounds well, so generally I'm reassured. I explain my past history, so to be on the safe side he refers me back to see a cardiologist. I'm lucky we now have some private health cover, and an appointment to see the cardiologist at a local private hospital comes through the following week.

***

Parking is awkward and I'm worried we're going to be late. We are at Pinehills in Hitchin, a small private hospital. Eventually we check in and we wait and wait. We are advised the cardiologist has arrived, but is struggling to park. We chuckle, we've probably been driving around with him earlier – maybe we could have undertaken the consultation in the car park.

When I see him, I explain about my past history and my recent faint. He gives me a thorough examination and has a good listen to my heart and lungs. 'Everything looks and sounds absolutely fine,' he reassures me. 'Although it was some time ago, you've had all the appropriate tests and there are no new ones, but I agree with you. I think your symptoms are getting worse.'

We nod in accord. I'm thinking, 'He thinks the same as me, there's not any more new tests I can have done.'

We discuss using beta-blocker medication with a pacemaker that was mentioned to me some years ago, but he initially wishes to redo some of the tests I'd undergone at Harefield before we consider that route. I'm booked in for tests the following week: blood tests; an ECG; a heart echo and an exercise stress test. I'm still concerned about having to have tablets and a pacemaker fitted.

In the meantime he advises, 'Drink plenty of water to keep well hydrated and put salt on your food. I know this is counter to every-thing we are told about healthy diets and salt, but it can help with fainting,' he explains. 'You may even need salt tablets to help you.' I don't really like the sound of this, but I agree to try and drink more water and put salt on my food and we would see how I get on.

**

The weather has turned hot. I keep on staring and staring. Staring at other people's ankles, then looking down at mine. Some people keep saying their hands and feet are swollen because of the heat and humidity. I feel relieved because I can believe that's why mine are swollen too. It's just that my own ankles don't seem to compare to anyone else's on the same scale. They're really swollen. My ankles and then my calves have turned into rolls that are folding onto more rolls of swelling. They're painful as though they want to keep on swelling, but they have nowhere to swell to anymore. I'm trying to keep more hydrated like I've been advised, but I feel so desperately tired with the heat.

I'm relieved to see the cardiologist once more and the first thing I tell him, 'It's just my ankles that don't seem right, they're so swollen.' He has a quick glance at my them and says, 'Let's run the tests first, shall we?' He leads me through for an ECG.

My ECG looks normal and I go for my heart echo next. The radiologist is kind and friendly and puts me at ease. I'd had an echo all those years ago, so I know it's nothing to worry about.

After a short while the lady says, 'Excuse me love, I just need to go to the toilet, I've been having one of those days.' I take it she means she has a tummy upset or something, think it a bit odd and curse to myself, 'Oh great I'm going to walk out of here with a tummy bug next!'

No sooner has she left the room, she appears back again. It dawns on me there's absolutely no way she's had time to go to the loo; it hits me that she's found something – something that isn't right.

My cardiologist follows her in, confirming what's going through my mind. I'm laid on my side with my face and body turned partially to the wall. I can hear their low voices, but can't make out what they're saying. The only snatch of conversation I hear is, 'I've not got it wrong, have I? That figure is definitely right, isn't it? It's not exaggerated, is it?' More mumbles, then the cardiologist leaves the room.

I'm told there's no need to perform the stress test and the cardiologist will see me soon. That confirms to me again something is amiss. Why was there no need to do a stress test? I don't think it fair to question the radiologist. I just know instinctively that something has been found and it should be the cardiologist who should deal with it.

Rob has been waiting patiently in the busy waiting room and is smiling away at me when I return. 'Where on earth have you been? I was getting ready to send out a search party,' he laughs, 'anyway, at least you're all done now.'

I whisper – I don't want anyone to hear me, 'They've found something.' He stops in his tracks, his smile dissolves. We sit back down subdued and wait quietly. It feels like an age, back to the inevitable waiting game. Waiting, waiting, waiting…

Four

My Tornado

(Summer 2010)

I stir from my unsettled sleep and, for a split second, all is normal in my world. The sun is shining through the cream coloured blind on our bedroom window. It's always bright and airy in this room, that's how I like it. I like to wake up to the sunshine. I can hear a soulful blackbird singing. My favourite. Peaceful – then the peace is shattered. A tornado is engulfing me, exploding all around me.

It's swirling up from underneath me, its hollow swelling rotating with the debris of my life, blurring the real world. It culminates above my head with fragments of my life flashing around me – everything disconnected. Shreds of my past mixed with sketchy images of my future – ebbing, flowing and throbbing amongst the reality of the here and now.

I'm stunned – frozen in shock – yet still able to move in this tornado. I can climb out of bed, dress myself and drive to school. Although it's like a thick swirling fog circling me, I can still see through it. No one else can see my tornado. It's invisible – everyone's expectations of me remain the same. It's business as usual and I carry on with my tornado shrouding me. Everything is still ordinary – just an ordinary day in a very ordinary week. Not for me anymore, my life has been changed and changed irrevocably, in one moment. I am worried this feeling will stay with me forever.

***

I arrive in reception class. I'm wearing a cream and orange flowered shirt, chosen deliberately to disguise the equipment I am wearing underneath it – a twenty-four hour heart monitor. Little children don't miss a trick – I don't want them to see – I don't want anyone to see. I don't even want myself to see. I want it out of sight, out of mind, so I carry on as normal. The consultant had fixed me up with it, after I had been back in to see him the previous day. He wants to obtain some readings on my heart.

It's the only thing I can do – carry on. If everything is normal, then it can't really be that bad, can it? If I carry on as normal, then it all will be alright, won't it? There doesn't really seem another way forward. The world is still spinning and everything is just the same around me, but I don't know how to behave inside my tornado. I haven't an inkling or clue how I should behave at all.

My heart. The life deep inside me that ticks every second, every minute, every hour, every day. The heart I know is in difficulty. The heart with its right side too seriously enlarged – dilated, he had said. The heart with the septum now too flattened out by the pressure it's enduring. The heart with the outrageously and abnormally high blood pressures inside it. The heart struggling with Pulmonary Hypertension – what is that even? The heart that's in serious failure. The heart that I've been told, even at this very early stage, probably hasn't long left to tick. I don't like that someone has told me this about my heart. *My* heart.

There is something significant to most people about a heart. For me it's at the core of your very being, life and soul. Everywhere you look you will see heart shapes – heart symbols encompass that feeling of love emanating from deep within. It's the hardest thing ever being told my heart isn't working. It's the hardest thing ever knowing it's broken, and broken it is, both literally and figuratively.

We drove back from the hospital in stunned silence. The consultant's words were bouncing off us, flying around, echoing loudly and choking our ability to speak. I couldn't quite manage to absorb them in any way. That's when the tornado began to form – information, thoughts, consequences. They refused to sink in. Instead they surrounded me. What was becoming clear to us, though, was that all the symptoms I had been experiencing were actually connected.

Our girls were smiling in anticipation when we arrived home. We had no choice but to tell them. We've always been honest with our children and we felt they needed to know it was serious, otherwise how would we begin to cope. It was something that we weren't going to be able to hide from them, although we were delicate with the truth.

I teach two reception classes whilst stuck in my tornado. We have fun and a good productive morning. None of the children spot the bulges under my shirt. I know they haven't, little ones are never short in coming forward, unlike adults – that's what I love about them – they will just ask you anything outright if they are curious with neither embarrassment nor reserve.

As soon as I finish in class, I slip quietly out of school. I manage to avoid seeing any of my colleagues. I really don't think I could cope if I have to speak to any of them.

***

I think this may be the beginning of a long journey with my tornado. I'm worried it might rage on and on, and I don't know how I'm going to live inside it as it twists and turns, taking different forms. I don't know how to tackle it, so I decide I will start in small steps.

I spend the afternoon trying to find out more about Pulmonary Hypertension. I need to start confronting this broken heart head-on and become calmer. The more informed I can be, the better I can understand things – understand what's happening and be more prepared for what is to come.

The consultant explained Pulmonary Hypertension in very general terms to us. It seems to be some sort of high blood pressure in the heart and lungs. He told me how it could be due to several underlying different causes, or could appear aggressively from nowhere. He wants to undertake further tests to find out why I have it. He told me it cannot be cured, and that the pressures in my heart are far too high. I'm booked in for an urgent angiogram test, which will give an accurate study of the pressures in all of my heart chambers and show if there are any other abnormalities.

I search the internet to find out what I can. Most of the articles are from medical research papers undertaken by clinicians. I know deep down, from what I've been told already, that it isn't ever going to make good reading. My consultant has warned me, 'Your lifespan will be shortened, you don't have decades left.' I'd pressed and pressed him for a finer prognosis than this, but he couldn't, or wouldn't, tell me. I'm obsessed with how much longer I've left to live. I discover a website called, 'PHAUK', a charity to support anyone affected by Pulmonary Hypertension ('PH').

There is a multitude of solid and accurate information on this website and I register to join the charity and request every booklet they have, so I can glean as much information as possible. I want to know everything I can find out about this blight that's fallen on my family and me.

Anxiously, anxiously, desperately, desperately, I wait for the post to come. Waiting for those booklets that might tell me somewhere that everything will be alright; waiting for some comfort and reassurance that things cannot possibly be as bad as I think they might be. Every single day I wait for the booklets to arrive in the post. I will them to pop through the letterbox before it's time for my angiogram. I want to be ready and prepared for what the consultant finds next, and be armed with some proper information so we can make decisions about my treatment. The angiogram is going to be very important to determine where we are going next, and it's all I can think about.

My consultant tells me to stop the salt and extra fluid intake immediately as he starts treating me for heart failure instead. He gives me diuretics, which help my heart and bring my ankles back to normal. I begin to find it difficult at school because I need the loo quite often because of them. I'm feeling physically well in myself, if not mentally, and the consultant has advised me to carry on as normal and it's safe to do so. I suppose I must look normal to everyone else.

I know I can't really carry on at school like this, with no one knowing what I'm going through. However, I'm having major difficulties telling anyone and retaining my composure. The hardest thing is that I've left all my close colleagues and friends behind in my old school. I've only been at my new school for about seven weeks, and although everyone has been really supportive, I don't feel I know people well enough to just blurt out what's happening to me. I'm becoming totally distraught at the thought of telling them. Telling people equals admitting it. Saying it out loud means it's real. Hearing myself say it means I can't ignore it, like I want to. I've already told close members of my family and a few friends, and that's been hard enough. It's been difficult phoning them. I know they are cheery and happy on the other end of the line, and that I'm about to drop a bombshell when there's an appropriate pause in the conversation.

I feel I'm letting the school down badly as they've just ap-pointed me, but I decide to phone the head teacher on my day off. That way I can come straight out with it so it doesn't matter if I lose my composure. She won't see.

I make the phone call and try to explain to her, but it doesn't go as planned. I'm utterly distraught trying to explain what's hap-pened, and don't even know properly what's happening myself. I manage to relay enough for her to understand it's serious. She's brilliant in giving me support and puts provision in place to help me through to the end of term. I feel empty. I'm beginning to realise this may be the end of my teaching career.

I want to tell other friends too, but it's a balance of trying to tell them enough so they understand, but not the real harsh facts. I'm struggling to understand them myself and still haven't reached the bottom of why I even have this cruel disease.

We carry on together as a family trying to act normally and on an even keel, but it's far from easy. Sarah has to continue and finish her A level exams and Rose her GCSEs, so we try to be careful what we burden them with. My girls aren't stupid though, they are well balanced and tuned in and well aware when things aren't right around them, so it's hard and stressful for all of us.

***

It's mid-July. Harley Street, with its black painted wrought iron balconies and tall attic rooms peering down at us. We arrive at our third hospital in four weeks to have my angiogram undertaken. My private health insurance has fast-tracked me to this grand Georgian house. I'd never imagined I would find myself in Harley Street, I thought it was the preserve of the rich and famous. Am I really important enough to be coming here, just ordinary old me?

We book in and wait with other patients. I see a lady with no hair and Rob whispers quietly to me, 'That lady must be really poorly.' I readily agree. I can see some very sick people waiting. I think I'm quite poorly too, but no one else can see it. I'm scared about my illness. I'm frightened of what the day's test results may bring.

It's my usual consultant undertaking my angiogram. He talks to me throughout the procedure, but I find it hard to listen. It's because I'm trying to conjure up a happy memory to take my mind of what he's doing.

I close my eyes. I'm in the Lake District. Rob passes me the paddles. I flop down into our kayak. He joins me. Paddles left. Paddles right. Left. Right. I watch the gentle ripples as we glide across the water towards the middle of Coniston Water. We look down the lake and admire the gorgeous view. I wonder if I'll ever be able to do this for real again.

My consultant completes his task. The angiogram will give him more accurate information about my coronary arteries and a meas-ure of how efficiently my heart is pumping, together with the blood pressure levels in my heart chambers. It will also show whether my arteries are narrowed or blocked and if I have any other irregularities.

I'm resting after my angiogram. – I have to lay flat and still for a few hours after the procedure – when my cardiologist and nurse enter the room to give me the results. My consultant is in full flow about how severe the pressures are in my pulmonary arteries, when a workman carrying some wood and a toolbox enters the room to start putting up a few shelves. I'm lying here flat on my back thinking, 'Is this really happening all around me, or is it some twisted dream?'

My mouth tries to tell the man to get out of the room, but words will not come. I'm so shocked. I don't want him to become part of my diagnosis and prognosis. I don't want him to hear my fate while I'm flat on my back and he's putting up shelves. I cannot speak. I'm speechless. It feels like my world is getting more and more bizarre by the minute. Rob shares my sense of disbelief, intervenes and tells the man forcibly, 'Hang on a minute, this is ridiculous, can you just leave us, please?' We start again. This time a private, but very frank, conversation.

I think I will always remember this man wanting to put up shelves while I'm in the middle of finding out the worst. Him going about his ordinary business while my life's tossed upside down. It makes it seem like it's an ordinary everyday occurence, that my life doesn't matter, that life is worthless. Who cares about life when there are jobs to get on with? It's sticking stark in my mind as the consultant delivers his news.

I find out I have very severe PH. My coronary arteries look good though, which is a bonus. The left side of my heart is working fine – another bonus – and there are no holes detected in my heart – yet another bonus. We have a clearer picture now. Nothing other than the PH has been detected, and the damage it has caused to the right side of my heart and septum. That means other avenues need to be investigated to find out what is causing my condition, before I can be treated specifically. I'm back at work the next day with one ridiculously bruised thigh from the angiogram entry site.

During the last week of term I have lung function tests undertaken at my local hospital. These seem very strange. I sit with a peg on my nose and blow in different ways into a tube, which is attached to a computer. The computer takes readings of how well I can blow, and can interpret how effective my lung function is. People telling me gently how ill I am, while people try to put shelves up on walls; people telling me to put pegs on and off my nose – it all feels surreal and overwhelming.

It's the end of term and we're no nearer to knowing why I have PH. We're feeling strained the more we find out about the disease. All I know is that I'm seriously unwell, with a poor outlook, but no definite prognosis. Once more it occurs to me that it's unlikely I'll be able to continue at work. My only hope is that we can find out the underlying cause and obtain the right treatment to stabilise me.

My head teacher says she will hold my post open until I come back with more information from a CT scan of my chest, which is due at the start of the school holidays. My cardiologist wants to check if there are any blood clots on my lungs, as this can be a cause of PH. I'm not on a permanent work contract as I've taken a supply teacher role, so I have no sick leave or entitlements like I had only a few months ago.

I take all my boxes of stuff to the car on the last day of term. There is a lovely premises manager who runs after me, innocently saying, 'You should have asked for help, we don't want you harming yourself, we want you back next term.'

I put on a big smile, 'It's not heavy really, I'm fine. Enjoy the summer.'

Climbing into my car, I bite my lip hard as I know deep down I won't be coming back. I drive off, knowing that it's the last time I'll ever stand in front of a class or have my own classroom. I've left my teaching career behind at Howe Dell. I want to cry, but the tears won't come. I've become numb.

Somehow the tornado has developed a hard shell, which remains separate from the real me, making it difficult for bad news to sink in. None of this is happening to the real me: it's happening to my shadow or someone sitting behind me – someone separate from me – it isn't anything to do with the real me at all.

I'm mightily relieved to arrive at the end of the school term and it feels like a weight has been lifted. Now I don't have to pretend anymore, and I can carry on with getting to the bottom of what's going on.

Perhaps I should have handled this all differently. Maybe I should have given up and resigned as soon as I received my diagnosis and saved myself the stress, but when unfamiliar and traumatic things are unfolding unexpectedly, you tend to fumble on through.

It's like I'm walking blindfolded and lost in fog, struggling inside the tornado that's blown my life away and trying to grasp my way forward in a world where I've no understanding. I keep trying to cling on to the world I know best: my family, my work and all the security and stability I'm used to. I'm trying to balance all this so I have hope for the future. I cling onto a small hope that my teaching will still play a part in it. I want to hang on to life as I've always known it.

The future which I'd foreseen at Easter has slipped away, and the reality of my new beginning is dawning. I knew this reality as I walked away from school. I had my new beginning as I drove home. It's a totally unknown future that will now be mapped out in front of me.

I always say things happen for a reason, and no matter how much we plan and direct ourselves, there is always some element of life over which we have no control. We are steered down paths that we don't anticipate. Sometimes it's accidental; sometimes it's coincidental; sometimes we manage to make our own luck.

I firmly believe that my decision to cut my hours and work part-time has been a blessing in disguise. Slowing things down has made me realise that the fatigue did not improve as I thought it would by reducing my commitments, and that I do need some help. I think this decision might just have saved my life.

Five

An Old Woman

(Late Summer 2010)

Two majestic red kites circle above. I watch them from our garden, thrilled that they have randomly chosen to soar and fly above us. It's a beautiful August afternoon – hot and sunny, but with a warm gentle breeze. I watch them in fascination as they rise elegantly and float overhead, twisting gracefully to change direction, their enormous rust-coloured wings spanning wide.

It's the first time I've ever seen red kites flying above our home and it's an unusual sight – something of a phenomenon to watch from our own garden. Red kites are still quite a rarity in this country and I feel it's almost a reflection of this unusual situation I've found myself in.

The kites allow my mind to be momentarily drawn away from the new world I've been blasted into with a force – the world of PH, the world of hearts and lungs, the world of doctors, nurses, hospitals and tests.

My CT scan results had revealed that there was a huge problem in my lungs. This had come as a big shock, as I hadn't ever once felt or even sensed any problem with my lungs. I'd had no signs whatsoever of any breathing difficulties until the last few months. They had found that my pulmonary arteries and vessels in my lungs were badly scarred and blocked and were much thicker and hardened than they should be normally.

It confirmed my diagnosis was definitely one of PH. Because of all the scarring, the radiologist who undertook the CT scan thought the most obvious reason must be blood clots. My consultant explained you can have small blood clots that can pass through the vessels in your lungs and they may not give rise to symptoms, but can still cause damage. Blood clots are a very well known cause of PH. At the same time, he explained, you can have PH without any known cause.

Although we had researched PH, as it is so complicated we still hadn't properly understood that PH is primarily a rare lung disorder. It is high blood pressure that affects the arteries and vessels in the lungs which, in turn, damages the right side of the heart. It begins when the pulmonary arteries and smaller capillaries in the lungs become narrowed, blocked or destroyed. This makes it difficult for blood to flow through and raises pressure within the lungs' blood vessels. The pressure builds up and the heart's lower right chamber (right ventricle) has to work harder to pump blood. This eventually causes the heart muscle to weaken and fail.

PH becomes progressively worse and can be fatal. There are currently various treatments for PH to manage and slow down its rate of progress, but in the vast majority of cases it cannot be cured. The treatments can vary depending on what may be causing the PH and its underlying severity, which can help to improve a patient's quality of life.

There can be several causes of PH, for example: congestive heart failure, blood clots in the lungs' arteries, HIV and autoimmune diseases such as lupus and scleroderma. PH can also manifest itself for no known reason; in rare instances it may be genetic. All the main causes of PH are classified by the World Health Organisation ('WHO') and the severity of PH is measured on a separate WHO classification scale. For diagnosis and treatment you require both of these classifications.

In between all the anxious waiting, I had gleaned this information from various sources, including the resources provided by the PHAUK. It was clearly obvious from what I'd found out that this is a very complex disease, and very rare.

I still didn't know why I'd acquired PH, but the evidence

seemed to be pointing to blood clots, or it had simply started on its own. In this latter instance, it is often referred to as idiopathic Pulmonary Arterial Hypertension ('PAH'). The incidence is currently a handful of cases in a million.

With PAH, the high pressure is caused because the cells lining the blood vessels of the lungs have begun to mutate, which in turn causes them to harden and block. This continues to worsen over time. It is not fully understood why this happens, but there are some known genes that may cause it, but even in those cases where the gene is identified as being carried, the triggers that then cause the cells to mutate are still unknown.

As I had read more and more about PH, I began to pick up on the fact that specialist expertise and medication is required to treat it and that there are only eight specialist centres around the UK given this responsibility, including the children's hospital, Great Ormond Street. PH affects people of all ages from babies to the elderly.

The red kites circle high above us, round and round they hover. I think again how unusual it is to see them here, as unusual as my disease. Backwards and forwards they go, like the troubles in my mind.

I'm still heavy with these thoughts when my mobile buzzes. It's my consultant. I'd left him a message as I wanted to speak to him because I was beginning to realise from the research I'd been undertaking that I should be having specialised care. We agree to meet early this week. The red kites have vanished, their magic gone, and abruptly I'm back in my harsh reality.

As my CT scan indicated blood clots, my consultant has placed me on the blood thinner, Warfarin. He's already given me Furosemide, Spironolactone and Digoxin to help my heart failure. These are all general treatments for PH, but none of them are actually targeting the raging pressures in my pulmonary arteries. This has begun to concern me, as I'm tired all the time – exhausted – and I'm passing out more frequently.

We had been supposed to be going to Spain, but I'd been told right at the outset that I wasn't fit to fly. It was disappointing, as we were to stay with friends, but they kindly suggested that our girls still joined them. It did them good to be away from it all, and less-ened my guilt that I'd ruined the family holiday we had all been looking forward to. It was a blessing I didn't go, as I'd had several more severe fainting episodes.

I'm becoming more and more anxious. The Digoxin and diuret-ics have helped my heart failure, which had been classed as severe when my PH was found. Several heart echoes and exercise tests later, the pressures in my pulmonary arteries remain severely high, and my exercise tolerance is less and less.

When we eventually meet my consultant, I don't need to broach the topic of specialised care, as he pre-empts me by saying that my case has gone beyond his remit and knowledge, and that it's time to refer me elsewhere.

For the first time in a while, I'm actually thinking I'm lucky – if you can say that – because three of the specialist centres are based in London and there's Papworth Hospital as well, near Cambridge – four options, all within an hour's travel. Choices. We have choices, but that means making a decision: trying to make the right decision. It's back to those all-important decisions again. Which way do we jump? Would it really matter whatever way? We're on the verge of opting to go with the Royal Brompton in London, purely because my consultant has contacts there.

Papworth Hospital. It keeps popping in my mind as we are talk-ing. I'd read quite a bit about Papworth already. When my consult-ant had talked previously about blood clots, I knew from my re-search that Papworth is the only hospital in the UK that performs an operation called 'pulmonary endarterectomy'. This is quite a seri-ous, complex and life-threatening operation to remove blood clots from the blood vessels in the lungs. If my condition relates to blood clots then Papworth seems a sensible choice.

The outcomes from this blood clot operation look promising. The operation doesn't always successfully clear the blood clots, as some are deep-seated in tiny vessels too small to be operated on, but it usually gives an improvement in quality of life for some time, or if patients are very lucky, their PH can be cured. I am still obsessed with my prognosis and how long I might have to live, so any option which gives me longer seems the most attractive.

My mind's racing around with all these thoughts and the possibility of transplant keeps popping up in there too. Uncannily, I'd been watching a programme on Sky about heart transplants, which had been on every morning in those first few weeks of the school holidays. It had caught my attention because I'd seen transplant mentioned amongst all the PH literature. I recall Sarah telling me off for lying around watching programmes that seemed to be about more doom and gloom when I should be trying to keep cheerful and on top of things. She'd made me stop watching it.

With these thoughts swirling around, I suddenly make a snapshot decision, 'Don't refer me to the Brompton, refer me to Papworth. They do the blood clot operation and they do transplants. They do the whole lot! I've been reading a lot of good reports about them and it's just as near to home and may be easier to get to, as it's in the opposite direction to London for all the traffic.'

Rob agrees. Papworth is the only hospital of the four which he has heard of, and he doesn't relish the prospect of frequent trips into London with me so ill, as it had been a trial bringing me back home from Harley Street after my angiogram.

My mind is in overdrive trying to grasp at all options, however wild they seem. It's stretching out, reaching into my distant future, trying to protect itself. I need to have a future. I'm pretty certain I'm going to be sorted out with some tablets, but perhaps I may need these options in years to come.

I have hope inside me. Hope. A simple powerful word. Hope. It gives a future to live in. I know my life is going to be different than before, but I hang onto hope that once I'm on the correct medication I will find some normality and stability once more. That's why I choose Papworth.

I still hope I'll get back to school. I'd given my notice in when I found out I was dealing with both heart and lung disease and knew I was deteriorating. I cling onto hope though, that I might be able to go back to work at least for one day a week in the near future.

My consultant agrees to refer me to Papworth urgently. In the meantime he prescribes me the drug Sildenafil to start targeted treatment for my PH, but when I take the prescription to the hospital pharmacy, they're unable to make it up, as it's out of their jurisdiction and can only be prescribed by one of the PH specialist centres. I stand there speechless and frustrated in the crowded hospital pharmacy, relieved I have brought a close friend with me to ask the questions.

Again, I can't make any progress. Again, my underlying condition isn't being treated. I'm realising how rare and complicated PH is – it's so specialised that even an experienced cardiologist isn't allowed to treat me. I want to scream, 'Please can someone bloody well help me!'

That said, I feel fortunate that my cardiologist knew enough about PH to have made an initial diagnosis and start me on treatment for heart failure, racing me through the relevant tests to provide a picture of the severity of my condition.

My research has revealed that there are many stories of PH patients taking years to become diagnosed or even being misdiagnosed. One of the main problems with PH is that it often goes undetected until it has done some serious damage, causing the patient to experience symptoms.

I realise that this is what must have happened to me, and that the PH must have been the trigger for my fainting symptoms. At Harefield, all those years ago, my condition just hadn't progressed sufficiently to reveal any damage. There wasn't ever anything to indicate a lung problem either, as I had no signs of breathlessness, which is a key symptom of PH.

***

I find myself despairing when I'm on my own in the house and everyone else is at work, my mind dwelling on my situation. I cry and feel hopeless for the future, I feel desperate I'm still not having my PH treated. I'm totally beside myself and don't know how much longer I can continue both mentally and physically. At times I stare blindly into space in complete shock and cry out loud from deep within me. I find myself with my face in my hands. This is happening often. There are no quick answers. I am in a silent hell with a silent killer, and there seems no immediate help forthcoming.

Other than Rob and the girls, no one really understands, and with seemingly no one to turn to, I decide to log on to the PHAUK help forum. Unfamiliar with social media, it all feels very alien reading about complete strangers on the internet, but I need to see and understand what others are going through.

I begin to read some of the threads. Many are dealing with the same issues and experiencing similar symptoms. Many, like me, had thought they were just unfit, but they weren't, it had been PH.

Symptoms can range from breathlessness, dizziness and fainting to swollen legs and chest pain. Over the years I had only been fainting, with the other symptoms being brought on with heart failure. I recall telling my cardiologist that I felt unfit. I will always remember his reply, 'You're not unfit, you're in quite serious heart failure and it's only because you are quite fit, that you have been able to get through your own front door.'

I realise what an adverse impact this is all having on my family. Sarah receives her A level results and has done really well in the circumstances, but she's had a lower grade than expected for one exam, which means she hasn't been offered a place at either of her chosen universities. We have a stressful day or two sorting out a clearing place for her at the University of Kent in Canterbury. Being ill doesn't shield you from all the other everyday problems that crop up.

We travel to Canterbury for a hastily arranged open day for clearing students. I'm not feeling too good, but I'm determined to go. While I can still be a mum, it feels important to do things that mums do. While we're listening to one of the speakers, Rob misunderstands some information about the university admission points and suddenly thinks Sarah hasn't enough points to secure the offered place. The stress of the last few weeks takes its toll on him and he passes out in the middle of the lecture theatre; I'm stressed too and can feel a faint welling up. Rose and Sarah step in as we cause a commotion in the lecture theatre. Rob manages to recover and we muddle on through the rest of the day.

It adds to the weight of what we're carrying, and I have crushing and desperate thoughts about what I'm doing to my family. It feels like we are being blown apart and I am the one responsible, yet can't do anything to stop it. I have to try and contain myself from being weighed down with guilt about what is happening to us.

Sarah decides to defer her university place at Kent for a year, mainly because of problems with accommodation, but I know she's worried about me too. I don't want to be affecting her life like this, but secretly and selfishly, I like the fact that she will be with me and I won't have to cope with partial empty nest syndrome on top of everything else.

Instead, Sarah steps up her shift work at Waitrose locally to full time – she had originally started there whilst at school to earn some pocket money – so she often comes and goes at various times in the day. Rose is in the sixth form and always home reasonably early, so now I'm hardly on my own and this helps get me through the day without thinking too hard about everything and getting into a state. Rob's still managing to work full time, but is becoming increasingly edgy about leaving me to go abroad.

The weeks pass while I wait for my Papworth appointment to come through. PH is having a major impact on my daily life, and if I try and do basic simple things it can take me ages. I'm beginning to faint more often doing the slightest things such as bending down to put a radiator on or getting out of bed during the night. I'm breathless in the shower and getting dressed – my breathing feels impaired if I'm walking or going upstairs.

I have to walk very slowly all the time and feel I look a bit foolish, but otherwise I might faint. It will start with feeling a little breathless and then a swell of sickness and dizziness rises up through my body before I pass out. There's little warning, but I continue to read the signs as well as I can and adapt my activities to avoid fainting more than ever. I'm also becoming anxious and terrified about anything happening to me when I'm out on my own.

I try to go out shopping and walk around the shops, but it's a struggle and I can't help thinking negatively. 'Is there much point in buying new clothes if I'm going to die? Is it a waste of money?' I stop and pretend to look in shop windows or sit on benches as I catch my breath. I carefully fold and put my summer clothes away, as it's autumn and turning cooler. Swimsuits, beach clothes – items I've not even worn this summer. I think more increasingly black thoughts. 'What if I can never travel abroad again? Will I wear some of these things again? Will I even be here to lift them out again when it's spring?' Agonising thoughts. There are many. Often, I'm just doing ordinary things when I succumb, but my situation feels extraordinary and helpless living with such a rare disease.

I shuffle up the street on a breezy wet day, coming back from the doctors' surgery, my head bent down to protect me from the rain. It's no more than a hundred yards. I'm halfway home, but have to sit at the bus stop to catch my breath back before I warily continue, staying near to the walls of people's gardens so I have something to hang on to. I use a walking stick. I've bought this to have something to lean on when I have to stop and rest to catch my breath. It also signals to people there's something wrong with me, as otherwise I look like a perfectly healthy woman who's just dawdling about and getting in people's way. I catch a glimpse of Sarah as she drives past on her way back from work.

Once again, like the night of the Indian restaurant, it feels like I'm climbing a mountain just walking this short distance. I pass one house, then another, then reaching my next-door neighbour's house, I think, 'Only a few yards left to go, will I make it?' In that moment Sarah comes rushing down towards me and then gasps in surprise. 'Oh Mum, it's you, I thought it was an old lady, I'd seen her struggling and I was rushing to help!'

That's how bad it has become. My own daughter hasn't even recognised me. She's mistaken me for an old woman.

***

I've been on my medication for a while. Although I'm only being prescribed four drugs, it feels alien to me as I've never been on medication before, and I don't want to be taking tablets or even admit that I'm ill. As each drug and tablet has been added gradually, I seem to be running out of one or the other every week. I'm making endless trips to the doctors to order prescriptions and back again to pick them up, and then more endless trips to the pharmacist to collect them. Walking back and forth and back again is becoming a burden. On top of my illness, managing all this new medication is an unnecessary worry.

One of my drugs is Warfarin, which involves having frequent blood tests to achieve a correct level of INR. INR is a laboratory measurement of how long it takes blood to form a clot. It provides a standardised method (International Normalised Ratio) of reporting the effects of an oral anticoagulant, such as Warfarin, on blood clotting. When you are prescribed Warfarin, if the dose is too high, then your blood can become too thin which can cause internal bleeding and be very dangerous; if your blood becomes too thick, then it may exacerbate the medical condition you have and be equally dangerous. It's taking a while to get my dose correct, so I'm up and down to the local hospital's pathology department a few times a week. There's building work going on and parking is chaotic. Together with long waiting times for the blood tests, it all adds to the stress when I feel so unwell.

Fortunately, my INR stabilises eventually and I'm able to attend the weekly Warfarin clinic at my GP's surgery instead. However, my first visit to the nurse isn't straightforward, as I don't have all the usual paperwork like most other patients. Apparently I'm missing a yellow record book and emergency card. It's becoming a bit of a circus and I can feel myself becoming more worked up as calls are made to my consultant. There seems to be one problem and complication after another, each one exacerbating my stress and desperation. The Warfarin nurse is fantastic though, and manages to sort out the paperwork. I feel like I'm an anomaly in my local medical vicinity.

Although much is beyond my control, there are some things I can still organise. I discover I can pay for my numerous medications by buying a pre-payment prescription form. This way I pay one annual fee, which is significantly cheaper than paying for each individual prescription, as I've been doing. I arrange with the pharmacy that my monthly-prescribed drugs will all be ready at the same time each month.

Although I don't like all this medication, I'm feeling a little better for being in control of the drugs and more accepting that they're needed. It feels like an achievement amidst my chaos and frustration.

***

I wait anxiously and desperately for the appointment letter from Papworth – day in, day out – the wait seems to stretch on and on. Day in, day out. My mind playing games. I'm regularly sitting in despair at where this is all leading to – where's it going to end? The answer to that is intolerable and I have to find ways to stop my mind going to these dark places. Time's moving on and I'm still not receiving the specialist treatment I need. My despair and frustration are mounting up.

I sit there agonising – shall I press the button or not? It goes against everything I've ever taught my children and the children in school. Talking to strangers on the internet. In some ways I'm shocked at myself for even thinking of it. I'm desperate. I press the send button.

'I'm newly diagnosed and I'm waiting for an appointment at Papworth. I don't know what to expect. What usually happens?'

There, I've done it. I've posted on the PHAUK forum. To my relief, I'm welcomed with open arms and given so much reassurance. Other PH patients start telling me that things will get better, and that I will be in safe hands once I arrive at Papworth. Many of them are quite stable and living a good quality of life. Some are even still working and travelling abroad. I begin to feel more encouraged by the stories and comments of these new people. Complete strangers, but already becoming friends. It feels liberating to speak with others who are going through similar issues and such a relief and comfort to speak with people who understand.

I see that I won't get through all this if I allow myself to think negatively. But I know what the reality might be, and have long stopped denying that this is a serious matter. I'm making tiny steps in beginning to come to terms with my tornado. There are still many things that feel completely out of my control and I'm not used to this. I don't like the not knowing. I don't like the waiting. I don't like this drifting sense and not knowing what's coming at me next. Everything feels so uncertain.

At this point only Rob and the girls are truly understanding of what's happening to our family. I know I look really well on the outside and I try to carry on as normally as possible. As a consequence of this and the fact that PH is so rare, neither my friends nor wider family know the real state I'm in physically, mentally and emotionally. It's so tough looking normal and well on the outside, but in the very core of your being you feel like a ticking time bomb waiting to explode.

I wish I would explode at times, then people would get it. Pulmonary Hypertension is almost a complete unknown, leading people to confuse the hypertension tag with high blood pressure. Rob says he has lost count of the number of times he's heard people reply, when he's tried to explain my condition, 'Oh, yeah my dad has high blood pressure too – he just pops a few tablets and he's fine.' Ironically, Rob knows exactly what high blood pressure is, he's on tablets of his own – hardly any surprise with what I'm putting him through.

Friends try to be understanding and I want to say more to them at times, but equally I want to carry on as normal. If I'm seeing friends, I desperately don't want to become the person who constantly drains people's energy with all their ailments and problems. I don't want to end up dying and them remembering me for being a constant moaner.

I don't know how long my situation will go on for – days, weeks, months, years? I'm clueless and no one can answer that one for me. I just want to enjoy my friends' company while I can and not weigh anyone else down too much. When people don't properly understand my predicament, I reason this is probably due in no small part to my own attitude, and the way I have chosen to handle my illness.

Having PH is very isolating.

I make up my mind it's better to take one simple step at a time and go from there. It's senseless to let my mind wander off to the worst places. I keep visualising the tornado, with me clinging onto it. I'm determined I won't let it sweep me away and that I will climb out of it. I'm subconsciously beginning to fight, the knowledge being born inside me that this is going to be my toughest battle.

I'm a common sense person, so I have reasoned that I might die, but I'm becoming determined to confront my future positively and with all the strength that I possess. But nothing can be rushed. I have to move forward in small steps. It's very much a case of getting through one day at a time. It's a case of valuing what I have; it's a case of living in the moment and not thinking too far ahead, because no one can predict what may or may not happen to me.

By popping on the PHAUK forum regularly I begin to see that hope and positivity are the qualities which will help pull me through, and I can already appreciate that reading about other patients and their own stories seems to be helping me feel much less isolated. I start to believe that I'm not on my own so much anymore as I discover, in the most unlikely place – the internet – a small band of wonderful, encouraging and inspirational people who I genuinely begin to see as true friends.

The phone rings. 'Hello, it's Papworth, can I offer you some dates so we can admit you and assess your condition?' The release from waiting has eventually arrived. It's been the longest few weeks. I'm to be admitted for three days of tests, so they can give me a proper and formal diagnosis and hopefully start the appropriate treatment. At long last help is getting nearer. I'm flooded with enormous relief.

Confirmation arrives in the post as promised, and I ready myself for my first overnight stay in hospital since Rose was born. I'm a bit unnerved about staying in hospital and having more tests, but at the same time I can't wait.

I'm pinning all my future hopes and dreams on a hospital I've never even been to and where I don't know a soul. Papworth Hospital is all I have left to cling onto. It will be better when I get there – won't it? It will be the start of a new journey – won't it? My hopes all rest on Papworth.

The new beginning I'd hoped for in spring has long faded; it's somewhere far away in oblivion. I'm yearning to move on and come out of all of this – to be mended.

Six

Safe Haven

(Autumn 2010)

We reach October and the air is autumnal and crisp. I'm in a wheelchair, which has been strapped down in the back of an ambulance. I'm clutching on to a black bag that carries all my notes and then we're off – off for the first test of the day.

I think yet again how bizarre my life is becoming. What on earth has it come to? Here I am being driven around a hospital site that I've never set eyes on before, strapped in the back of my very own personal ambulance, with my own personal driver and feeling totally unfamiliar with my surroundings. Disorientated, bewildered and bemused all at once.

I should be standing in front of my class this Monday morning and teaching my little year ones, doing all the things that are familiar to me, but instead here I am in this strange and unacquainted place. 'Where the hell is he taking me? What on earth is happening to me?'

***

I'd arrived at Papworth hospital. It was the fourth hospital I'd visited in just short of four months, each one with its own identity and peculiarities, each one new to me, me new to them and, at each one, my story so far being recounted over and over again.

I was so relieved this day had come. I'd believed my luck was going to turn but we'd been delayed by a bad accident near Papworth Everard – the roads being shut. It felt like the world was against us. I'd worried that my tests would be cancelled and I'd have to go through all the waiting again. I began to despair, but I needn't have worried, as even though we arrived late, I was immediately given a thin pink folder containing my medical notes at the reception desk and directed to Duchess ward.

Duchess ward – the Pulmonary Vascular Disease Unit – I'd landed in the right place at last. I'd only managed a quick glimpse when a porter whisked me off in a wheelchair to an ambulance to go for an echocardiogram – my first test. I hadn't even had time to take off my coat or go through the usual admission procedures.

There was a sense of no nonsense, speed and efficiency with a we-will-get-to-the-bottom-of-things and sort-you-out type of emphasis; a sense that everyone knew what they were doing and they'd do their best for you; a sense that I was in the hands of the experts. I had needed and longed for this so much. At last!

Finally I was going to find out what's what; what I would have to face; what I would have to deal with. It was going to be a relief in itself whether the outcome was good or bad. The tests were scheduled throughout each day of my stay.

I was familiar with the tests: an echocardiogram: a right heart catheter (very similar to the angiogram I'd had previously, but this time studying the right side of my heart); lung function tests; a walk test; an ECG; a three-day heart monitor and a lung perfusion scan (similar to a CT scan). All these tests together would give the specialist PH team the information they needed to diagnose what type of PH I had, and its severity, which would then enable them to prescribe the best treatment.

***

My senses are heightened. It all seems vivid. I'm on a small ward of six people. Everyone looks far more ill than me, and once again I feel something of a fraud. Although I know I'm ill, I'm able to function reasonably well at times and I'm adapting my routine around the fainting, breathlessness and fatigue. Being in hospital, there's plenty of rest time and no stairs to contend with, so I feel better than usual. I sense I'm amongst others who seem to be contending with much more than I am.

'Do you need a commode in the night?' asks a nurse, who is concerned about my fainting.

I'm horrified at the thought and refuse point blank. There is absolutely no way I'm going to use a commode. 'Good grief, what is she thinking!'

I'm not in denial. I know and accept I'm ill, but when I glance at the other PH patients around me, I believe I look very well in comparison. Some patients appear to be very poorly and struggling. It makes me believe I will obtain my diagnosis, be given tablets and then I'll be able to carry on with my life.

It's Tuesday, time for my right heart catheter. While waiting for this procedure, I have my first encounter with a transplant patient: a lovely gentleman who received his heart transplant many years ago. He's waiting for a right heart catheter too, as part of his follow up care. We chat about our respective health history but I find it hard to imagine what he's been through.

By the afternoon, the team has assimilated sufficient results to diagnose me properly and discuss treatments. I've already gathered considerable information about PH: being armed with this gives me some control in a strange way. It doesn't stop things happening, but it does help me to understand things better and make more sense of the tidal wave of emotions, which are being whipped up by my tornado.

I prepare myself for the worst, that it may be really severe and I may need intravenous medication. I also hope and pray the news will be better and I may be given tablets, such as Sildenafil, which had been mentioned by my previous consultant.

Rob and I are given the news my diagnosis is idiopathic Pulmonary Arterial Hypertension and is assessed as WHO class four, which is very severe.

I will need a treatment called Iloprost, either inhaled or administered intravenously. My PAH is being classed as severe because of my fainting. Although I'd hoped for just tablets, deep down I'm not completely shocked, as I know the pressures in my heart and lungs are severe. I'm relieved I've undertaken research beforehand as it helps to take the edge of our devastation.

The diagnosis makes it all incredibly real, yet it brings with it such relief. Of course I'm not really relieved, but at least I have a diagnosis and the proper medical support now. This is a new start for me, another turning point. A point where I know what I'm up against, know I must try hard to fight and not let this illness take me over.

A PH specialist nurse comes to explain everything to me in more detail. 'I'd recommend you try the inhaler first, as once you go onto the intravenous drug, there's usually no turning back and being able to come off it.' I decide to follow this advice. I know they are the experts, have seen all this before. It makes perfect sense to me to try the inhaler first.

Wednesday arrives and it's decided I need to stay in hospital for a few days longer, so I can learn how to make up the medication for the inhaler and the staff can monitor my progress. I learn the ropes quite quickly: there are little phials of Iloprost and buffer that have to be transferred via a needle into a nebuliser. The nebuliser is called an I-neb, which is specially designed for administering the drug. There's a bit of a process for cleaning it with filtered water, which adds to the preparation time.

The major drawback, which I dislike the most, is that the drug only stays in your body for a few hours and then wears off. The process therefore needs to start early in the morning from about six o'clock and repeated seven times each day (every three hours to inhale and then ten or fifteen minutes for preparation and cleaning). Rob says it reminds him of years ago when we had to sterilise the girls' feeding bottles, as the cleaning process is similar.

During the rest of my stay I become friendly with another patient who has a Hickman line, so she is having her PH drugs administered intravenously. We have loads of time to chat, and our conversations help me understand what my next stage of treatment might be, should it come to that.

A social worker who has a good knowledge of PH comes to visit me on the ward, and gives advice about claiming my private pensions, as they both offer ill health benefits, given that it's unlikely I'll be able to work again. A pharmacist also visits to go through my medication and possible side effects in more detail.

Later a palliative care nurse arrives when Rob is with me. She explains that she is like a Macmillan nurse, and offers counselling. It begins to dawn on us both that this level of specialised care and support is unlikely to be given unless you are seriously poorly. We're very grateful it's being offered. At the same time we're still numb from the diagnosis, so don't feel we are yet ready to bare our souls to a stranger, but suspect this time will come.

I think back to when we joked about getting out alive after the priest came to bless me in Harefield. Suddenly it doesn't seem funny anymore. Ironically the Papworth priest comes to visit me shortly afterwards. I ask him for a blessing. How things have changed.

After five days I'm discharged. I'm given large box-loads of equipment and drugs to take home. I can only thank goodness that I'm going home so soon; quite a few other patients are in for a long stay. I feel I'm the lucky one. I have some answers to my worries, and at long last I'm receiving specialised treatment, not necessarily the treatment I'd hoped for, but I'm relieved to be having the right treatment alongside my more general drugs.

I'm pleased I'd managed to organise these general drugs earlier, as I now have to cope with a whole new medication regime. One of the positives with my new drug, Iloprost, is that it will be arranged centrally by Papworth and delivered via a health care company, so at least I don't have to worry about having to go through my GP.

***

Once home, I'm determined that this drug is going to work for me. I want to feel safe again and hope my symptoms of fainting and extreme tiredness will be alleviated. I know I need to make some big adjustments to my life, like accepting I won't teach again, being more cautious than ever when going upstairs, and making sure I build in rest periods so I don't get too exhausted. The more I think about it, I will have to make so many adjustments to my whole daily routine, and start to rely on Rob and the girls more heavily for their help and support. I'll also have to make considerable time to administer my new drug and care for the equipment.

Somehow over days, a routine does emerge. Rob helps me by making up my Iloprost for the early morning and evening doses, and the girls take on more of the daily chores around the house. Although it's good to be balancing our family life around my illness, I'm not really feeling any better. I'm still fatigued. In addition, it's onerous, day in, day out, having to use this nebuliser every few hours except when I'm asleep. It's tiring me out starting with it at six in the morning until eleven at night. I realise I have to adjust even more and build in daytime sleeps to cope. However hard I try, and want this medication to work for me, there seems very little benefit from this strict regime of inhaling Iloprost every few hours.

Although the illness and medication routine are both seriously impacting on my life, I don't want this to stop me getting out and about, but it's not easy as there's only a couple of hours in between doses. I can't prepare it in advance as the Iloprost only has a short shelf life and, once it's prepared into liquid form in the nebuliser it can spill out when carried. In addition it has to be prepared in clean conditions.

I am determined to overcome these problems. I buy a tiny ceramic tray and a makeup bag in which to carry all the equipment, including hand wipes and gel. So if we have the car with us, I can go back to it and clean my hands, sterilise my little tray, make up the drug and have it in the car. This works well and enables me to stay out for longer. Although it's not without its difficulties, it gives me a sense that I'm feeling my way positively.

***

I'm waking up – frighteningly my arms and legs are thrashing around out of my control, as if I'm having a seizure. There's a loud ringing in my ears – a ringing that sounds like a large wave crashing and receding against the shingle on a beach. An angry and rough sea that's inside my head. It's the middle of the night. I'm hazily remembering getting up to go to the loo. I'm on the bedroom floor.

Rob has a bad cough and is sleeping downstairs so he won't disturb me. I call out, but he's already here. He's heard the dreaded loud thud. He doesn't know what to do for the best – phone for an ambulance, phone Papworth or wait until I come round properly. He opts to phone Papworth and once I'm properly conscious, he takes me to A&E.

We can't continue like this. It's becoming terrifying for us both, and I have to grudgingly admit defeat that my new drug isn't making any difference. I've pinned so much hope on this. I'm deflated, confused and frightened. What does the future hold for me? Do I even have a future?

We check in at the reception at A&E and explain my circumstances. The nurse breezily informs us that her uncle has hypertension too. 'Here we go again,' Rob mutters a little too audibly.

I'm ushered fairly promptly to see a doctor – a young trainee – who seems efficient and arranges an ECG test and notes down my history. I explain about the PAH and show him a twenty-four hour helpline and emergency card given to me by Papworth. Although it's early Sunday morning, he assures me that they will try and phone Papworth. I feel quite encouraged that I'm going to be helped.

A bed is allocated to me and I'm supplied with a trolley to make up my medication as it's time for the nebuliser regime to start. I'm surprised to hear a patient who is being discharged shouting abuse at the staff about how badly he's been treated, and think him rude.

I'm moved to yet another bed and then a consultant arrives. He goes through my medical history. He's rather dismissive and doesn't appear prepared to phone Papworth believing he knows better, 'I think it's the diuretics that have caused this, you need to come off them and I'll write to your GP.'

I'm insistent that I won't be changing any medication until it's been checked with Papworth. I know the diuretics are key to my

PAH treatment. Eventually he concedes and then sensibly suggests I provide a blood test to ensure I haven't had a heart attack.

In the meantime Rob phones Papworth to keep them in the loop, and they confirm there should be no changes made to my medication. This sequence of events is a stark reminder to me that my condition is so rare it requires specialist treatment and knowledge – even experienced medical professionals don't appear to understand it properly.

Rob leaves me to feed the car park meter. While he's gone, I'm told my bed is needed and I have to wait in the public waiting room by the ward. The room is far from clean after a busy Saturday night. When Rob arrives back he's fuming there's no proper place for me to rest after being so unwell, or anywhere clean to make up my medication. Although he complains, we are forced to go and make up my medication in the car and I have it in there instead.

Twelve hours after I'm admitted, we finally receive the all-clear on the blood test results and I'm discharged. I'm exhausted, having had to sit in this uncomfortable room feeling unwell for so long. As I walk out I've no sense of relief, being so poorly and shattered. I slow myself down. As much as I want to get out of here, I think I might black out again. I don't want this to happen – not here.

**

It's Monday morning and we're still anxious my medication isn't having the desired effect, so Rob phones Papworth to speak to the specialist nurse about the weekend's events.

She pre-empts him. 'We're already discussing Kathryn's case and we'll phone you back shortly,' but she still allows Rob to explain in detail what has happened. Before we know it, the phone rings and Rob is advised there's an ambulance on its way.

Rob insists he can drive me there instead, but the nurse is more insistent that an ambulance will come. We gather my things together while we wait. Guilt washes over me that they're making such a fuss, but at the same time I'm full of relief I'm going to receive the proper help I need.

We speed along in the ambulance as Rob follows in our car. I notice through the frame of my window differing scenes covered with frost – moving pictures as we race by. They look enchanting – the trees glisten in the early December light. I notice the life-saving medical equipment in the ambulance, the fact I have two people with me, one driving, one accompanying me just in case. Inside I'm in turmoil – a mixture of guilt mingled with angst and unease. The beautiful glittering frost. The clinical oxygen tanks, masks, first aid boxes. Inside. Outside. Contrasting images.

I'm back at my safe haven. It looks different in the white of the ice – peaceful compared to the chaos of the day before. I'm given my own room. I notice the cleanliness, spaciousness and how spotless it looks – again I can't help but compare this to the experiences of yesterday. Staff pop in and greet me, familiar faces offering some surety that I will be looked after properly. I know physically I'm in a bad place, but medically I'm in the right one.

There's a sense of calm, but I'm scared and fearful for the future. Really scared. Where is all this leading to? The future? Do I have one? My mind turns to Christmas – one of my favourite times – will I make it to Christmas? It's nearing now, but I sense for me it's far away. I contemplate the white frost and the glitter of the trees we drove past earlier and mentally will for Christmas to pull me towards it. I have to see Christmas.

Seven

The Premier League

(December 2010)

'Help me! Help me!' I'm crying. Everyone comes running, the ringing in my ears is humming, vibrating. I'm slumped in an unfamiliar chair. I try and rouse myself, hesitantly. 'Where am I?' My mind searches and reaches for an answer. Slowly, it comes back – Papworth – making my last medication up for the night. I'm in Papworth. It's happened again.

I'm aware I'm causing a disturbance. It's late at night and everything is otherwise calm. The nurses help me to safety. A doctor arrives. Swiftly and cautiously he checks me over. I'm moved to my bed and hooked up to a heart monitor immediately. I'm not allowed out of bed, not even for the loo. I have my own bathroom, but I'm advised I must use a commode – the same commode I was quick to dismiss only a few weeks ago. I suddenly don't care anymore, it feels safer being on the monitor and knowing someone will be watching me carefully.

The doctors come early in the morning and prepare me with a cannula. There's not much talking, not too much discussion. When the consultant had come round earlier, she'd explained they needed to start me on a permanent intravenous drug called Flolan right away.

I listened to her, resigned. 'I haven't any choice, have I?'

'Not really,' she replied quietly, but I could tell she meant 'No'.

An echocardiogram is undertaken at my bedside, as it isn't safe

65

to move me. It's explained my heart is struggling, and there are two pericardial effusions showing on the scan (an abnormal amount of fluid between the heart and the sac around it). I'm told they are worried about my heart. It's lunchtime when they come to do the deed. They use the cannula to fix a line in my arm; the line is attached to a syringe, which is fixed on a pump. The pump has an adjustable flow rate and it delivers the drug through the line, into my arm and then through to my heart and lungs.

The drug Flolan is a prostaglandin drug, which causes the blood vessels to dilate. This allows the blood to flow more freely, especially in my heart and lungs where my blood vessels are too constricted and blocked. This intravenous medication is the only choice left to help me. I don't have the luxury of weighing up the pros and cons about whether I want it or not. My life is in immediate danger – there isn't time for my mind to consider the implications of being permanently hooked up to a drug for the rest of my life.

As I lie here I suddenly appreciate why an ambulance was sent for me and what danger I've been in. I'm shocked that I blacked out again last night. I had felt safe back in Papworth. I wasn't even exerting myself. It's hitting me hard, how poorly I am. I don't feel like I can keep up with all that's happening to me. So much is occurring to me physically, but mentally my mind lags constantly behind every event, unable to play catch up.

The side effects of the drug are explained: nausea, headache, flushing skin and jaw pain. I'm asked if I'd like some anti-sickness to help me.

'How will I know if I need that or not, when I don't know whether I'm even going to have side effects?' I don't like any of this medication. Paracetamol is all I've ever had in my life until recently. I'm being tried on all sorts of unusual concoctions that I'd never heard of until these last few months. I decide rather flippantly to wait and see if it affects me. There's no point having more drugs than I need going round and round inside me.

I'm rather self-conscious that I'm making a grand entrance. I'm being wheeled onto Duchess ward in my bed with all the machinery attached. Everyone gives me a smile as we come through. Some patients have visitors and there are children. Rob arrives – he's been searching for me, as the side room I've been in is now empty. He's shocked to find I'm already on the intravenous medication, and when he hears about the events of the night before. I haven't been able to contact him because of poor phone signals.

Within minutes I feel nausea wafting over me and I'm badly sick. That's how my body welcomes my new drug. If I'd any doubts beforehand over being ill, I'm rudely awake now to the fact that I'm actually very seriously ill. I can't pretend to myself or put an act on anymore. My illness isn't stable. My life is actually in danger. My heart is struggling and my lungs are diseased.

The sickness doesn't ease up. I'm embarrassed, because the ward is busy and everyone can hear me. The nurses and Rob are running around finding bowls and cleaning me. It isn't pleasant being sick, but at least at home you can do it in private.

The sickness becomes worse and worse. Eventually a ward sister comes dashing to help and, without discussion, places another cannula in the back of my hand to administer some intravenous anti-sickness drugs. Tablets are not considered an option, as it's hard for me to keep anything down. I can't eat anything. I struggle to even have a sip of water and take my routine tablets.

The night is restless. My thoughts are distracted, and my body is uncomfortable attached to machines. The morning arrives, but with it no change. I feel sick, but there's nothing to be sick on anymore. The syringe holding my drug needs changing every twelve hours. After twelve hours the strength of the drug deteriorates and loses its potency. When it's time for the drug changeover, I'm told the drug needs to be increased on each change until I'm on a suitable dose to control my symptoms.

The team is working hard to achieve the correct dose for my weight and size. I'm asked if I need anti-sickness again, and this time without hesitation I nod wearily. I'm feeling truly rotten. I wish I hadn't been so naïve yesterday, instead of having to learn the hard way.

I try to eat and drink, but as the drug is increased, so my sickness increases. It becomes a ritual. Every day an increase, every day

I'm more sick and nauseous. It feels like torture. I know they will come to increase it; they will ask if I'm ready and I will have to brace myself again and stay strong.

I have to find determination. I don't think anyone else can see it, but it's there in no uncertain terms, somewhere deep inside me. I'm not sure if the doctors think I'm being precious or acting as though I'm some drama queen. But I make up my mind once and for all I won't be beaten by this. I will survive and do whatever it takes. A bit of sick for a few days will be well worth it in the long run.

Trying to stay strong, I focus on reaching the correct dose – whatever it takes – so I can be better. The team encourages and reassures me – egging me on. I can see even the nurses feel bad when it's time for an increase. I try to laugh and joke about it as they come each day. A sense of humour can take you a long way in difficult situations.

The arduous days and nights continue. I'm hooked up to a drip, as I become dehydrated. I keep trying to drink at least, but can only manage a few sips. Rob brings in an assortment of fizzy drinks and squashes to try, but I struggle with each and every one.

Water. It's a vicious circle – I can't even face a sip of water, but it's imperative I take my oral medication, so I'm forced to drink it. The more I'm forced to drink, the more I feel sick, and the more I hate the thought of it. I develop a complete aversion to drinking water.

The green trays. They bring them before every meal with the cutlery, napkins and cups. I can't even cope with them – let alone food. They smell of food. I despair at the green trays. Three times a day they bring the green trays. The young girl with the food trolley approaches. 'No, don't even come near me!' She smiles and it becomes a standing joke between us.

Headaches. Severe ones like migraines. My skin flushes red over and over. The nurses tell me it's a sign that the drug is working. This feels encouraging. I'm surprised I feel delighted I'm flashing like a belisha beacon. I am going to beat this.

Death by Flolan – that's what I call the dreaded increases now. If I don't laugh and joke about it, I will cry and I cannot do that. I cannot allow myself to start that. I don't think I'll ever stop if I do. I know if anything is ever going to give my health some stability, then it will be the Flolan. I've developed a love/hate relationship with it. I'm unlucky, as I learn from other patients that they haven't reacted so adversely to this drug.

I'm aware it's most likely I will always have to depend on the support of this intravenous medication. I know now I will be on Flolan for the rest of my life if I want to survive, and it's quite difficult to take this fact in. The drug is flowing through my arm, but once everything has settled down, the plan is to have a Hickman line – a type of catheter – implanted in my chest. This is to enable the drug to be infused directly into my heart and lungs.

I'm never going to be physically the same again. I'll have this line permanently in my chest, and carry the syringe and pump which administer the Flolan with me all day and night. The line needs to be cared for and managed, together with making up the drug, which will become part of my daily life. On the positive side of things, though, at least I'm going to still have a daily life.

Days come and go, and I start to improve slightly like everyone has been telling me. The headaches still pound, but the sickness and nausea recedes. I feel encouraged. I'm beginning to turn a corner. Rob is putting a good front on, but even though he's been given time off work, I can see he's strained. It has sunk in with him as well just how poorly I am.

He comes in every day and helps wash and change me. I let him, rather than ask the nurses, because I can see he feels helpless and wants to appear as though he's doing something for me. The weather is against him. There is heavy fog, frost, snow and ice, but he appears every day relentlessly. It's a freezing cold December. One of the worst we can remember for a while. The girls are deeply upset, and come as often as they can in between work and school. I'm lucky in this respect, as most other ladies on the ward don't have visitors at all, given they live too far away. Rob has begun to visit everyone and get goodies from the hospital shop and other things they need. He soon gets used to the patient who tries to short-change him every time!

***

The forecast is for heavy snow. I persuade Rob to leave early and go home quickly when it begins to fall, as I want him to arrive home safely. I watch the snow float down and cover everything it touches. It causes its usual wintertime chaos outside, but for me in here it's surprisingly calm. The ward is quiet and there's a soft glow reflecting from the whiteness outside. I'm remote from the goings on in the world. I'm snuggled up, cosy and warm in my bed with no need to go anywhere. A brief respite, a moment of peace.

I begin to manage some food and drink, just very plain food and soft drinks. I still can't manage water. I have searing pain in my jaws when I eat or drink. Luckily, it's only on the first sip or bite and then it's gone. It's a strange side effect of the Flolan. I remain bright red much of the time, but I'm feeling less nauseous and the headaches are subsiding. My body is beginning to accept the drug. The medical team has been right, it's taken a while but my body is settling down at last – another turning point.

Syringes, glass bottles, needles, buffer, freeze dried Flolan, orange-coloured plastic lines, line connectors, dressings, saline solution. My new toys. I have to play with them, so I can learn practically how to use them and make up my new drug and look after the line. Day in, day out. Pushing syringes up and down, moving different solutions from one bottle to another, then another, then into a syringe. I smile at the thought of getting into a stew during the summer about organising and taking oral tablets. I smile at myself for moaning about making up the Iloprost and having to use an inhaler. This is a whole new league of drug taking. The Premier League.

A whole new way of life – a new life on a pump is emerging. I've made a friend – my Flolan Friend – to help me though. There aren't too many patients on this type of treatment, but unusually there are two of us on the ward going through the same procedure simultaneously. This helps enormously.

The nurse gives us a dummy of a chest and head, nicknamed Chester, on which to practice, and we have a great laugh with him.

We have fun practising changing a dressing, which goes over the entrance to the site of his Hickman line. It's good to laugh and share this with someone else who really understands.

Later, my own Hickman line is inserted in my chest, although I still have the drug being administered into my arm. It's a fairly straightforward procedure, and I have a local anaesthetic. It's a long thin silicone tube, which is guided through a large vein in my chest using ultrasound. It takes a while before I can bring myself to look down at where the line is now protruding from my chest. It looks and feels totally alien.

Despite this I'm encouraged, as I'm getting nearer to going home and Christmas is approaching. I feel very emotional at the twin thoughts of going home and my permanent mechanical device. It's going to help keep me alive and I'm trying to treat it as ordinary, but it's anything but.

I'm resting quietly afterwards when I hear the sound of carol singers. Suddenly a group of children appear singing on the ward. They're primary aged – I think probably year five or six. I watch the other patients' faces light up in delight as they start to sing.

I lie propped up in my bed watching the children singing, but I'm watching it all differently from the others. I see the teacher's purposeful glare at the pupils who try to overstep the mark. I see myself doing the same with my own year five pupils. I've taken children to hospitals and nursing homes in the very recent past. It suddenly hits me hard what has happened. It's as though I'm watching everything I've lost and left behind. It's all staring back, confronting me. I haven't even had the chance to grieve for my old life, yet here it is. Being played out in front of me. In hospital.

It's the most poignant of moments, stark on the day of my new life with a 'line'. It cheers me up and saddens me in equal measures. I bite back my tears.

The Hickman line is connected up to my Flolan, and the cannula in my arm is removed. It sets off all the difficult side effects once more, as the drug is now flowing directly into the vessels of my heart and lungs before hitting my bloodstream and leaving an unpleasant metallic taste in my mouth.

***

Christmas Eve is fast approaching, and it's a frantic rush to go home in time if I'm well enough. Before I can be discharged, Rob and I have to be assessed whether we are competent enough to manage my new drug regime. As well as learning how to make up the drug, we are warned about the dangers that could occur. It's dangerous and life threatening if we don't fully know and understand what to do properly. We are reminded constantly that this is an intravenous drug and there can be no room for error.

The drug has to be made up and changed in strictly sterile conditions to avoid infection. We are shown the procedures to undertake this. Infection can rapidly lead to sepsis, which in turn can be fatal without immediate intervention. It is drummed into us to carefully to watch out for signs or symptoms of infection – high temperature, feeling more unwell than usual and/or any signs of discharge from the entry wound.

We have to ensure that there are no air bubbles in the equipment. They can cause the drug to stop flowing freely, which may cause a quick onset of dangerous symptoms returning, as well as being life-threatening if they reach the circulatory system. We are taught the importance of being precise with the drug doses – too much or too little can have severe implications either way. It is very daunting for both of us.

We both know what to do and can manage it successfully, but we both make a mess of doing it each time we are observed. Rob manages to pass the test after several attempts. I'm finding it harder though. I'm exhausted and fragile from the last few weeks – still recovering and finding it hard to concentrate for long.

Eventually on Christmas Eve morning, after the umpteenth go, I'm assessed once more and it's agreed I can go home. It's only been three weeks, but it's been both a life-saving and life-changing three weeks.

***

I gingerly climb out of the car and step into a winter wonderland. The remains of the early December snow lay hard and frozen to the ground. It's twilight and the front of the house is lit up with white lights ready for Christmas. The day's frost and icicles from the melting snow are sparkling among the trees and bushes, competing with the Christmas lights. Patches of snow are luminous in the dusk.

A holly wreath adorns the front door, as it always does at this time of year. Rob says, 'Stay still while I unlock the door'. Home. I look up at the house and see the warm glow of lights spilling from the windows. I can't wait to go inside. Rob makes me close my eyes and leads me through the front door and then through every room, one by one – each one trimmed up for Christmas. The Christmas tree with its array of multi-coloured and familiar baubles twinkles from its same corner in the dining room; the boughs of red berries hang festively from the ceiling beams like usual. Christmas ornaments and decorations are all around me, all of them – and where I always put them.

I've always loved decorating the house for Christmas. Rob and the girls have trimmed it painstakingly, just how they know I like it, to make my homecoming special. My homecoming. It's the best one I've ever had in my entire life.

It's taken eight months. I've been on a long detour and was even lost for a while and couldn't see my way forward, but here I now stand on Christmas Eve, my home transformed and illuminated. I'm transformed too. A changed person – a new me. I've found my new beginning at long last. My new future. It isn't the one I'd planned and expected, or hoped and dreamed for, but it's still a future. A new journey is about to start with a fresh new year around the corner, one that beckons with hope. Hope. Hope will accompany me from here.

It's Christmas Day tomorrow and it's magical. I've already had my Christmas wish.

I'm alive.

Eight

Harry

(Christmas 2010 – March 2011)

Christmas Day. Our family's favourite time. My love for Christmas has rubbed off on everyone. We all sit for dinner. Happy. Smiling. Together again. Tucking into our roast turkey dinner – in our pyjamas.

It's my first full day home and I've tried hard to make an effort. We've successfully managed the rigmarole of making up the medication, and we've opened our presents and phoned family. I'm very weak and tired, but decide I will bath, wash my hair and get dressed into something special.

The effort of climbing in and out of the bath and working around my new attachments, which I must not allow to become wet, is gruelling and takes ages. I have to rest in between getting dressed, drying my hair and putting on some makeup. I feel more human when I look in the mirror. I've attached the pump and syringe on a waistband underneath my clothes out of sight – I glance down and reckon the bulge isn't too obtrusive.

By the time I'm downstairs, however, I find that I'm totally drained and exhausted. Fatigue washes over me. I feel uncomfortable, as I've been used to wearing pyjamas for nearly a month. I can barely sit up. 'Why don't you change into your new pyjamas, Mum? We all have new pyjamas, why don't we put ours on too, so you don't feel left out?' Before I know it, the whole family has joined me in wearing their pyjamas. We laugh and hope no one looks in through the window or knocks on the door. Christmas is even more special and peaceful than ever. We count our blessings.

***

Harry Hickman. That's what we call him. He's a little like a new baby. His presence always felt, always between us. He needs looking after every day, day in, day out. Syringes need making up and changing twice daily; lines and connectors need changing every other day; dressings need changing and the constant site wound cleaning every week. He sleeps with me, bathes and showers with me and is supposed to hide under my clothing, but he does a good job of peering out most of the time.

Sometimes he's a nuisance and beeps or cries, causing us to go into a panic; sometimes he likes to create drama and we end up transporting him back to hospital so he can have even more attention. It's stressful on occasions as we climb the steep curve of learning to look after him. I still have that love/hate relationship. He's a part of me and I'm a part of him. We depend on each other. I didn't want to choose him – who would? But it's either him or the unthinkable. Here he is holding my hand on my journey into the unknown – attached to me for the rest of my life – keeping me alive. That's why I have to accept him.

Life is very different, but life is all that matters. Every other worry we've ever had in our lives pales into insignificance. We've been pulled roughly into this new world, and it's a harsh lesson on what's important and what's not. I'm grateful to be in my own home; grateful to be with my family; grateful to watch the birds through the window. Simple pleasures. That's all that matters.

Surprisingly I adapt to Harry quite quickly and he doesn't seem such a baby anymore, probably because I'm starting to feel better. He's become part of my daily routine, like brushing my teeth and washing my face in a morning. An extraordinary little line and piece of machinery, but ordinary in my eyes now. I've become used to him; him used to me. I've been given a brand new start and hope. I still can't think long term, but I can see an immediate future waiting to be enjoyed.

Rob has taken a month off work as we build our new lives together. After such a rude awakening we're putting our affairs in order, updating our wills and looking at finances. I receive good news from the DVLA that I can drive once more, after advising them about my health issues. I start to go out independently and regain my confidence. Our lives begin to settle into a pattern and Rob manages to return to work.

I need plenty of time to bathe and dress and take adequate rest in between activities, but I'm able to potter around the house and carry out some light housework and cooking. I slowly clear out my teaching paraphernalia and begin to put my past away, as I know I have a new life to live now. Rob is always planning outings for me, and friends visit and take me out.

Life is feeling settled and more positive for the future. I'm enjoying my new-found peace and tranquility after the upheaval of last year. I keep telling myself, 'Just find ways to adapt around this illness and all will be fine.' I feel much more secure with the support from Papworth and the PH specialist nurses. They often phone out of the blue to check how I'm doing. I've a growing number of new friends on the PHAUK forum, who offer endless support. I'm finding I'm able to help others as I've been through the process of having some of the end stage treatments that many patients worry about.

*****

Ant and Dec's Saturday Night Takeaway. It's on at full pelt. Blasting out. Sometimes there's a need to be quite tolerant of others and their little idiosyncrasies on a hospital ward. Sometimes patients are elderly and deaf; sometimes they are just plain selfish and rude. We have to rub along together and mostly it's really pleasant to meet and chat with others, but my pet hate is television on at full blast.

It's my second day back in hospital and I'm wired up to the heart monitor and having my second increase of Flolan. My head's beginning to hurt as I watch my former Flolan Friend being wheeled off the ward. She's in some distress and I know things aren't right – in fact it looks pretty serious.

I can't think straight with the noise of the television. I'm worried about what's happened in the last week or so. Just when I'd felt much better and begun to adjust, I became much more breathless. I'm breathless from doing the slightest things. It's a worrying sign that my health may be deteriorating. It happened again – another faint. I'd collapsed on the bed after coming upstairs. I'd been climbing the stairs even more slowly: both feet on each step, with a rest in between and another rest at the top of the stairs, then another sitting on the bed. A new regime in place, but to no avail. It's back, and back with a vengeance.

I've been brought into Papworth as an emergency and, coincidentally, so has my Flolan Friend from December. We spent an hour or two chatting and catching up on news in between all the admittance procedures. We were then both wired up to heart monitors, so were unable to carry on our conversation. We'd looked across to each other a few times, waved our blue finger oxygen monitors, shrugged and smiled. Here we were again – just like before. Same time. Same place. Old times.

I'm not too worried about the increase, my system's used to it now. I'm disappointed my body has let me down again though, just when I'd reached some normality and a state of acceptance. It's only been eight weeks and here I am again. I can feel the flushing on my skin starting.

I worry about my friend. Where are they taking her and why? We haven't had a chance to finish our chat. I wish the others would turn their TVs down. I can't cope with it. I toss around on my bed this way and that. I try reading my book, concentrating hard to shut out the noise. My head hurts.

Sunday. I wake to the feeling of nausea once more. I'm not ready for this. I thought I was used to this drug. I notice my friend isn't back. Her bed is still empty. My Flolan is increased once more. My head hurts more. I have anti-sickness medication to keep the nausea at bay. I manage to eat and drink a little. Hopefully, it will only be mild this time.

I ask a nurse about my friend. I'm aware about patient confidentiality, but I can't help myself. We'd become quite close, having gone through similar together and I'm worried. The nurse says, 'When the doctors come to see you, ask them.' I worry more now and the bed across stays empty. I don't ask the doctors, I don't feel it's my place to pry. I just wait and listen.

Monday morning, and there's the usual hustle and bustle as a new week starts. Mine starts off with a bang. As soon as I wake I'm violently sick. I'm unable to eat anything and can barely get my tablets down with water. I'm cast back to December. It all rears up: the smell of the green trays, the taste of water, the sick bowls, the intravenous anti-sickness drugs. It feels desperate. I'm only just over last time and it's all happening again.

The doctor is sitting with me, gently telling me my friend passed away on Saturday night. I'm totally stunned. I knew something was wrong. I thought she might be in intensive care somewhere being looked after, but I hadn't let my mind stretch as far as this. I'm violently sick again.

The consultant arrives next. She says they're concerned about my heart, so they're going to give me a second drug – a tablet called Sildenafil – once they've finished increasing my Flolan. I'm a little taken aback. In the next breath, before my mind has even begun to process this, she says, 'I'm going to refer you to the Transplant team about a double lung transplant.' I'm stunned. Totally stunned. I can hardly speak, as I'm already shocked with the news of my friend, and Rob isn't here to share the burden.

I don't know how to process and absorb any of this. There is no preparation; no handbook on how to deal with it. The nurses are clearly shocked about my friend. They keep my curtain partly closed around my bed. They come and sit with me. As professional as they are, I sense that some of them need to sit and take in what has happened just as much as me. My mind swirls. I can't even cry. I'm numb. Grief, transplant, drugs. Grief, transplant, drugs. My head throbs, more sickness. More throbbing, more sickness. Her death is my first encounter with the cruelty of this disease. I have read much about it, but this time I'm witnessing the very worst at first hand.

I know Rob will be arriving smiling and cheerful. I try and text him but he has already set off. He arrives smiling, just like I'd thought. He's visibly stunned and shaken at the news. We sit in despair. Rob – a young nurse – me. We just sit in grim silence. *Ant and Dec's Saturday Night Takeaway* – it won't ever be the same when I watch it – there's a hook now deep in my memory.

***

I beg the weekend doctor, 'Please don't restart me on Sildenafil yet, I'm feeling dreadful.' The increases in the Flolan have finished at last – they've had to be stopped, because it's making me so ill – but then the new drug, Sildenafil, has been introduced. It hasn't been a good start.

It was only supposed to be a quick weekend visit to have my Flolan increased, but days have passed into a week as events and the nausea and sickness took hold. Starting the new drug has taken the sickness to another level. I'd taken my first dose, been monitored on the heart monitor for an hour or so and all looked fine. The consultant had even confirmed I could go home. I felt unsure about this, as I still felt utterly dreadful. The palliative care nurse came to visit me, but I could hardly speak when the sickness came back with a vengeance. She quickly administered more intravenous anti-sickness drugs.

I wanted to give up, ask them to take me off the drug and stop. I couldn't though. I always knew if it wasn't for the Flolan, I wouldn't survive and not surviving wasn't an option. Getting myself to a safer place was the only answer and I was determined to get there – eager for nothing but survival. I just had to survive. I had too much to live for – too much to lose if I didn't.

A drip had been connected, as the sickness became so bad I was dehydrated. It was decided I needed respite, so the Sildenafil was stopped for a day. I was desperately disappointed in myself, and that the treatment wasn't working. I longed for it to work; I longed to get better and go home again. I was frightened after what had happened to my friend. Selfishly, I worried if it could happen to her, then it could happen to me. I was scared about this talk of transplant.

I'm relieved. The doctor has been given permission to let me have another day's respite from the Sildenafil to see if it helps me settle. However much I want to be stable and safe once more, it doesn't make sense to force a new drug on my body when it's still reacting badly from the increases that have been made to my Flolan. I believe it will settle down, like it did before and I'm determined that I will be able to continue with the Sildenafil once this happens. I know the doctors want me to have the dual therapy to stabilise me, but my body can't accept any more right now. Physically, I've hit the point where enough is enough; mentally I know I need stability as well.

The days continue. Feeling a little more settled, I manage to eat and drink. Success. I keep down a small dose of Sildenafil as well as my Flolan and then another and another. I'm thrilled and even more thrilled when there's talk of me going home soon.

The lovely girl with the food trolley delivers my lunch. I'm not feeling one hundred percent, but I should be eating again to build myself up. I've chosen quiche.

Rob tries to coax me into eating. He takes one look. 'Good grief, that's a bloody brick of quiche, they must be trying to fatten you up.'

'We can always use it to break a window to escape, if they don't discharge me soon.' It's been a two and a half week long weekend and I've been here long enough.

***

The waves of nausea are coming over me more and more as we head home in the car. I make it, but then the sickness returns. Rob and Sarah run shifts around me – nursing me, cleaning me up. Rob phones the hospital. I'm advised to stop the Sildenafil but that I can attempt it again once things are settled. I know I've given it a good try, but I'm so disappointed in myself and worried that I'm still not on a strong enough dose of medication to keep me stable.

I don't feel I'll ever be the same again after this hospital visit. I haven't really been after my December visit when Harry was fitted, but this one seems to have taken another piece of the real me away. Physically I feel nauseous and unwell from the Flolan – it's either nausea and sickness or upset stomach with diarrhoea. It feels hard to cope, but I've no other medication options. The side effects that had disappeared during my December hospital visit are in full swing again after this latest increase. The jaw pain is excruciating; my skin is flushed red and mottled on and off constantly.

I'm disappointed and worried about it all – how will they ever manage to keep me stable when I react like this? I'm disappointed because I've spoken to quite a few patients on the PHAUK forum who have all done so well with Flolan, and so many who have no problems with Sildenafil either. What's wrong with me? Why does it make me feel like this? So many others have been stabilised on these drugs and have been doing extremely well for years. Why can't it be the same for me?

I despair at what may happen. I constantly think of my friend, losing her life so rapidly, just twenty-four hours after we had been laughing and joking. This disease is a shocking killer. I don't feel safe anymore. I toss and turn in my sleep, my mind in turmoil.

***

There's a new monster to face, which has been thrown at me amongst everything else. Transplant. I hadn't even had the strength to think of this while I'd been poorly in hospital. Transplant? I can't process the thought. Double – lung – transplant. I say these three words out loud to myself. They just feel like words. I am numb.

I'm still reeling from having a line permanently stuck in my chest; I'm still reeling from discovering that I'm sick with some strange disease; I'm still reeling from all the upheaval and change PH has caused in my life and my family's lives. We are all still reeling. Transplant cannot find its way into this mix of trauma yet. I'm not ready. I push it towards the hard shell that's formed around me, my tornado's protective shield. It can circle me there with the rest of the debris of my illness until I'm ready to confront it.

We start to measure everything in terms of life and death, because I've come so close to the edge and because there's still the case of survival in front of us. Instinctively we learn to prioritise what's most important. There's no space for mulling over and grieving for events of the past. We've only energy left for finding ways to move forward.

I can't change what's happening to me, but I can determine what I can still do each day and how I can feel. In this way, I can see I might move my life forward. Rob decides to take more time off work – his role has quietly slipped into that of carer as well as husband. We deliberately set about enjoying as much quality time as possible. If we put in the effort to maintain my health, emotionally and physically, then maybe we might get through all this. How, we don't know, but we're determined to give it our best shot.

Adapting around my needs, we go out for lunches and dinners and visit places of local interest. We go to our favourite Lake District and enjoy driving around in the early spring sunshine. I see it all in a different light: every flower, every cloud, every view. I'm glad I'm seeing it all once more, visiting places we'd always visited, visiting new places. It all helps to settle me – settle us. I feel stronger and the medication feels more settled. There are good days and bad days, every day needs to be paced with what I can or can't manage, but it's uplifting to be enjoying life and its simple pleasures.

Rob keeps encouraging me, telling me I have a new job now – the job of keeping alive and well. He's walking every step of the way with me. 'Your illness is our illness,' he keeps on saying. Over the weeks we establish an uneasy stability and I'm able to forge a fragile alliance with my disease.

The letter drops through the post box – one I want to ignore. It's been on a backburner floating in a recess in my mind. I have to face up to it. It's time. Transplant Continuing Care Unit. I turn to Rob and say, 'I know we've some peace and calm at the moment, but why do I think this journey might be just beginning?'

PART TWO

Living on a List

'Oh make this heart rejoice, or ache;
Decide this doubt for me;
And if it be not broken, break—
And heal it, if it be.'
William Cowper

Nine

Kathryn

(April – June 2011)

We're having trouble finding it. At last, here it is, hiding in a corner tucked away at the rear of the hospital, just as if it knows I'm reluctant to find it – reluctant to step over its threshold and enter its world. Transplant Continuing Care Unit. Surely this is a world that belongs to other people? It's not my world. I'm not ready to enter this world. I don't want to negotiate these uncharted waters.

I want to turn and go, but it's not an option in my survival game. I have to step through the door. I need to find options for further down the line. Flolan is the only card I have to play and it's not a strong enough hand in my game. It's keeping me alive – but for how long?

This is my primary assessment appointment with the Transplant team. A transplant coordinator whisks me off to make a list of all my medications, then weighs me and takes my blood pressure. We have a general chat about my background and what's been happening with my health, before being taken through to see a locum thoracic consultant.

The consultant briefly explains to us the general principles of lung transplantation. He keeps it simple so it won't send us into overload. I hear the words, 'end stage treatment for lung disease'. It feels painful to hear this said out loud but, in many ways, I need someone to tell me what's what in this direct fashion. I want to be treated gently, of course, but on the other hand I'm craving some brutal honesty. How can I know what I need to deal with and prepare to face, if people don't tell me the hard facts? Rob and I both need these facts to push our way forward.

It's as though we are in a business meeting where I'm merely a detached observer. I'm Kath. Kathryn is the formal me. The consultant is speaking to Kathryn. Kathryn is my intermediary, my agent. I remain safe and protected, happy that Kathryn is the one having to deal with this on my behalf. Our business meeting is very matter of fact and on an even keel. Hospital procedures are discussed. There is no alarm or panic, nothing emotive. It is a blunt discussion about fixing something – like it's just a broken leg.

Kathryn asks about survival rates. 'Eighty-five per cent of patients survive the first year of lung transplantation and fifty per cent survive the first five years.' The consultant then discusses my medication situation with her, and concludes there's still scope to improve it. To my great relief, he says it's too early for a full transplant assessment. But before I can even breathe a sigh of relief, he adds that he will review this and see me again in two months' time. I grip the chair tightly. For a split second I thought I'd been dismissed from the world of transplant, but no, I'm going to have to step into it again and very soon.

***

I'm given my first dose, only a very low dose, of Sildenafil – the drug I was unable to tolerate a few months ago. The consultant is fantastic and thinks we need to try it cautiously and in small steps. I'm pleased with this idea. I want it to work so much, then hopefully my PAH symptoms might improve. I take it warily and hope for the best. I am much more settled with my Flolan increase now, but I don't want to go back to all the sickness again with the Sildenafil.

Following chest pains and yet another emergency admission to A&E at my local hospital, I've been admitted back into Papworth to try Sildenafil once more. To my surprise I'm coping. So far, so good. It's increased again. I'm coping well. A higher dose. Again I cope. Relief. Huge relief. I'm successfully on dual drug therapy treatment.

I'm walking, walking, walking as hard as I can – determined with a passion to prove I can now walk better than last time. I try so hard and I know this is going to be a better one. The six-minute walk test. The simple little test, where I walk up and down and around a few marked cones in a hospital corridor, while someone times me and monitors my oxygen levels and heart rate. The aim is to walk as far as I can in the allotted six minutes.

Although it sounds simple, it's a benchmark test in the ongoing monitoring and management of PH. The distance walked serves as comparable data to how far I walked last time, and is a measure of how my condition is progressing. I have to do it at each clinic visit. Now I'm successfully on dual therapy, the consultant has said she expects me to be able to perform better than my last test, when I only walked for two hundred metres or so, which was considered poor.

It's finished and I'm certain I've done well. Three hundred and ninety metres. It's a significant improvement. I say to Rob, 'Good, I've got myself in a far better place. I'm beating this. When I go back to the Transplant clinic in a few weeks time that'll be the end of the transplant talk for a while, thank goodness.' I feel very chuffed with myself. It's as if I'm on some manic mission of proving to everyone I'm actually doing quite well. I will just continue like this and there'll be no need for any more of this prodding, poking and intervention. Enough is enough for now.

I have the other usual range of tests and I'm discharged from hospital after only a few days this time. Life feels brighter. I feel safer now I'm able to tolerate both of the specialist PH medications together at last. It's June. The weather is good and I feel better in myself, still very limited, but somehow brighter and more optimistic.

***

We know where to go this time. I'm feeling very hopeful as we sit and take our seats in the Transplant clinic. I wait for my turn. I know I'll be called to see a nurse first to be weighed and so on. I happily explain to her that I've managed to tolerate more medication after struggling so much previously. The consultant is next. It's another new face, the lead thoracic consultant. We go through what's happened over the last few months since my diagnosis.

Despite my improvements, he seems very concerned about my symptoms of breathlessness and chest pain. He begins to discuss the options of transplant once more. Fortunately, Kathryn moves in from behind to step in on my behalf as he abruptly stops midway conversation and says, 'You don't seem to be very keen about this?'

It's probably because I am sitting here in sullen silence. I'd thought he'd say, 'Oh that's great, you've managed the new medication, now we'll just wait and see how you get on.' I had thought that would be it and we'd just walk out of here and not go back again for another year or two. Sometimes I can be stubbornly stupid.

My mind wants to reply to him, 'Who in their right mind would be keen?' Instead Kathryn says politely, 'I'm just trying to absorb all the information you're giving me. There's so much to take in.' Kathryn realises I will need him to be on my side, an ally. The realisation is sinking in that this is not yet done with.

The conversation continues and I hear the words 'severe disease progression'. I shuffle myself upright like a startled animal that has just heard a distant sound. I hear fragmented words said out loud, 'eighty-five per cent survival after one year; fifty per cent survival after five years for a lung transplant'. I hear myself repeating them in my head, trying to absorb each fact as he swiftly moves on to another. I hear the words 'poor prognosis category' and 'two years of quality life'. They go round and round in my head as the consultant talks away to Kathryn. I'm just an onlooker sitting here with my husband, trying to make sense of it all.

Hearing these facts, I begin to despair, but Kathryn calmly nods and starts to mentally compare them with an earlier letter from my PH consultant, 'With current medication the five years survival rate is sixty per cent, Mrs Graham falling into the poor prognostic category'. Kathryn weighs this all up quickly and can see the odds for transplant look better, because I fall into the forty percent with a poor prognosis. I'm glad she's there to work all this out for me.

The consultant concludes I may be a good candidate for transplantation and that, on balance, he believes this might give me a better quality of life for my remaining time. He recommends I should have a full transplant assessment fairly quickly. Rob and Kathryn concur, and I accept their decision that I must go along with it. They both want what's best for me. I have been brought back into my survival game. I have to go along with it. I need to have options. More options than I have at the moment.

The transplant coordinator, taking my bloods, says reassuringly, 'You've another team to help you now, you can ring us whenever you need.' She is friendly, caring and her words sound comforting. I suddenly feel more supported – reassured. Maybe it isn't so bad being here after all.

The waiting game recommences.

Ten

The Iron Door

(August 2011)

We are surrounded by a scene from a typical and beautiful summer's day, but the contrast between this and the angst and turmoil inside us is dramatic. No one else can see it, but for us it's tangible. It's the tornado again – this time spinning devilishly with doubts and decisions.

Wimpole Hall Estate. A National Trust estate that we have visited many times when our girls were little. We used to take them to see the lambs in springtime and to the shire horse shows in autumn. The girls loved the walled garden with its display of scarecrows. I used to bring my year one classes here for school trips – we had guided tours of the walled garden, summer picnics and enjoyed the play areas and farm animals. We pass it by often on our journeys to and from Papworth.

There are no children with us today, but there are many children playing, shouting, running around and having fun with their families. It's the height of the school holidays. We're in the courtyard having a cup of tea – Earl Grey – my favourite. We look like any other ordinary visitors, amongst the busy hubbub. A gorgeous summer's day marking the occasion we leave the ranks of the ordinary.

A beautiful show of plants in the courtyard catches my eye – purple verbenas, grasses and late summer flowering plants. The gift shop across from me has colourful blankets and cushions displayed in piles and, to one side of me, wares are sprawling out from the garden shop – iron-work benches and garden ornaments – with rows of second-hand book stalls to my other side. People are browsing; dogs are tied to benches and chairs sitting patiently; children are eating ice creams.

It is all such an ordinary and typical summer sight. We're part of it and yet we aren't. We are detached. It's all happening around us. How we long to be part of it – to be the carefree mum and dad with their kids; to be one of the people just choosing their next book to read, present to buy or making simple decisions.

***

It's Monday, the first day of August. We're greeted by one of the transplant coordinators, who goes through the itinerary. 'It's going to be a busy three days,' he says and goes on to discuss the numerous tests I will be having: blood tests, lung function tests, walk tests, X-rays, heart echo, and an ECG. 'You're quite lucky,' he tells me, 'as you're already a Papworth patient and we've fairly recent CT and lung perfusion scans and an angiogram, at least you won't need those.' I nod my head, finally more at ease with what to expect.

'Smile,' he says as he takes a photograph for my file – so all the team will be able to recognise us.

Okay, so they're seriously making preparations already for this transplant thing, then? It feels weird smiling cheerfully for a photo sitting by my hospital bed – but then again nothing feels very normal to us anymore. I'm just riding along on shock. It's been one shock after another, and shock is normal. I've become a shock absorber. However events try and shock me, they're deflected into the debris of my tornado.

'You'll meet a transplant nurse, who'll explain about the follow up care after transplant, then you'll see a consultant to review everything again. If there's a surgeon available, you'll be able to discuss the operation and its risks. We'll then gather all your test results together and discuss your case at a multi-disciplinary team meeting before we can let you know the outcome.'

It is stressed that there may be several possible outcomes. I may be considered suitable for transplantation; I may need further investigations to be deemed suitable or I may be deemed unsuitable, in which case they will discuss possible options for me. I have a strong sense – I don't know why – that it's almost decided I'm suitable. I don't like the thought of being 'unsuitable', in which case the option might include some form of palliative care – I don't want this option.

A transplant doctor sees me and asks questions about my quality of life and the severity of my symptoms.

'I've been having a lot of chest pain, I've recently been in hospital, it worries me.' I babble on, 'It's probably indigestion.'

'I don't think so, it's probably your condition and your heart.'

I like that this team is frank with me. When people are frank, it helps me to make the proper decisions.

I go off for tests. They are all familiar to me. Routine. Normal. I just get on with them. I'm on automatic pilot – like I'm doing the washing up or something equally mundane. My PH consultant comes and sees me too. I've only recently seen her, but it's good she's so supportive. I tell her about the side effects I'm still having with the drugs, and how I'm struggling with them.

She can already see my skin is blotchy and bright red, but there's not much to be done about that. I explain about the constant nausea and diarrhoea. She chats with the pharmacist and they decide to prescribe me regular anti-sickness and diarrhoea drugs. 'Hopefully they'll help. We want you to get out there; you have a life to live.'

I'm relieved the side effects I'm having are being taken seriously.

We're taken down to the Transplant clinic and meet with a transplant nurse, who explains more about the procedure on the day of the transplant. We're in a tiny side room and she brings us a cup of tea while we chat. You know it'll be difficult when someone brings you tea. It's as though I'm already having this transplant thing.

There is talk of the complicated drugs I'll have – they mean nothing to me just yet. I'm still grappling with the ones I have, I'm still learning. We talk of sedation drugs and painkillers during and after transplant. I've never had a big operation. I think back to having the event recorder fitted and removed at Harefield – that's the most I've ever had done. I laugh inwardly, 'Well, in for a penny, in for a pound. If I'm going to have an operation, then let's go for the big one.'

There is talk of the complications that I may encounter post-transplant – this is hard to imagine, as I'm still just trying to imagine actually having a transplant. I haven't overcome the hurdles in my mind on that yet, never mind the problems that may come afterwards. It's very clear I need to know what can happen though. It's part of the whole process on deciding what to do. There are many disturbing things to consider.

She starts with 'unexpected poor function of the new organs'. This is a tough one, however much the donor organs are checked, there are still risks that they may not function properly once transplanted. It can mean complications and an extended stay in intensive care. There is the further possibility of excessive bleeding and having to return to theatre for more surgery. Some patients are not lucky enough to survive. She continues…

We hear about ventilators, which help you to breathe until you are able to manage breathing on your own … feeding tubes, catheters, drains, intravenous infusions, pacing wires and boxes … it's difficult to keep up with it all. It's all calmly delivered and made to sound the most ordinary and routine of procedures.

We are given all the time we need to ask questions, but really I'm still trying to assimilate all the information. Once again I am Kath, and Kathryn takes control on my behalf. Kathryn processes the information and gives it to me simplified. The information flows on and over me. I can tell from Rob's reactions that he's trying hard to take in everything too. He's frantically scribbling down notes in a book so we can refer to them later.

I'm struggling to understand. I'm frightened to understand. It's all new information. I'm given a folder entitled Lung Transplantation, which explains everything. I'm glad Rob is with me, it would be too much to absorb on my own. Families are included and encouraged to be part of this process. The talk is all rather dark at this point, but it's imperative that all the risks are laid bare so that we fully understand what we'll be entering into.

I'm back in my safe haven once more, Duchess ward, and settle down for the evening, meeting my fellow patients. There's a lady with PH I've met a few times before – we are both on the same IV medication and have been for some months. I learn she's very poorly and too ill to have her transplant assessment. There's no more that can be done for her.

It's with this harsh news that I realise that I desperately need to kick this transplant door open wide while there's still time. It's as if the transplant route is being paved for me – each time I'm in hospital I find I'm the lucky one.

Back with the transplant consultant, he sympathetically tells us, 'We still need to hold our group meeting to confirm, but I think you'd be suitable for transplant. I believe that if all goes well, transplantation will offer you a much improved quality of life. We've looked at all your test results and think a heart and double lung transplant will be the most suitable way forward.' Rob looks like he's been punched – this is the first time a heart transplant has been mentioned.

He explains that I have markedly dilated pulmonary artery and branch pulmonary arteries, so it would be more complicated and riskier to join them up to ordinary sized arteries from donor lungs – that's why a heart and lung transplant is considered preferable. He shows me the X-rays of my lungs and pulmonary arteries and demonstrates on the computer what the size of normal pulmonary arteries look like in comparison. I try to imagine those are the damaged lungs inside me, but it's hard to rationalise. Surely they can't be mine?

There's more difficult news. 'It usually takes an average of two years to find a donor for heart and lungs, and it may take longer. It's advisable that we list you fairly quickly as there's a fine balance of being well enough to withstand transplant and then falling too unwell.' More information follows, 'There's a one year survival rate of eighty percent and a five year survival rate of fifty percent for heart-lung transplantation.'

We try to make sense of this daunting information. 'Can you just tell me the comparable survival rates for PH once more?' asks Rob. We need to know the likelihood for my survival if I continue as I am with my existing treatment.

'It's very difficult to be certain about this using existing data. Historically we've always quoted a three year survival of fifty percent with idiopathic PAH from the time of diagnosis, but with newer medications this may have significantly improved,' he replies. 'You're clearly limited and have ongoing disease. You're a long way down the diagnostic pathway, having been diagnosed late on and having severe PH.' It's evident I fall into a poor prognosis category, and my quality of life is likely to become more impaired and decline further in the next two years. That's if I'm lucky.

It's a frank discussion and, although it feels grim, in many ways I welcome it. I want to hear it, because to hear it said out loud helps me accept what's happening. It's the beginning of enabling Rob and me to make some decisions about our future – not just about whether to have a transplant, but about what we want for our future now we know for sure that it will be limited.

Nobody can say the future is definite though – every patient is different – there are always exceptions to the rule – some patients can do better than initially thought. I dwell and doubt over and over, 'What if I fare better than they think with my PH medication? Is there the time to wait and see how I do? What if I decline more? The last few months haven't been that steady, have they? What if I become too unwell to cope with a transplant? Will my only chance of an escape from this have gone? What if time runs out because it takes so long to get a donor?'

The questions in my mind are endless. It's no different for Rob. He just wants me to have the very best outcome – nothing else and nothing less – just the best. He's quite keen on the idea of transplant, as he's very much focusing on the words, 'an improved quality of life'. He is best placed above anyone else to know how much my PH affects me on a day-to-day basis, both emotionally and physically.

The conversation moves on to the transplant drugs. My consultant notes that I'm struggling with harsh side effects from my PH drugs. He discusses the long-term impact of immunosuppressants – in particular that they may cause high blood pressure, diabetes, kidney failure and high cholesterol and carry high cancer risks. He explains, 'To be clear, transplant is *not* a cure. You'll be swapping one set of problems for another, but the hope is that you'll enjoy a better quality of life, although I cannot guarantee that you won't suffer from some side effects of the drugs like you're having now.'

It's more to consider. It's overload on my brain. It feels bleak either way. But I know it's an option I am lucky to have.

I imagine walking along a path. It's the path I've been treading down for over a year. At the end of the path is a heavy iron door. Something urges me on towards the door, but I stop in my tracks when I reach it. It's slowly closing and I can't see what's on the other side. I'm terrified. The door is going to shut soon and once it does, I won't be able to open it. I will have to stay where I am. Have I the strength and courage to push through it and see what's on the other side? Will there even be anything there? Will there be a new path to go down? A new future?

I cannot answer these questions. No one can.

Back on the ward I pack my bag, ready to leave before returning again on Friday to find out the outcome of the unit's multidisciplinary team meeting. We say goodbye to the other patients. We know we won't see the other lady again. We walk to the hospital lift feeling deep sadness for her and her family, entwined with hope for our own. Desolation. Elation. There never seems to be any in-between any more.

***

Friday. It's already familiar coming here. It's a quick meeting and the consultant confirms what's already been said. Subject to us meeting a surgeon and having up to date mammogram and smear tests, I'm to be listed for a heart and double lung transplant. I'm required to have the tests to ensure they don't throw up any abnormalities. Once on immunosuppressants, transplant patients have a higher risk from cancers.

'Should you begin to deteriorate while you wait, we'll still have the option to switch to giving you a bi-lateral lung transplant,' the consultant explains. 'We prefer not to do this in your case, as it carries more risks. It would be much more complicated with the joins to your pulmonary arteries.' It's also explained to me that, once on the transplant list, it opens up funding for a third PH therapy – PH therapies are incredibly expensive and various conditions must be met to obtain funding. This is good news. I now have more options. I'm relieved. We're both relieved.

***

Wimpole Hall Estate. A beautiful August day. A day marking the occasion we leave the ranks of the ordinary. We've called here on our way home from meeting the consultant at Papworth.

I glance back over the times we've previously enjoyed here and see myself carefree and unsuspecting of the future. I would never have imagined we'd be sitting here facing this impossible decision. Suddenly every other decision we have ever had to make fades into insignificance. They were all easy compared to this. None of them even mattered that much when I think properly about it – mere lifestyle choices – choices that could be undone or changed if necessary.

I think back to all the soul searching I've done in the past – all the rationalising and reasoning that goes on making decisions to change jobs, move house, buy a car – all of it so trivial now. This decision we face now is beyond the pale and has no place in our normal world.

This time the choice is stark: life or death – or both. Making a choice where there will be no going back – ever – whatever the outcome. There will be no going back. We sit and drink our tea and wrangle with the hardest decision we have ever had to make. Wrangling – I think there are going to be many, many days of wrangling.

We buy ourselves an ice cream and wander around the gardens in the sunshine. If we do ordinary things like everyone else, then maybe we can just pretend to be the ordinary people we crave to be. I'm looking at all the plants and flowers, but I'm not seeing. The tornado is rising up again. It's not going to go away. I fear it's going to be circling me – circling my family for ever.

Eleven

My Chariot

(September 2011)

I'm sitting on a wall overlooking the sandy beach at Southwold in Suffolk. The waves crash to the shore beating a steady comforting rhythm. I love the soothing sounds of the sea, but I've a sinking feeling deep in the pit of my stomach that this cruel disease is creeping and coursing its way through me, slowly robbing me of more and more.

I'm watching people walking. Everyone's at it. People of all shapes and sizes – young people, old people, children, toddlers – they don't even realise they're doing something that is so wonderful and special – something that's so fundamental to their lives. Some are marching along purposefully; some dawdle at their leisure; some are walking dogs; some are pushing prams. Toing and froing wherever they are going to, or coming from.

I'm conscious I've only made it a few yards from the car park and cannot manage to walk any further. I'm too breathless and walking is making me exhausted and dizzy. The ground keeps spinning below me. Every time I take a step, the ground spins upwards to meet my feet. Walking isn't something I'm able to do very well any more. The muscles in my calves ache desperately when I do.

We are trying to enjoy a few days break in Suffolk and Norfolk after all the turmoil of the last few months. In fact we've made a very conscious decision to try and make the most of every minute.

We've decided this should be a memorable time – a time when we'll look back one day and say, 'Remember all those wonderful things we did while I waited for my transplant?'

During my transplant assessment, one of the transplant nurses had said to us, 'The first year of transplant is usually very tough but, when you've got through these twelve months, that is the time we say to you – go off and do all those things you've ever wanted to do. It's the time when you may be able to go abroad again. What do you think you might want to do?'

My mind had tried to process the information, and I felt I should be full of dreams in response. I muttered some reply, but in my mind I thought, 'I'm not waiting until then to live my dreams – it may be years – we cannot wait that long dreaming – we need to be doing things now – trying to live some of those dreams while there's a chance – there might not be the chance later.'

I feel sad today though, and wonder if we should give up on this holiday, pack up and go home. Going out for the day or on holiday is supposed to be relaxing and enjoyable, but it is surprising how much energy you need, and I've simply none. I've managed two days of the holiday so far, gently pacing myself, but it seems that's all I can cope with. We have reached day three and it's got the better of me. I don't want to be defeated like this. I don't want to give in. I don't want to end up stuck inside for months on end just waiting for the phone to ring.

Some people are riding along on scooters and in wheelchairs – they are all managing to do so much more than me. Rob suddenly says, 'How about when we get to Norfolk, I'll have a look around and see if I can get you a wheelchair?' He's surprised when I readily agree, recognising the advantages it would bring.

We give up on Southwold and arrive at our hotel in Norfolk. Luck is with us as Rob finds there's a mobility aid shop just a few hundred yards away selling wheelchairs. He returns promptly with a very comfortable, lightweight wheelchair – we instantly christen it my chariot. Many people may say using a wheelchair is giving up and giving in to my disease. That thought doesn't enter my head – my only thought is, 'I can't wait to use it, now we'll be able to go out for so much longer and do so much more.'

I embrace it as a positive step, and having it won't stop me walking for as long as I can manage. The wheelchair will enable me to pace myself. Rob will find it useful too. It's not good for his fitness when he has to walk at a snail's pace every time we go out, so pushing the wheelchair means he'll be getting some decent exercise at least. Rob picks a few more items up from the shop that might help me while he's there – various bathing aids: a low bath chair, a step for the bath and a shower stool. I'm struggling hard with bathing and showering because of my Hickman line and pump device, combined with my breathlessness and exhaustion.

These adjustments help considerably with my simple daily routines, even though it still takes me a long time to organise myself in a morning. Some side effects of my drugs, such as nausea, are worse early on and the diuretics mean dashing to the loo every five minutes. Whole mornings can be lost while I work through these daily problems. From late morning onwards, the days always improve and we're able to get out and about and enjoy ourselves now we've got my wheelchair, before it's time for the next intravenous drug change.

We are patiently waiting as we try to enjoy ourselves – waiting to hear that I'm officially on the transplant list. We try and push it out of our minds as we go about with my chariot discovering new places.

***

We'd been back to Papworth to meet the surgeon and undergone the 'listing' meeting. We'd gone over all my health issues once more as well as all the particulars about having a transplant and living life post-transplant. It was still difficult for us to hear out loud someone telling us that my future looked bleak. It was done in the most sensitive, gentle and positive manner, and we were grateful for this.

I'd tried hard to sit impassively, keeping what was being said on the very straight and level, staying detached, keeping my face blank, without feeling. I needed to stay composed, as I didn't want to allow my emotions to get the better of me.

I'd had thoughts of ordinary straightforward procedures – plaster casts on broken legs, bandages on thumbs. Then I'd conjure up what they were really talking about – someone actually taking my heart out and removing my lungs and then the rest that would follow – putting someone else's organs back inside me – not even taking into account the events then would need to have occurred to allow this to be possible. It was too extraordinary; my mind wouldn't, and still won't, reconcile it. I try to prevent my mind wandering away with the enormity of it all.

Bandages, plaster casts, hearts, lungs, bandages, plaster casts, hearts, lungs – all wrestled in my head. I managed to get the thought of a broken arm and its plaster cast to take precedent, suppressing all others, staying calm to take in the facts. I could cope better sitting there in front of the surgeon, thinking of it as a simple 'procedure'. Choosing this allowed me to ignore the words 'heart and double lung transplant'.

We discussed how it might take as long as two years to obtain a donor match as a result of a huge shortage of donor organs. It's much harder to find a donor where all three organs together are functioning well enough for transplant, and if heart and lungs are available, they are usually split. This enables a heart transplant to be carried out as well as either a bi-lateral lung transplant or two single lung transplants. This way two or three people can be saved instead of just one.

The surgeon explained, 'At Papworth, we are very committed to doing what we think is the best for the patient. If it's both heart and lungs that you need, then we will do our best to achieve this.'

It felt reassuring. We agreed amongst us that I would be listed for a heart and double lung transplant. The consultant then went through more details of the operation, in particular all the risks that were explained during my assessment.

I signed the consent forms – on the day itself it might be too much of an emergency, so all had to be prepared in advance. We'd agreed. We'd come to a decision. The decision. The one that might change so much, but have so many possible outcomes. A decision, but one that held so many uncertainties.

Rob asked, almost casually, 'How many heart and lung transplants have actually been done this last year?'

'Just six in the UK,' replied the surgeon, 'and I did them all.'

I smiled and joked, 'You'd better not be on holiday when my call comes.' It made us realise how rare the operation is. What are the chances of even getting it? Less than winning the lottery? What really are my chances?

We discussed a little more about the average two-year wait period. The coordinator said how impossible it was to predict, but that she had known at least one case where a patient had received a transplant donor match on the way back home from their listing meeting. So we had to be ready at all times. Rob looked visibly shocked. He said later how he'd nearly fallen off his chair. Suddenly my transplant had become all the more real and imminent.

After lunch, we returned to meet with our coordinator for the 'listing' meeting. It was explained about living on the list. There are certain things we'd need to adhere to while waiting. She said, 'You must telephone the Transplant team beforehand if you're going away and it's more than three-quarters of an hour away from home. We need to be able to contact you at all times. You'll need to have a case ready for hospital, as it'll be an emergency situation once the call comes.

'All there's left to do now is get all your data keyed on the system, and then you'll be live on the waiting list within the next few days. We will phone and confirm when you're definitely listed.'

It felt almost momentus and far reaching, as if we were embarking on a special mission. Another decision made – another landmark in the journey – another new beginning.

***

After my listing meeting there was more need to make further adaptations to the life we'd been thrust into. It had been weighing heavily on our minds that I may decline, and we would regret not having spent more valuable and special time together as a family. We'd always dreamed of enjoying a retirement in our sixties, but we were now less certain what the future would hold.

As Rob was taking on more and more the role of carer, he decided to give up his career so he could help me as much as possible and we could try to enjoy some sort of a 'retirement' now. We decided we wanted to make the absolute most of the situation we had in front of us, and embrace our future and that of our family's positively, whichever way things turned out. With an acceptance of our situation came the ability to count our every blessing, and we looked for all the good things in life that we did have.

We were still adjusting and adapting our minds to thinking of transplant – to entering the world of a pre-transplant family – becoming a post-transplant family felt another world away. A world unknown. It had been a busy year grappling with the uncertainties and instabilities of PH – grappling with so many unknowns and grappling with one adjustment after another after another.

Each consultant's letter to my GP would be out of date – by the time my GP received it, I'd always been back to hospital and there was a newer letter on its way. I kept having three monthly hospital appointments in the diary, but never quite made them, always having to return to hospital or clinic sooner for one thing or another.

The 'never-knowing-what-was-going-to-happen-next' scenario added weight to our decision to take that leap and change things completely. It was as if we were putting a survival strategy together. The doctors and hospital staff were all doing their level best on the physical front, but it was a case now of coping emotionally and mentally as well as trying to hang on to my health and well being. Not just for me, but for Rob and the girls.

We'd never have believed eighteen months beforehand that we would both end our careers this abruptly, but when it came down to the basics in life, which it had for us, keeping me healthy and alive had become our new priority. I read somewhere that three people die each day while waiting on the transplant list. The thought made me shudder.

MY CHARIOT (SEPTEMBER 2011)

***

We're enjoying Norfolk with my new found freedom – with my trusty chariot. Today we're at Holkham Hall trying it out again. We're having some fun and games, as Rob isn't quite used to handling it yet, even though we've been using it for a few days. I've learned it is a complete 'must' to use the seat belt. With Rob in loose control, I'd be propelled into busy roads or over cliff tops and into the sea if I didn't use it! I probably won't even need a transplant, as he'll finish me off the way he's going. Maybe that's his intention? I wouldn't blame him!

This time he's jammed my wheelchair trying to cross a cattle grid. I feel ridiculous with the rear wheels of my chair wedged in the gaps of the grid – I'm completely stuck. There's an open-air buggy vehicle full of foreign tourists hurtling towards us. With great exertion, Rob manages to lever me out of the way just in time. When he regains his composure, we chuckle at the thought of a bunch of foreigners snapping away at the sight of our ridiculous predicament.

We head to the café and sit outside enjoying the fresh air with a well-earned cup of tea. We then go to the beach and Rob tries his hand at pushing me along the boardwalk, through the pine trees and towards the sand. We are still laughing about our cattle grid experience. The boardwalk is easier to negotiate, much easier than when we reach the sand. I walk where it's soft for a while and Rob carries the chair to the hard wet sand, where he can just about push it and I can use it to support myself.

My mobile rings. I stop and look at Rob, 'Might this be it?'

'Hello, is that Kath? Just to confirm you're live on the list now.' I come off the phone, Rob has understood. That's it. It's done.

It's a clear September day – fresh, bright and breezy – the twenty-first of September to be exact. The tornado is hovering shakily around us. We are inside it treading warily through the sand, avoiding puddles left behind by the sea. Some of them are deep. We don't want to get our feet wet or sink. We are living on a list. The first day of living on a list and we are stepping cautiously.

We reach the tide's edge – the breeze has suddenly whipped up with the incoming sea. Three people somewhere will have died today, because there aren't enough organ donors. The sea ebbs back and forth at the shore like my seesaw of emotions.

Twelve

Raining Sheets

(October – December 2011)

The phone. I'm jumpy. Every time it rings, the thought flickers there in my mind. Every time it rings I pick up the receiver with some trepidation. I'm almost reluctant: if there's anyone in the house with me, we'll look at one another in silence while I answer it, and then almost breathe out a loud sigh of relief when it's a friend or family calling. It feels even worse when we are out and the mobile goes off, especially if we don't manage to answer it in time and it's a withheld number.

We're trying hard to live with this phone call fixation. We can't help it being an obsession, as it will be a phone call that will change our lives. How can a simple phone call cause such immense change? A change that carries so much uncertainty – that can alter the course of fate for better or for worse? It's a phone call I so dearly want. It's a phone call I'm terrified of. It's a phone call I never want to hear, but desperately want to hear at the same time. How can you want something so much and then not want it in equal measures?

Nothing in my life has prepared me for the confusion of lingering feelings in me which rise up every single time the phone rings. We try to keep on with our usual routines, clinging to some sense of normality, but when the phone rings we are reminded. Normality is shaken.

It reminds us just how sick I am. It reminds us of what may

happen – will it be good or bad? It makes me feel stuck in the middle, as if I'm in my own personal no-man's-land – drifting and roaming helplessly – waiting for something to happen, waiting to be rescued. If I drift in one direction, the disease will take over me. If I drift in the opposite direction, there may still be hope. If my disease succeeds, I'm frightened of dying and how it might happen. I think, 'Will it be slowly? A slow deterioration, more and more of the old me disappearing, my breathing becoming more laboured? Or will it be quick? My heart suddenly saying enough is enough?'

I have to put these thoughts away. Pack them up in a box in my mind. Not let them out, but the phone reminds me. I try and learn not to open the box when it rings. It will just be a phone call – that is all. Just another ordinary phone call, not the call I'm waiting in hope for, not the call I dread.

This is how it is – the extremes of living on a list.

***

I slowly wake and can hear Rob in the kitchen making up my Flolan. It must be early. As soon as I raise my head above the pillow, it starts to spin, I think I'm going to black out. My heart pounds fast like I've never known before. What is happening to me? The room spins, my heart beats faster and faster. Fast. Fast. Fast. Out of control. I see my worst fears being played out in front of me. Is my heart giving up? My heart must be giving up.

I must remain calm. It's the morning of my sister's wedding. I must remain calm. I cannot die on the morning of my sister's wedding. I must not die. I try to breathe myself out of my panic. My heart is still racing. If I move in the slightest way I think I will faint.

Rob comes back into the room cheerfully with my Flolan and the usual welcome cup of tea. I must not panic him. I lie still and say to him steadily, 'Change my pump over and when you've done that, I want you to dial 999.' Of course he panics. I dare not move and lie still as he goes to feel my heart. But he's no need to feel it. He says he can physically see it jumping in my chest. He dials 999 immediately.

We're staying in a cottage in the Ribble Valley in Lancashire. We're all here together – Rob, the girls, Oli – Sarah's boyfriend, and me. My sister's wedding – an occasion that we've been looking forward to for months. The girls are to be bridesmaids.

We arrived the previous evening laden down with stuff – bridesmaids' dresses, wedding outfits, hats, bags, presents, luggage, boxes for my medication, my transplant hospital bag and all the groceries to get us through the weekend. We'd met my sister and her fiancé along with his family and their friends for dinner. We had to drive cautiously through gusty winds, sheeting rain and flooded roads to make it to the restaurant. The wind and the rain had carried on without interruption through the night.

Rob runs to wake the girls and Oli: they all come dashing into our room fraught with worry and are verging on panic at the sight of me. I try to stay calm, the calmer I remain, the better it will be for us all. I hope and pray for the ambulance to come quickly and then they can be relieved. Rob and Sarah start to sob. They go to look out for the ambulance, as they've been instructed. It gives them some respite, some purpose. My heart pounds and my head spins, as Oli and Rose hold my hands and try to comfort me. I have to shake my hands free and away from them – I'm clammy and hot and don't know what to do with myself. I've no control over my body playing these games and tormenting us all to despair.

'I wish I'd had my transplant call.' The thoughts wash through my mind. 'It can't come quick enough, we can't carry on living like this.' I'm frightened it may be too late now. I fear the worst is happening – all my fears of the last eighteen months coming together and acting out in slow motion before me. I'm scared. We're all scared, more scared than we've ever been.

It feels an age before the ambulance arrives, although it's not really long at all. I'm relieved for my family that they can leave things in the hands of the experts. The relief is etched in their faces. There's only so much my family can do for me. They aren't trained medics. They need them here as much as I do.

The paramedics decide to keep me still as they don't want to set my heart rate racing even faster. They assess the best way of moving me onto a stretcher is to improvise, rolling me over to it, using a sheet from the bed. I'm wrapped in the sheet. I begin to worry about it. This sheet doesn't belong to us. What if we lose the sheet? I silently chastise myself. Why am I worrying about a sheet at a time like this? It's my sister's wedding day, I might be dying and it's just a sheet.

The paramedics take some routine readings before taking me out into the fine, yet heavy rain – the kind of rain that soaks to the core. I still worry about the sheet, which is becoming drenched. If I focus on the sheet, then I might forget about what's happening to me.

No blue light is needed, as it's only just after seven o'clock on a Sunday morning – there's no traffic at all. I can't see where we're going. I have no sense of direction or time. My only thought is, 'I can't possibly die on my sister's wedding day, any other day, but not my sister's wedding day.' I listen to the constant 'shush' of the pouring rain and sigh in relief that I am in safe hands as Rob looks anxiously on holding my hand.

I don't know who all these incidents are more frightening for – my family or me? Or is it the same for all of us locked into this unwanted world, all in our different ways? Sometimes it is too much for Rob – he's the most caring of carers, but he isn't a doctor. At times I think he wishes he were. At times I know he wishes he could just wave a magic wand and it would all be over. At times I worry I've ruined our lives and feel guilty. At times I know Rob wishes it were him, just for my sake, just for a day even – to give me a break. I'm glad it isn't him, though. I can cope with it being me: I couldn't if it was him or the girls.

I am wheeled through doors and corridors and brought to a stop at a small cubicle. As we head towards it, there is an overwhelming smell of stale alcohol lingering in the air and I can hear the crackle of police radios. I see policeman after policeman standing in doorways. I think they've made a mistake and I've been brought to a police station, but then it registers that I'm at Preston Royal Hospital. Preston is a very large town and I'm witnessing the aftermath of a long Saturday night in A&E.

More tests are undertaken, nurses and doctors seen, then I'm taken to the acute assessment ward. Rob is in tow, dragging my hospital bag – thank goodness we had that with us all ready packed – and struggling to balance a box of my medication while he fumbles through doors trying to keep up with us. I can see the wet sheet is folded precariously on the box.

The consultant eagerly phones Papworth to discuss my condition and treatment. Rob phones them too and speaks to both my PH and Transplant teams to advise them what's happened. I'm pleased and relieved they're all liaising with Papworth. The Preston medical team can't do too much to help and make me comfortable.

I'm admitted so that they can keep an eye on me while I'm hooked up to a heart monitor for safety. I'm still dizzy and my heart is beating slower, but still too fast. My hopes of going to my sister's wedding are well and truly dashed, but I have to put my feelings to one side and stay calm. Deep down, I know I'm in the safest place and it would be ridiculous to try and go to a wedding under these circumstances.

Rob lets the family know that things are more settled. Sarah and Rose are relieved, but obviously still worried. They have carried on with the day as planned and have readied themselves for the wedding – it's been a tough start to the day for them, to say the least. My brother has taken over the 'father of the bride' speech duties, which Rob had been going to undertake on behalf of my dad. Although my dad is very poorly, he and my mum are still able to go to the wedding.

As the hours pass, I'm trying hard not to be tearful about missing out on everything, especially not being able to see my sister get married and witness my girls being bridesmaids for the first time. I'm worried I will have spoiled my sister's wedding day, but I take some comfort in that I haven't taken a further turn for the worse.

There is many a commotion amongst my fellow patients: some are elderly and suffering with dementia – desperately calling out, and some are weekend drunks or drug addicts, sobering up slowly and shouting incomprehensibly. Suddenly, amongst all the chaos, the girls and Oli appear to surprise me. They're dressed in all their wedding finery. I'm surprised and thrilled to see them – I've been able to see the girls in their bridesmaid dresses after all.

They tell us both all about the day as Rob makes up my medication for the evening. It cheers me up. I'm wired up for the night to a heart monitor, although my heart is no longer racing and the dizziness seems to have eased. I feel safe even amongst all the frenzy around me – safe and in the best place. I'm resigned to the fact that I've missed the wedding celebrations, telling myself it's part and parcel of being ill. It is tough, though. I force myself not to cry. Instead, my eyes search for the sheet to check it's still there safely folded amongst my belongings. I must return the sheet.

Rob arrives early in the morning to make up my medication – the team is relieved because they don't know what to do with it. I'm glad they've let him, as it's specialised medication – one mistake with the dose and the consequences can be dire. I only ever allow Rob or the PH staff at Papworth anywhere near my medication, line, pump and catheter site and I'm adamant to keep it that way. It's self-protection.

The consultant and doctors come to see me after speaking to staff at Papworth. They've concluded that my heart is suffering from the strain of my PAH. I'm still having a few dizzy spells which feel like the start of one of my faints. I don't really know what to think other than this incident has really shaken me up and frightened me. On top of all this, I'm desolate about missing my sister's wedding and not being part of a happy family get-together. Again the two situations are stark. Happiness and despair. There is no balance. Once more, there is no in-between.

I'm discharged. The doctors wish me well and say they hope my transplant comes soon. Crossing to the car park, we step back into the relentless rain that shrouds everything in its dismal mist. Rob dodges the frantic cars battling for non-existent parking spaces, pushing me in my wheelchair with one hand, balancing the box of medication and dragging my case with the other, negotiating the puddles and flooded potholes. We are laden down. Laden with the weight of my illness and its continuing consequences. Laden with soaking wet rain. The heaviness is bleak.

Back at the cottage, Rob points to the folded sheet, carefully guarded amongst all my hospital bags and exclaims, 'Why on earth have you nicked a sheet from the hospital?'

'The sheet belongs here, that's why. I've been guarding it all the time I've been in hospital, worrying I would lose it!' He'd been too distressed to notice they'd used the sheet from our bed to move me onto the stretcher. It dawns on him why I've been clutching to it all the time I've been away. The sheet is safely back. I'm back.

Night comes. I'm terrified of going to sleep, scared I might wake up and it will be the same again, with my head spinning and my heart beating too fast. I'm terrified if it happens again, I may not come round or spring back. I want to run away from this place. I want to go home. I want my transplant call to come. Above all I just want my transplant call to come. The thought of continuing like we have for the last eighteen months for much longer is an unbearable thought. I just want rid of all this from my life – to be rid of it, rid of the symptoms and drug side effects and rid of the fear that underpins our lives every waking moment.

I restlessly manage the night and we wake to the same rain. Still the same dense and ruthless rain saturating my family, as they brave it to the car over and over. Suitcases, hatboxes, bridesmaids' dresses, suits, flowers, in they all go – sodden. I sit helplessly as they clear the cottage, venturing in and out of the rain. I feel more useless than ever. They won't allow me to do anything. I daren't anyway.

We set off for home. The sky is black and reflects our mood and emotions. Its downpour beats a harsh refrain. Every time we think we've managed to haul ourselves into the sunshine, it rains again with a vengeance. The rain is a distinct reminder that all isn't well in our lives; no matter how hard we try and overcome our obstacles, it always comes back. This time it's been pouring constantly for days and our spirits have been drenched. It's an arduous journey home in this rain – the most burdensome journey. It's a reflection of our reality.

We reach home safe and, after the unpacking is done, Rob and I sit and look at each other in silence. We have nothing to say, we feel speechless. We have finally, after eighteen months of trying hard to remain positive and hopeful, reached rock bottom. Usually one of us is there to help the other back up, but today we have both fallen down the black hole that we've been trying to avoid for so long. There isn't anyone to rescue us from it. Isolated from the world that carries on around us while we plunder this way and that. We are alone.

***

Fortunately, when you hit rock bottom, there is only one way to go – back up. It's a new day and it starts with a bouquet of flowers arriving unexpectedly. They're from a thoughtful friend just wishing me well, who knows nothing of the weekend drama. The timing is perfect – it lifts my spirits.

Next, one of my specialist nurses calls, 'We'd like to admit you back in so we can check you out properly after the incident at the weekend.' Suddenly we begin to bounce back – we aren't on our own – the support is there when we most need it. I pack my hospital bag once more and off we drive up to Papworth. I notice that the sun is shining and the sky is deep blue, crisp and clear. It's a beautiful bright October day, in sheer contrast to the previous few days. It lifts me further.

We arrive at my safe haven. Today it feels like a five star hotel compared to the chaos of A&E. No policemen. No drunks or drug addicts – only drug addicts like me – those of us on drugs of the healing kind.

I have the usual tests, am admitted for a few days and kept on a heart monitor. The palliative care nurse comes to see us, as she's heard about our weekend – she understands that it's all been traumatic. We have a good chat – it is reassuring and helpful to know that she's always here. I have no more episodes and the team is eventually happy I'm stable enough to be allowed home. As always, I'm told to phone for help should I have any further problems.

After all the tender loving care from Papworth, Rob and I feel much better and reassured. We return home feeling much brighter. We've bounced back and the sun is still shining.

***

Life continues steadily on towards Christmas – visits to both of my clinics, visits to my GP, visits to hospitals – sometimes hospitals other than Papworth. Like many patients with a severe and chronic disease, I've started having secondary issues to my main illness. I've begun to develop allergies and skin problems, so I'm visiting Addenbrooke's Hospital in Cambridge regularly to see a dermatology consultant. Since October, I've continued to experience dizziness and have developed a ringing in my ears, so I'm under a consultant audiologist at my local hospital to rule out any ear issues. Hospitals, doctors and drugs seem relentless.

In the middle all this medical mayhem, we've managed to settle down into the rhythm of family life. Rose has been made Head Girl and is planning to go to Uganda for Christmas with her school. Sarah is settled working full time and has moved in with her boyfriend Oli. Rob and I are trying to venture out and about as much as I'm able.

Oli is quickly becoming part of our family and offering us much support. He's also becoming a firm favourite every time I stay in hospital – he likes a chat and will talk to all the patients who haven't visitors.

On one occasion when I was being discharged, a lady said in a disappointed voice, 'Oh are you going?'

'Yes, later on today hopefully,' I replied, thinking that's so sweet of her to be sorry I'm leaving.

'It's just that I've been looking forward to your daughter's boyfriend coming again, that's a shame.'

I laughed and thought, 'Well that's put me in my place! I know where I come in the order of things.'

Christmas Eve, and I have to rush to clinic with another allergy issue relating to the dressing over my Hickman line. I'm given the necessary treatment and luckily not admitted. The staff know me well by now, and many of them stop by to wish us a Merry Christmas, while others joke about me being here on Christmas Eve again and that I must be desperate to have Christmas dinner with them.

Once home, we relax in relief ready for Christmas Day, pleased my visit has just been a blip and not a crisis. We put hospital and illness firmly out of our minds. I'm elated we're ending the year with some steadiness and stability. I know I've an ever-growing handful of secondary issues, but appointments for these will be in the New Year, so no need to worry for now.

We are watching TV when a newsflash pops up and there is Papworth Hospital. Prince Philip has been flown there by helicopter from Sandringham Estate suffering from a heart problem. Every news bulletin, every day over the Christmas holiday, and there is Papworth Hospital. There's no escaping it!

Rob quips, 'If it's good enough for Prince Philip, then it's good enough for you.'

***

New Year's Day. Another year behind us. An achievement we've made it so far. An achievement to celebrate – we celebrate any achievement we possibly can these days. Today is another year – what will it bring? Will our lives change?

The phone. I'm still jumpy for the call I'm dreading, for the call I'm desperate for. Today I've been waiting for this phone call for one hundred and two days. It's a sobering thought that, in that period, three hundred and six people will have died waiting on the transplant list.

Thirteen

All in the Genes

(January – September 2012)

'Blogger'. I search around, work out its systems and nuances and then – I write. I write and write and write and write. I cannot stop writing. I pour it all out – all that has happened. Cataloguing. Processing. Putting it into some order – all those events – all those happenings – making them orderly. They might make more sense if they're orderly, but even if they don't, it feels so good to write them all down. Cathartic. Therapeutic. That's how 2012 starts. An unloading. Positive.

I've always loved both reading and writing from being a small child. As a teacher, it was teaching writing that I loved the most. Now it's time to start doing some of those things I love. A time to develop new interests and foster old ones. A time to give myself some new challenges – challenges which I might enjoy amongst the imposed challenges of my health.

Not being the most technical person, I'm quite proud of myself when I manage to organise my blog all on my own without pestering Rob or the girls for help. Rose often rolls her eyes at me when I'm stuck with media and technology, but I've no need to harass her. Having written all my entries up to date, I explore my way tentatively around the software and learn how to add in links, pictures and videos.

Writing about my journey in the form of a blog is one of my new goals. It feels like an achievement since I've lost most of my independence. Sometimes I feel I'm not really doing anything other than staying alive and trying to keep out of hospital. So much of the busy and proactive person I'd once been has faded away. It's time to move myself forward, give myself some new goals I can achieve within my limitations.

All the settings on my blog are kept to 'private', so no one can see. It's just for me, my own thoughts, records and musings. An indulgence. A therapy. An escape. I aim to write every week, keeping a log of all the ups and downs that have become part of our daily life.

I set myself a reading challenge with 'Goodreads', an online book review club. This year I've challenged myself to read fifty books. Reading is good for me on those 'off' days – the days when my energy is spent and I need rest. I may not be able to achieve much physically, but I can read and read to my poorly heart's content.

My reading allows me to visit so many places. I float in the Pacific Ocean with Pi watching out for sharks and ducking from flying fish. I live in Afghanistan and run through the streets flying colourful and eclectic kites with the other kite runners and I toil with the missionaries struggling in the depths of the Congo jungle. I may not be able to travel abroad, but my mind can wander all over the world.

Both my reading and writing emerge as excellent coping strategies. Reading gives me escape and writing gives me therapy.

The garden is another great pleasure. I can't do much gardening any more, but Rob lifts the compost and plants onto a garden table for me so I can sit and manage to make up a few baskets and pots. It enables me to feel I've contributed. We plan new borders and collect a variety of plants while we're out and about on our travels. Not only will I be able to see the plants grow and bloom in the garden, but I will have a lovely reminder of a place where we've enjoyed ourselves. Just the simple act of deliberately planting bulbs, shrubs and flowers in order to watch them grow in the future gives me hope.

Photography is also becoming a passion – photographing the

changing seasons, plants, wildlife and places – photography captures memories of the good times and the uplifting experiences of nature.

I don't have a traditional 'bucket list' like many seem to do in my circumstances. My list is rather more an ongoing list of plans, people and places to visit. A never-ending one. My life won't finish at the end of a list – of that I'm determined. I don't have an end to my list.

We try hard and relentlessly to turn our situation around, count the blessings we have and not dwell too much on our unknown and foreboding future. The getting out and about, photography, writing, reading and enjoyment of our garden contributes enormously to keeping me inspired and motivated. In turn this helps my emotional and mental well-being, and keeps me positive. We are determined to live life to the full. I keep on saying, 'I want to look back on this time of waiting for my transplant as a lovely and enjoyable time. I don't want to end up even more poorly and look back with regrets.'

I don't want to waste what life I have left waiting for a telephone call – a telephone call that may not even come. Of course I'm wistful and wishing for a better future – that never leaves me – but at the same time I've learned that living in the moment is also key in getting through all this.

We make plans constantly – things to look forward to – cramming as much as we can into what might be my short life – taking our minds off the bigger picture of reality. We know the odds are against us. We go out for days – anywhere we can find locally of interest. We venture on holidays – the Cotswolds, Norfolk and Rutland, as well as visits to our favourite Lake District.

Our plans don't always work out: sometimes we have to give up on a planned day out, because I'm too poorly. Sometimes I'll be ill while we're away and will end up in bed for days at a time, and we'll wonder if we're being ridiculous trying to do too much. We persist all the same – hungry for life. For the times that are bad, we make many more memorable moments that are good, and this is what we cling on to.

In between the health and hospital issues, I write my blog about all the places we've been visiting and add many of the photographs I've taken. Writing my blog gives me more and more motivation to venture out and visit new places and take more photographs. It's become a new and fulfilling hobby – in fact it marries together many of the things I love doing. Where can we visit this week? What good photo shots can I take that might be interesting? Travelling, writing, reading, photography – all knitted together and keeping me inspired and motivated each day enabling me to forge a positive life from something so dire.

***

Looking around the clinic, all the other women are pregnant. I feel a little embarrassed. I'm sure they're looking at me and thinking, 'Blimey, she's a bit old to be expecting!' I look down at myself and feel conscious I even look like I might be pregnant with Harry bulging underneath my loose clothing. This is a positive step for our family today though – a way of gaining back a tiny element of control over our circumstances. There is so much about this disease that makes us feel completely helpless.

Ever since I've been diagnosed, it's been in the back of my mind about why I have this rare and dreadful disease. What has caused it? Where did it come from? And why? Because of these unknowns, one of my biggest fears is whether my girls might inherit or develop PH. My mind goes to dangerous and dark places when I think about my girls.

So far we have coped with this thing, this monster, but it's been troubling me more and more about our girls. The girls want to find out more if they can too. They want to be prepared, ready to catch it. We all want to be ready to catch it and stamp all over it, if it so much as dares to rear its ugly head within our family again.

We are at Addenbrooke's Hospital waiting to start the process of genetics testing. I reason that's why there are so many pregnant women here – they must be going through various genes testing themselves. We are shown through to the consultant.

It is known that Pulmonary Arterial Hypertension, which cannot be attributed to a specific identifiable cause, is idiopathic. Idiopathic PAH can be caused by genetic misprints or mutations in several genes that regulate the dynamics of the arteries that supply blood to the lungs. Approximately twenty percent of patients with idiopathic PAH have a genetic misprint or mutation in a gene called BMPR2. A smaller number, around one per cent, have a mutation in a gene named ALK1.

The consultant tells us, 'Given that around a fifth of patients with idiopathic PAH have a genetic mutation that can be identified by genetic testing, it's important that we consider this for you, as it may have implications for your children and your wider family.

'Someone carrying a mutation of gene BMPR2 has a one in two chance of passing it on to each of their children. However, only approximately twenty per cent of people who inherit a gene change – this includes twice as many women as men – go on to develop PAH. This can be precipitated by environmental changes including pregnancy.'

We nod in understanding, trying to keep up with the stream of information we're being fed.

'If a genetic mutation is identified, then we'll have a predictive genetic test for your other family members, which will tell them whether they've inherited the gene mutation and have an increased risk of developing PAH.'

Obviously predictive testing has pros and cons, so he goes on to recommend that my family would need to seek further advice and help should they identify any genetic mutations. We listen quietly, but feel optimistic we've made some affirmative steps to try and pinpoint why all this has happened. Equally we feel some trepidation.

There's always a conflict of emotions – the turmoil never stops. We're positive that we have put the process in motion because it's well known that the earlier a diagnosis of PAH can be made, the earlier treatment can be administered and the better the prognosis can be. It's a process the four of us have agreed on as a family and we've agreed to review it together as more information unfolds.

We know we can't control whether our children may or may not develop PAH, but at least we can be prepared and armed ready should they do so. We can hopefully pre-empt the situation, and ensure targeted treatment is provided to restrain the development of end stage PAH. Of course, we're hopeful it won't come to this and that I don't carry the mutated genes.

We're acutely aware that findings from the testing may result in confronting even more uncertainty. The thought of my girls having to endure any of this is agonising – knowing what it's like to have this illness myself – the thought is intolerable. On top of everything else, again, it is overwhelming. Yet, at the same time, this testing feels a positive step forward.

We sit down in the clinic once more waiting for my blood tests – back with the pregnant ladies. We're not that dissimilar. We're all anxious about what grows inside us. We're all expectant for new life – for the miracle of a new life.

The girls are keen with interest when we arrive home. We relay all the information we've been given. I explain, 'At this stage they've just tested me and then the results will determine what the next course of action will be: this may involve testing the both of you, if it's found I carry any of the mutated genes – that's only if you want to go ahead. We can talk about it again if it comes to this and make our decision then. There's a good chance that I don't carry any of the known mutated genes anyway.'

We agree once more that this process needs to be done cautiously and one step at a time. If either of the girls were to find they carry a mutated gene, they may spend their lives worrying about whether they may develop PAH or not, and it could affect their future decisions when the gene might not even be triggered.

We're going to have to wait months for the results of the tests. There's no proper genetic screening provision for PAH, but there's a new PAH genetics research study that's being partially funded by the British Heart Foundation (BHF) and led by a BHF Professor of Cardiopulmonary Medicine, who is also the Research Director for the National PH Service at Papworth. We've been lucky to enquire about genetics at the very same time this project is being initiated.

Only around six thousand five hundred people are affected by

PAH in the UK, and in about twenty per cent of those cases the cause may be genetic. This research work will focus on these patients, and hopes to be able to establish the frequency of all the known genetic mutations and also identify new mutations that may be responsible for causing PAH. There is expectation that, eventually, from this research, it may be possible to introduce a screening programme that can identify those at risk, provide better information to families and identify new ways to treat the condition.

I willingly give some DNA to take part in this study too. At least things have been set in motion for my own genetic testing, but I'm also delighted about this study. I don't think any results will be in time to help my situation, as it's predicted it will take several years, but anything that may in the future prevent another family going through what we are, would be fantastic.

The research may help me understand why I have this disease – help me make more sense of it. I just need to have some logic to it. If I have this, then I think it may help me somehow – help me settle. I constantly wish to know why – I can't help it. Not 'Why me?' But rather, 'Why do I have this disease?' At the moment it seems such a great puzzle.

***

I find myself at Addenbrooke's over and over again during the course of the following months to continue with allergy testing. I'm having so much trouble with allergic reactions to the dressings, which cover the site of my Hickman line. In between we make frequent trips to Papworth. My skin around the Hickman line site area constantly reacts to various dressings. It blisters and is red and itchy. I need to be checked to ensure it's not infected. Blood cultures need to be taken and tests performed to ensure there is no infection in my blood stream.

Eventually several allergies are identified and my PH team manages to find dressings that my skin can tolerate. The Transplant team take note of the dressings which I'm able to tolerate in preparation for the 'big day' – if it ever comes.

***

We seem to have slipped into an easy peace and period of acceptance, with hospital visits and clinics being a part of our everyday lives. We're in some ways becoming more and more immune to all the events that keep emerging out of the depths to confront us every way we turn. It's become almost a normal way of life – but a parallel normal rather than a proper normal. I'm not sure we even know what normal is anymore.

The good news is that, with my medication and major adjustments to my life, my PAH has become reasonably stable. It hasn't improved and I'm still extremely severe, but I haven't become any worse. We're more used to its way of life – the ups and downs – we're becoming hardened to its blows – taking them in our stride and more accepting of them. But while we're becoming impervious to shock, it's still all shocking somehow.

We're used to gauging when we should be panicking over incidents and seeking help – or when we shouldn't be panicking. I'm managing to make it all the way to three monthly clinic appointments, rather than being admitted to hospital before I reach the next one. It feels like an achievement to attend a clinic without an incident since the last one. It provides some respite – not quite enough to catch ourselves up totally from all that's happening, as PH and waiting on the list always hovers around us, but we're able to draw breath and take enjoyment out of life and count our blessings.

Counting our blessings – we're always doing this now. We've witnessed first hand on many occasions how illness and death cruelly ravage others and their lives. We appreciate that luck has been on our side in many ways. I feel blessed I've reached this stage in my life, and at least I can say I've achieved many of my dreams. I have Rob and the girls, who support me relentlessly. I've been lucky enough to have children, to have had two rewarding careers and a comfortable home and lifestyle. Although I struggle with being ill, I don't have to look so far to see others who are having it so much harder than me.

We've met so many types of patients: younger adults, teenagers, children and even babies. Those who wish to have families like us, but are stopped in their tracks due to illness, and young mothers and fathers battling against the odds hoping to survive for their children's sake. Then there's the elderly suffering on their own and, harrowingly, families torn apart because individuals can't cope with the devastating effects of illness. The list is endless.

Things are hard for us in many ways, but we're left in no doubt they're easy for us compared to others. We often feel grateful for all we've ever had and had the opportunity to do. I thoroughly appreciate I'm still alive – we both do, and this makes us want to make the most of every moment. Seeing what others are going through is often very inspiring. We see others coping where all the odds are stacked against them. If I ever feel sorry for myself, I soon jolt myself out of it just thinking of what others are enduring. It's truly humbling and inspiring.

I have immense support from my PH team – the nurses phone me often between appointments to ensure everything is still going well. I chat regularly to PH friends on the PHAUK forum. I've already been through quite a long PH journey in a very short space of time – from oral medications to inhalers, to intravenous medication, then the transplant list. I'm finding myself more and more in a position to help others who are facing some of these difficult stages. We all support and help each other. We start attending the Papworth PH Matters Support Group and meet a fantastic group of other patients and their families who are going through similar experiences.

Often patients with PH look really well. I certainly do – my PH comes with the healthy red glow of Flolan. Many people comment on how well I look and ask if I've just come back from holiday. My clinic letters describe this as high colour, which makes me laugh. High colour and sun tans? In reality it's flushing on and off all day and night long – flushing on the inside and out. The dilating blood vessels make me so unwell, especially when I'm tired – from the top of my head right through my whole body to the tip of my toes. Every blood vessel in my body dilating. It makes me feel so ill.

Most people never see me using a wheelchair, being 'blue-lighted' to A&E or have sight of the catheter and pump beneath my clothes. They don't ever see me first thing in a morning trying to pull myself round from the nausea, sickness, headaches and jaw pains and all the struggles to get bathed and dressed. They don't see our faces and the judders each time the phone rings or the rigmarole of making up the medications and pill popping. When I'm sitting in a chair or just gently walking about in my own environment, things can appear pretty normal.

We feel grateful and supported having another family of friends where we can truly discuss how we feel. It prevents us from being so isolated, which is slowly happening as I become less and less able to join in with ordinary simple things.

I know I'm getting out and about, but it's with Rob at my side and usually in a wheelchair. He knows exactly when I'm struggling; he knows when I can't cope; he knows that sometimes we have to drop everything we're doing and come back home. It's hard when friends offer to take me out or invite us to visit them – I don't always know what I can manage from one minute to the next. Sometimes I'll feel well enough to go out, but then I get there and don't feel well enough to manage any further. It's hard to say yes to the kind offers I have from friends, when I know I'm so unpredictable, so I'm withdrawing from many social activities.

Looking pretty normal does have its upsides. We can easily get away with appearing completely ordinary and melting into the crowd, although our circumstances are getting more and more extraordinary. We can carry on going out using the wheelchair and stay away from home looking like just normal people on holiday. I don't fit the typical person's picture of a sick person, so sick that I need a new heart and lungs. I'm grateful for this.

In older days my vision of someone like this would have been a person lying in intensive care, attached to tubes and machines. This, I think, is most people's vision. The reality for me, though, is very different. In my individual case, if I reach that point, I don't think I'll be fit for transplant – I will have gone beyond it.

Again, I know I'm lucky in comparison to others who need to be hospitalised and can't wait for their transplant in the comfort and freedom of their own home. There's an urgent heart transplant list for patients in this position, as they do literally sometimes only have days to live. Once more, I'm able to count my blessings.

***

NatWest Bank. This thought flips through my head as we drive through the green and tree lined grounds of Heythrop Park in Oxfordshire. I've left those days behind long, long ago, but it all looks familiar – as if it was yesterday. This is one of the places where NatWest used to hold its staff training. The last time I'd been on a course here was over twenty years ago when I was in my late twenties, young, carefree, no children even – a creative problem-solving workshop.

I think of my old self back then and imagine this younger innocent self watching me, returning here today and knowing why I'm here. How shocked I would have been. Heart and double lung transplant – seriously – me?

Memories re-emerge – the fun we had, the formal dinners, the presentations, the nights in the local pub. Rob and I are both curious to see what this mansion house is like these days. I remember the rambling corridors, the old dim rooms lined in dark wood. We arrive, it looks very similar, but with new additions. It's now a hotel and conference centre. We check in.

We are attending the PHAUK's Conference. It's a conference where PH patients can socialise, share their experiences and also have informative sessions on the latest PH developments. There are fun workshops, lunches and dinners, so there's plenty of time for getting to know others who share similar issues and striking up new friendships.

I already know quite a few patients from Papworth who are attending, and I'm hoping to meet up with many of our PH friends whom we've been chatting to online. This may seem a little strange – chatting to people who you don't know online and then actually meeting them. Some may also think that spending a weekend at a conference for sick people would be the last thing they would want to do for a weekend. Not so for us.

Our new world is a strange one and we've been thrust into so much unknown territory and are wading our way through it blindly – not knowing what each day may bring – being isolated in many ways. For us, this weekend does not feel odd at all. We are excited. We want to learn so much more, meet others and it may help us cope even better.

We want to talk to others who instantly know what it's like. We want to stop pretending and stop acting. Acting. We're doing this for much of the time now – putting a brave face on things, pretending our lives are normal. We keep trying to fit back in our old world, but in reality we're slipping further and further away as our lives have changed so much.

It turns out just how we'd hoped – meeting special people, who share our anxieties, fears and dreams; having the chance to speak openly and freely about our illnesses and restrictions; being totally relaxed in good company with no pretence – it's so damn good not to pretend!

We leave feeling completely uplifted and encouraged in the knowledge we have more support behind us than ever.

***

I sit and falter for a while, but then I press the button. There. I've done it. I've opened myself up to the world. All my Facebook friends will see it. In fact it's out there on the internet for anyone to see.

It had been speaking with other patients during the conference that I began to reconsider whether to keep my blog private or not. My friends there had been intrigued to hear more and one had said, 'You should publish it, so we can all see it, it might help us and it might help other PH patients too.'

I felt inclined to do it and wrestled with the idea because, if I did, other friends unaffected by my condition would see it – I didn't know whether I wanted this. It was Rose who finally encouraged me to go public. She said, 'Mum, a lot of people just don't understand what you're going through, they've no idea. If you publish it, then they will see and, if they see, they may understand a bit more and well, if they don't want to see it, then they don't need to read it, do they?'

So I press the button! It's official. I'm blogging now, not only for myself, but to try and help other sufferers see that there's some life after diagnosis of this dreadful disease. I hope it may help give some understanding of what happens when you go through each stage of the medication process and what happens when you go through transplant assessment and beyond.

For others who don't suffer from PH or who aren't affected by transplant, I hope it will raise awareness and give an understanding of some of the issues surrounding rare disease and transplantation. Personally, it's giving my writing much more drive, knowing others are reading it, which helps me feel I've more purpose in life again. I'd felt I'd little self worth when I lost my teaching. I can feel a little of my old self returning.

I'm suddenly inundated with good and positive feedback from both our friends and the PH online community. Rob starts tweeting about it and begins to acquire quite a few Twitter followers from the PH and transplant world. It just seems to happen – almost accidently – we fall into campaigning to raise awareness of both PH and organ donation. From having little social media skills twelve months ago I'm becoming media savvy.

A whole year on the waiting list has slipped by. At times it's been fulfilling, uplifting and inspiring; at times it's been draining, frustrating and arduous. I feel I'm still awash, in the lap of the gods and the doctors, but my life has become so enriched during this time too.

Transplant always holds that ray of hope inside me – a light shining, beckoning and enticing me in the optimism that things can be different. I'm still terrified of walking through the 'iron door' though; taking that leap onto the unknown path once I step through it. Will there even be a path? Will I be plunging into an even darker and deeper black hole than the one I'm trying to avoid presently? Will I plummet into murky waters? The burden can feel enormous.

It makes me angry to have to face this unknown, but in its own peculiar way the uncertainty sits comfortably in a niche it has found amongst our ordinary and daily lives.

I know I'm lucky to have survived this first year on the transplant list, to have reached this milestone. Three people a day are still dying waiting for a transplant. The realisation is totally shocking and outrageous. One thousand and ninety five people won't have survived this year while I've been waiting. I know I'm one of the lucky ones.

Fourteen

Acorn

(October – December 2012)

Any hope of a quick transplant has dispersed and quietly dissolved. We turn our thoughts to the next year of waiting, and brace ourselves for the possibility that any hope we have may be false hope. It's a reality check every time we read or hear that three people a day die while waiting on the transplant list. Only around thirty per cent of the population is signed up to the organ donor register, yet ninety per cent of people say they would take an organ if they needed one. It makes for difficult reading when you are one of those waiting.

I think of the one thousand and ninety five people that have died while I've been on the transplant list this last year – ordinary people with families and friends – people just like me. If there had been some sort of disaster in our country and this many people had been killed, it would be in every newspaper and there would be questions demanded at the highest level. These figures go quietly unnoticed though, passed over, rarely mentioned. I know too well that I might be one of the patients that die.

The anger stirs in me. Something needs to be done. It builds up and up in me that something needs to be done. Not particularly for me – there are thousands of us – over seven thousand, and we are all in waiting. Some of those waiting know they only have days to spare.

I momentarily catch the headline on television, 'Chronic shortage of organ donors...' says the voice of the reporter. I stop, sit down on the edge of my seat and watch with a keen interest.

There is a young man's face gazing from the TV in my living room. He is waiting desperately for a new heart. He hasn't long to live. The family is frantic, and ITV has kindly taken up his cause and the cause of organ donation. Suddenly organ donation is all over the news. I'm so pleased that ITV has devoted their programme *Tonight* to the immense problem of the shortage of organ donors. It's refreshing – the media are actually taking notice of the issues we are facing in our daily struggles. People are becoming more aware. It brings us hope amongst our despairing thoughts.

Again I see I'm lucky. This young man hasn't the luxury of time or being at home like I have. We are genuinely moved by his story; we truly hope he receives a transplant in time.

***

Autumn brings a flurry of new beginnings as ordinary life always does. Rob is contacted by his old workplace to see if he's interested in going back. They offer him a project to help manage where he can work part-time, or at home should he need to. We decide it will be a good thing for us and especially for Rob. The job is ideal with its flexibility so, once again, we know we're lucky.

Having to give up my career and life as I knew it had been difficult enough, but I always hated that Rob had to be forced to give up his career and be thrust into this world of PH and transplant because of me. The offer of part-time work seems an ideal compromise – he will have time to spend with me and the family and an opportunity to have one foot in the real world once more.

Meanwhile, Rose starts her first year at university in Bournemouth studying psychology. As Sarah has already left home, we're left with the notorious empty nest syndrome, but for me it doesn't feel like that. Of course a part of me misses my girls, but an even larger part is thankful and grateful that I'm able to experience ordinary life – life-changing events perhaps, but those ones that come in the natural course of a lifecycle. It means I'm still living and experiencing ordinary emotions.

I enjoy watching Rose make her first steps to independence and take great delight in seeing Sarah setting up her first home with the partner she loves and growing in confidence in a new job. I don't have the pangs of emptiness and the void that many mothers feel in these circumstances, just the joy in seeing them take these big steps in life. My pangs and voids are those of not knowing how many more steps I will see them take. That is my heartbreak, not an empty nest.

My appetite to live life to the full grows and grows. Autumn approaches. We celebrate our twenty-second wedding anniversary – as always nowadays, each event that can be celebrated is celebrated, and every one of them is another milestone I manage to reach. Rob gives me a silver necklace with a small silver acorn. I can see, as a family, just how much we've managed to move our lives on, despite our circumstances. I look down at the acorn on my necklace. I think of all it symbolises – a new life, a new beginning but, above all, strength.

***

When you are sick, real life goes on and real life presents its ups and downs – you aren't spared from the downs because you are poorly.

'I'm ringing about Dad; he had a bad turn and couldn't get his breath back. Mum dialled 999, but they haven't been able to save him. We're at the hospital now just waiting to know what to do next.'

My brother is delivering the news that I knew was bound to come sooner rather than later, but nevertheless it's devastating. It's devastating for all the reasons that anyone would feel when they lose their father. For me I feel another devastation: that he didn't ever see me become better – that he died thinking I might die. I'm relieved too in some ways – relieved he's no longer suffering – relieved that I didn't die before him. It was painful to watch him suffer with COPD – his inability to catch his breath, his lack of mobility, his loss of independence, his struggles. Selfishly, every time I visited him I could see my own future potentially playing out. It added to the sorrow – to the despair of the situation.

The weather has been bleak over the last few days – wind, rain and fog. It's a cold November morning, the frost is harsh, but at last the sun shines bright and the sky is vividly blue and clear as we ride in the funeral car to the crematorium. Dad's funeral is a lovely and fitting service.

The last time I saw my dad, we'd had a quiet minute together and he'd pressed a little black plastic box in my hand. It contained a silver cross and chain with a small disc that had the Lord's Prayer engraved on it and the Soldier's Doxology. 'This was my father's, he wore it through the Battle of the Somme. He wasn't religious, but he thought it might help keep him safe. I want you to have it. It might help keep you safe too.'

I think it was my dad's way of saying goodbye and his quiet unspoken way of acknowledging my illness without having to say anything about it – he wasn't good with emotions and feelings, but he'd given me a token of hope.

I told him, 'If it got Grandad through the Somme, then it might get me through this illness and my transplant. I'll put it in my transplant bag that I've ready and waiting for when I get the call.'

It's a massive relief to manage the funeral; I never know what I'm going to be like from one day to the next, and I've been anxious that I wouldn't be fit enough to go. It brought back having to miss my sister's wedding all over again. I absolutely hate this illness at times – hate it with an absolute vengeance – hate it – hate it – hate it. What if I'd not been well enough to go to my own father's funeral? It's always PH that makes the ultimate decision – on this particular day it decides to be lenient with me. I don't know how I would have coped if it hadn't.

***

We carefully plan how we are going to manage. It has been two and a half years since I've been into London. London is too big, busy and overwhelming for me since I became ill, but I'm going to do it. I'm going to do it come what may – bad day or good day, now I've made up my mind I'm going to do it. I'm tired of all this waiting. I'm tired of all this complacency. I'm tired of this useless feeling that everyone is ignoring the plight of people waiting on the transplant list. I'm tired of feeling useless.

Rob climbs flights of steps with my folded wheelchair, bags and me in tow. He negotiates crowds and turnstiles and tickets. King's Cross. It's all new since I last saw it – I cannot recognise it. It feels like an adventure. I'm riddled with nerves already. My life is getting more and more out of the norm – I never dreamed I'd be doing something like this.

We arrive at our hotel. It'll be an early start in the morning and I need time to relax, ease my nerves and recuperate my energy levels – just getting into London has felt a major endurance test.

Westminster Bridge. Big Ben looms tall as Rob wheels me over the Thames, steering his way in and out through the traffic of tourists that seem to flow perpetually towards us in the opposite direction. I'm desperately apprehensive and cannot really believe I've said 'yes' to doing this. My nerves. I think I'll forget the speech that has been swirling round my head – thank goodness I've made some cards – I don't think people will mind me using cards in my situation.

We search for the Cromwell Place entrance and stop and ask a policeman for directions. Then we have to go through security. I am conscious of all the tubes and equipment beneath my clothes and am concerned how the security machines may interpret this. I tell the security team, 'I'm on drugs! Oops – I mean the intravenous stuff. I'm all connected up for it go through my heart and lungs and I can't take it off!' I needn't have worried. They are lovely and guide me through and tell us what to do next. We are escorted hurriedly through hidden back-corridors, tired looking areas that others don't see. Staff are radioed from one floor to another to lead us through more lifts and corridors.

We had stayed with my mum to help for a week after my dad's funeral. During this time I had a message from one of my PH and transplant friends saying she'd been asked to give a speech at the House of Commons about what it is like waiting on the transplant list. She'd only just been placed on the list herself at this point and was quite poorly, so didn't feel up to having to do it. Because of my blog, she thought about me and asked if I might step in. It didn't take me long to say yes – it felt like something constructive to do which might make a difference. There wasn't much time to prepare. We wrote our speech in the car on the journey back from Lancashire – the journey has never gone so quickly.

So here we are straight from the aftermath of my dad's funeral, ready to speak in the House of Commons just a few days later. It is for an All Parliamentary Party Group meeting hosted by an organisation called Transplant 2013. It's a campaign group of clinicians, patient groups and industry designed to raise awareness of organ donation in Parliament, to ensure politicians are aware and can influence some of the issues affecting transplantation and organ donation. In particular they wish to raise organ donation consent rates and help increase the number of transplants that might go ahead.

We meet up with my friend, who's persuaded me to do it, and her father. After each member of the panel for Transplant 2013 has introduced themselves, it's time for us to speak. Rob introduces us, then I speak about what it's like living with PH and waiting on the transplant list. It's a wonderful opportunity not only to speak openly about what it feels like to live on the transplant list, but to explain about PH and the devastating effects it has on your life.

There are many people there, and afterwards we meet fellow patients who have been deeply affected by transplant, clinicians involved in the transplant process and politicians and peers. Coincidentally we meet the aunt of the young man who had been featured in the ITV *Tonight* programme and is still desperately waiting for his transplant.

It makes me feel fired to keep on raising awareness – more people need to understand about PH, and we definitely need more people to think about donating organs should they have an untimely death. It's hard to know that most people aren't against organ donation, that they would willingly have a transplant or want one for a family member should they need one, yet they don't get around to signing the organ donation register.

Being on the register signifies to others what your wishes are, and makes it easier for a transplant coordinator to approach a family in the most desperate of circumstances. It's easier for a family to give consent to donating their loved one's organs at a traumatic time when they are barely able to think, if they know their loved one's wishes.

I can understand this complacency, though, as unless you are really affected by these issues, then it isn't something you go around thinking about. There is much work to be done on raising people's awareness and trying to show them how giving the gift of life to someone is such a life-saving and life-changing thing to do.

We exchange emails, Twitter accounts and the like with many people, so we can keep in touch with various other organ donation campaigns and help if we can.

Afterwards we nip to the café in the House of Commons with my friend to have lunch. If that isn't unusual enough for me, I show her my pump device and Hickman line, discretely taking it off my waist and explaining all the bits and pieces. In a few days time she is being admitted into hospital to be put on the same medication. She is really anxious and I try to reassure and allay some of her fears.

I think of the bizarre scene. I couldn't have ever imagined myself speaking in the House of Commons, let alone sitting here in this unusual place showing someone the intricacies of a complex drug that's flowing from pumps, syringes and catheters straight into my heart and lungs. How life can change dramatically. Being able to help someone else helps me in turn to feel better about myself. I feel I've lost most of my purpose in life at times and my independence. Suddenly, today I feel I've been of use and taken some control of what is usually an uncontrollable situation.

Today, I've met many inspirational people taking their own personal strides to make a difference: a gentleman working tirelessly in his local community to encourage people to sign the organ donation register after his daughter lost her life waiting for a transplant; a dad, campaigning tirelessly after a complete stranger gave part of their liver to save his baby girl's life; and then the young man's aunt – desperately trying to do all she can while her nephew only has days to live unless he can receive a new heart.

We all think we are too small to make a difference, but that's wrong. If we shout up loud enough and take all the opportunities we are given to do something, then those tiny steps we take can begin to add up. Today's the day I begin to fully appreciate the scale of the wider transplant community, and that it's a force to be reckoned with. It's the day when I realise I need to try and do more – both to raise awareness of PH and organ donation. If anything I can do might help someone else like me, then that's all that matters.

Whatever the size of the sea, it's what you do while you're swimming in it that counts. Maybe an action might just save one life if one person signs the organ donor register; maybe someone can be given hope when they are frightened of what treatment lies ahead; maybe someone can be diagnosed properly and receive targeted treatment for PH. There suddenly feels many ways to make a difference. I feel inspired about what I can achieve to help others while living on this list.

We leave the House of Commons – Rob pushing me in my wheelchair and my friend's dad pushing her. We laugh at the pre-dicament we're in as we try to fight our way through the barrage of tourists meandering, marching and just plain rudely trying to walk through us as we cross Westminster Bridge. Apparently we are invisible. We have a competition, who can get across the fastest? It's better to make light of our situation. If we dwell on the constant struggles, we will despair. In an over-zealous attempt to win the race across, Rob rams one or two truly ignorant people in the an-kles, sweetly apologising with faked innocence.

***

Through social media, we hear of others receiving their transplant calls; some are false alarms, some go smoothly, some don't. When we hear a transplant doesn't go well, it shocks us back into the crude reality of the transplant world. But hearing about others receiving their transplants at least turns the transplant into real life – that 'yes' the phone call does actually happen.

To us, after waiting over a year, it's become some sort of mythical thing – something alluring, hiding somewhere in the future. As each day passes, the mythical thing moves forward another day with it – never within our grasp, but always keeping us moving on forward.

We begin to understand what it must be like for a family waiting for news during the transplant operation. I'm becoming aware of how hard this is going to be on Rob, the girls and our immediate family. It's hard enough waiting to hear about friends – it's going to be total anguish for my family if, or when, it happens. It brings it home that it's a high-risk operation that can result in death. It brings it home that it can be a miracle too – a total transformation of life.

It is prominent in my mind that every time a transplant takes place, someone must have died an untimely and unexpected death and that there's a real family grieving somewhere. This thought is difficult to dwell on, yet I cannot help but think of it. It's a difficult concept to know there's a family in despair and a family who is overjoyed. The bridge between these extremes is where hope finally meets the gift of a new life hewn from sorrow. A miracle emanating from something so tragic. It's a hard concept to assimilate, but it's there amongst everything else in our lives.

Hearing news of others makes the whole process palpable. Authentic. We've been trying to normalise everything – trying to make it as though I'm going to have a simple and routine procedure. My feelings are becoming all muddled again. Do I want to go through this? Do I want to put my family through this? The daily questioning rounds are back again. They haven't really ever gone away.

The waking in the morning and those first thoughts of, 'No phone call again, that's another day and night gone by.' The little bit of hope and the fear rising up inside me when the phone rings. These emotions are all symptomatic of waiting a long time for something – waiting too long. Reasoning and reasoning things out –

it's a rigmarole I seem to need to go through again and again – we both need to go through: the answer always comes back the same – if I want to change things, I need to do it. I know it doesn't help me to dwell on these things, but how can I not?

***

My mobile by my bedside pings with a text message – I must have fallen back asleep again after Rob left saying, 'Behave yourself, you know what you're like!' It's Rob telling me he's arrived safely in Bournemouth to pick up Rose for the Christmas holiday. The spinning again; the sick feeling rising up inside me; the dizziness; the drowning; my heart beating fast, far too fast. I can hear it. The fear.

I'm on my own. I'm frightened. My common sense kicks in and I stay calm. 'Get back on the bed and prop yourself up and see if it passes,' I instruct myself, as though I'm a medic who's looking after me. 'If it doesn't stop, pick up the mobile and dial 999.' I can feel my heart begin to slow, I've stopped myself blacking out. My phone pings once more – by some fluke it's Sarah – within fifteen minutes she and Oli are in the house with me. I ask them not to tell Rob. I don't want him driving hell for leather up the motorway to be back with me.

I think my intravenous line must have kinked itself in bed so the drug infusion had been cut off while I'd been sleeping. It's frightening to understand how much my body relies on this drug; how I can't function or even survive without it now.

Monday morning and I'm taking my usual slow process of sitting and getting dressed, yet it begins all over again. It's clearly not a kink in my line as I'd thought. We drive to Papworth cautiously. They're going to admit me. I know I'll be safe here. It's only a few days before Christmas. 'I'm at it again,' I think, 'trying to have my Christmas dinner at Papworth.'

The consultant tells me to prepare to stay in for Christmas. I'm not disappointed. I want to be safe. Just safe. I feel safe here. My family will be relieved of the strain of caring for me. I hate the worry, concern and fear I keep on causing for them. It feels like it's easier to be me – the patient – than it is to be them – the carers. The carers who are frightened and bewildered, not knowing what to do for the best, terrified to leave me or turn their backs even for a few minutes. It feels as though it gets harder and harder for them with each new incident. This disease is so unpredictable. I still feel like a bomb waiting to explode and they are waiting to clear up the devastation it will cause.

Luckily, after many tests, I'm stable enough to be discharged and allowed home for Christmas, but I am to face the prospect of another drug increase early in the New Year. There's fear lurking inside me after the last time. For now, at least, I'm home and wrapped in cotton wool and love.

***

It's New Year's Day, I've been waiting on this list for four hundred and sixty eight days. At least one thousand four hundred and four others like me will have died while they waited for their transplant.

There are all the others too – those that have had to come off the list because they've waited so long and have become too unwell for transplant. They're forced to go down the palliative care route. It's happened to more than one of my friends – that devastating double blow – all that hope you're fired with and inspiration you take from others who recover and get their lives back – then wham! All the hope removed and wiped clean away.

The numbers and figures that keep being churned out don't mean much to many, they're just numbers, but for us they're people – real people. We know some of these people. They're our friends. I'm one of these people. I'm one of the seven thousand plus or so people waiting for new organs to survive. I'm not a number. I can almost feel people dismissing organ donation, not wanting to know, not needing to think about it even. Complacent they will never be affected by it, smugly dismissing the small number of us affected. The numbers aren't big; it won't happen to us. Why bother? I can feel it and I want to scream.

If only there were more people signed up to the organ donor register. If only more people would share their thoughts on organ donation with their families, then perhaps more of us could survive.

Out of the blue, we hear the most wonderful news. The young man, who featured in ITV's *Tonight* programme has received his new heart. There is hope. Every time we hear of a transplant, there is hope.

Fifteen

Mind Games

(January – August 2013)

I don't know how to feel now we're starting this brand new year. A new year signifies a fresh new start, but I feel as though I'm lingering reluctantly with one foot still left planted in last year. I'm scared to stride confidently through. Maybe it's safer to stay where I am. I'm still alive. I'm still well enough for transplant. We're still coping. We have a new normal. We have a new way of life. Maybe it's better if time could just stay still and we can stay here. No risk taking.

***

The crew arrives at the house. I've been pacing about a little. I guess it's a peculiar situation and not one I'd expected to find myself in. They start by setting up the camera equipment and we chat about our predicament. Rob and I had joked quite recently how we needed someone a bit more prominent in the media on the case of organ donation, and today we are lucky enough to have the ITV's Science and Health Editor in our living room.

It's all very surreal. We're preparing for an interview for ITV's main national news in our own home. They film us – I ramble on and, at times, it becomes a bit emotional. They film Rob making up my intravenous drugs. It feels a great opportunity not only to raise awareness of organ donation, but to raise awareness of Pulmonary

Hypertension and its complicated treatments.

We feel so delighted that a main TV channel is supporting our cause, giving us a voice and valuable airtime. It gives us such a boost to know that somebody somewhere is standing up for us, and that people are getting together in a hugely coordinated and concerted effort to try and help us in a big way.

ITV is planning a very special week of activities all related to organ donation. The subject is going to be featured on all the main news bulletins, both local and national, on breakfast shows and talk shows and there will be a special concert with well-known celebrities endorsing our cause. Many transplant patients, both pre and post, are going to be telling their moving stories to raise awareness about the lack of organ donors.

The national news crew will be reporting live from Papworth Hospital daily for a week, and this is how I've become involved. It has all originated from the news story on the *Tonight* programme last autumn about the young man desperately waiting for a new heart and his family's determination to raise awareness about organ donation.

Significantly, the campaign has been named 'From the Heart' and is screened aptly during Valentine's week with all its connotations about hearts. We watch and follow it avidly and take much positivity from the amount of people who are not only discussing organ donation, but also actively signing up to the organ donor register.

We sit together as a family and switch on the news – the Pope has just abdicated, so a big story has broken. Often in these circumstances, smaller stories will lose priority and may not be screened. We wait to see.

The Pope is flashed up on the screen, then a picture of me flashes up next. That is it – enough shown already – Sarah falls into the biggest fit of giggles. It's contagious – seconds after, we're all falling around in giggles. This is supposed to be a serious matter but seeing me flash up in some abstract manner with the Pope heightens our nerves and the strange situation and reality we live in. We use laughter as a mechanism for coping. My family also likes to remind me that I'm just an ordinary mum. Whatever my circumstances, I'm there for them to tease and have a laugh at.

'There is no moment of glory for me then,' I say, 'you lot certainly know how to keep me down to earth.'

Composing ourselves, we watch the bulletin. It's very poignant and features a young girl suffering desperately with Cystic Fibrosis and in need of a heart and lung transplant too. It tells of the reality of needing three organs at the same time and how we face difficult futures. I'm shown speaking of my future: how I want to see those things that mums always want to see – my girls making their way in life; perhaps getting married.

It's screened on both the six o'clock and ten o'clock national news. On the following evening, I'm surprised to see myself pop up on the TV once more, as my piece is integrated with another article filmed at the Transplant unit at Addenbrooke's on ITV Anglia News.

My Facebook, Twitter and mobile go wild, as people contact me to ask questions about signing up to the organ donor register. It goes on for days. People who I haven't seen for ages get in touch because they have seen me on the news. It has made a massive impact. I have comments on my blog from a local journalist wanting to interview me. My campaign to try and raise awareness of organ donation and PH appears to have mushroomed overnight.

The young journalist arrives at the door. I think I'm probably going to need to explain in detail all the facts surrounding organ donation to her. We sit down and then she surprises me outright, 'The girl you were on the TV with, the one with Cystic Fibrosis, is my cousin.' It clicks straight away that she is passionate about raising awareness for organ donation too. It is, indeed, a small world. She produces an excellent article for us in the Welwyn Hatfield Times, which leads to more interviews with other local papers and our local radio station 'Bob FM'.

One of Rob's colleagues who saw the news article kindly donates five hundred pounds to the PHAUK charity after seeing how PH can devastate people's lives. This is such a generous gesture, and I'm pleased that not only did the news article make an impact on people to think about organ donation, but it's made them more aware of PH and its consequences too.

We receive news from NHS Blood and Transplant (NHSBT) that one hundred and forty seven thousand people signed up to the organ donor register that week – it is such uplifting news to hear. At last people are talking about organ donation. I feel proud to have played a tiny part in this massive campaign. It makes me feel more purposeful again and that I'm attempting to do something about my situation, however helpless it feels.

Rob says, 'Since you said you wanted to raise awareness about PH and organ donation, look now – you've been to the House of Commons, been on the local radio and in the local papers and even been on the national and regional news. That can't be bad going!'

I pass five hundred days of waiting. The toll is accumulating – one thousand five hundred people will have died. It is hard to know this. The waiting is feeling harder and harder.

***

Each stage in all our lives is becoming more and more meaningful. We try hard to be positive, to not worry over next week, next month or next year for we know that life holds no guarantees. We're becoming accustomed to living in the moment. If the sun is out, and I feel well enough, we'll make the most of each day. If there is a special occasion looming, we'll make plans to celebrate it in a special way. We celebrate Sarah's twenty-first, we celebrate my fifty-second birthday. Both are events I thought I might never see.

We even manufacture and create things to look forward to. Looking forward to enjoyable things is better than just waiting for what might never come. I adamantly, wholeheartedly and desperately do not want to feel that this long wait is a time of waste. I know I'm deteriorating slowly. I know I'm not going to get better and I know my call may not come, but we are equally and steadfastly determined that, whatever happens, whichever way our luck turns, we'll be able to look back and say we made the most of every precious moment.

I don't want this period to be just some test of endurance. None of us do – Rob, our girls, me – we don't wish to wait and worry for something that may never happen. We don't want to wait for our future dreams to come to us; we want to steal them all now, while there's time and chance.

When everyone keeps saying to us, 'Wow, you guys are always out and about doing things,' or 'Gosh, you lot are enjoying yourselves a lot recently, we cannot keep up with you,' we just smile and shrug it off.

I'm not entirely sure people understand. When you know your life and your world is going to be shortened, then you have to try and embrace the situation you're in and grasp every simple moment. When you see all those future milestones like birthdays, weddings, anniversaries, slipping more from your reach, you have to try and summon the strength to open your arms wide and snatch them back.

I'm glad and grateful to still be alive. Sarah was just eighteen when I was diagnosed and I'm still alive and trying my hardest to be kicking. It's a massive achievement to see her reach twenty-one. It has much more meaning attached to it than a usual twenty-first birthday. I'm still hungry for life, whatever may be happening to my body, I'm not prepared to let myself stumble further away from all that I love in life.

Everything has a heightened significance.

The positivity carries us on. Sometimes plans need to be cancelled – the physical illness takes over. My body simply cannot work the way I want it to. Some days can be really bad. On these days the positivity is measured by the achievement of getting showered and dressed or finishing a book or simply getting out of bed. The positivity can arise just because I've allowed myself the time needed to stop, rest and recuperate. Part of my coping strategy is accepting and admitting there are certain things I cannot manage anymore. It's not actually a crime to take time and space to do little or nothing on a bad day, or even let people down if I'm unable to manage.

We have reached five hundred and thirty-five days of waiting:

one thousand, six hundred and five people who've been on the transplant waiting list alongside me have not survived. I'm still lucky.

***

There's a wait on our hands whatever we make of our situation; this unknown and indefinite wait. I don't want to give up hope though. I believe totally it will happen: that one day it will be the right time. As long as I can stay well enough for my transplant, then it won't matter when. I take both hope and comfort from this. I think of the cliché every time when I think of my wait, 'the light at the end of the tunnel', but it has a resonance.

There is always a light dangling in my imagination – a glowing ball, deep yellow in the core, radiating paler shades of light, sparkling, always beyond my reach, yet enticing me forward through an opaque tunnel. I sense there are dangers all around if I stray from my path and so I have to trust this light, put my faith in it, that it will guide me through to a better future.

With all the discussions in the media on organ donation, come all sorts of opinions. The hardest ones to listen to are those that say people like me are just waiting for someone to die, so we can grab their organs as quickly as we can and get our lives back. Nothing could be further from the truth, but some people truly believe this.

Thousands of people die each day for all manner of reasons; many deaths are untimely and most unexpected. Both illness and death can strike anybody, anywhere at any time. It's a harsh fact – we all know it, but try not to dwell on it. People don't die because I've got heart and lung disease or my friend has liver disease or a little boy or girl somewhere needs a new kidney.

When people die, most are never in a position to retain healthy organs and donate them. However, here in the UK, we are fortunate to have modern science, skilled and advanced surgeons and, most importantly, an organ donor register so there are circumstances where, on their death, a person may be able to donate their organs for transplant.

A transplant patient is not willing people to die so that they can selfishly have their own life saved, nor does someone have to deliberately die so we can have their organs. It is simply that there are generous and kind strangers who are willing to help others in desperate need. Strangers who think about leaving a lasting legacy of life; families of strangers who courageously consent to organ donation. Strangers selflessly reaching out to others who are losing hope. Our organ donor register confirms there are good people out there who wish to do this for us.

As a transplant patient, I'm only hoping for the kindness of a stranger. A stranger's last wish to help us. A stranger's last gift. The greatest gift of all. Life. That's all my family and I hope for. We just hope for a kind stranger. Nothing more, nothing less. A kind stranger. We do not run around every day wishing for people to die, and people do not die because we need new organs to save our lives.

The thought of a family losing a loved one, while my family might gain new hope, is always a very difficult one to entertain. We will be poles apart, yet united in a special bond forever. It is painful to think of and a sensitive issue that triggers all extremes of emotions in one go: happiness, despair, elation, numbness, delight and sorrow. It has to affect two families: one in misery and one in joy. It is difficult to reconcile, but all I can do is simplify these complexities in my mind and come back to the thought of compassion from a stranger.

***

I'm resting in my hospital bed ready – well as ready as I'll ever be. I'm frightened. Last time I naively thought I'd be all right and I wasn't. Now I've lost my innocence. Today they are going to increase my intravenous drug.

I don't refuse any offers of additional anti-sickness medication. The nurses are gentle and caring. Many are the same lovely people who have looked after me time and time again and anticipate what may be in store.

My consultant has also been understanding, and kindly allows me to choose my time to do this. I'd wanted to enjoy Sarah's special birthday first – just in case the increase would make me poorly. I'm ready now. Prepared to be in here for a while if needs be. Prepared if it takes another piece out of me once more. It is time.

The process is started. So far, so good. The drug is increased each day. The device is slowly turned up – to pump the drug at a faster rate through my veins – one day at a time. I wait for the torture to start. It doesn't. I'm relieved. I cannot believe it. Neither can Rob. Everyone is relieved. I'm delighted. Everyone is delighted. I am allowed to go home on my new dose of drugs. It is another achievement. A huge one. A success. I'm elated.

I have more hope. I've never been sure how much more of this drug I will be able to tolerate. Now I know there will be another chance to try again if it comes to it. The iron door is still open. Relief. Pure relief. I have to stay well.

***

I pick up the letter on the doormat. The postmark on the letter is Cambridge, it doesn't look like the usual Papworth envelopes that I'm now so accustomed to. It must be something else. I steel myself as I open it and read. It starts off, 'I have the results of your BMPR2 gene test...'

Hurriedly, I scan the letter through, my whole body tensed. I let out a long slow breath of relief as I read, 'No genetic misprints (mutations) were identified in your BMPR2 gene. Genetic misprints in this gene are the commonest cause of inherited PAH. This result makes it unlikely that you are a carrier of a change in this gene which you could have passed on to your daughters.'

I shout out the news to Rob – in fact I want to shout it out to everyone. We're so elated. This is a good day! The girls are relieved. I'm relieved for other members of my family: my brother, sister, nieces and nephews. Continually living with the disease, the risks have been very real and possible consequences far reaching. We'd tried hard not to dwell on it too much, but it has been a weight and dark cloud over us. In one moment, it has evaporated.

The genetics team does, however, have to look for genetic misprints in another gene, ALK1, although mutations in this are a less common cause of inherited PAH. I receive another letter weeks later to inform us that no mutations in this gene have been found either, so there is now minimal risk the girls or other members of my family may develop PAH because of our family history. It is a fantastic result and a chapter we can finally close.

**

Sarah cannot quite believe that Rob and I are going to meet up with people we've found on Twitter. After all the years of doling out advice to our children about meeting with strangers on the internet, ironically here we are, Rob and I, welcoming a couple into our home. But given our new circumstances, it feels remarkably natural.

Initially, we had both started using social media to chat with other patients with PH. This had progressed to chatting with others in the transplant world when I was listed – people waiting for transplants, people who'd had transplants and even some families who'd lost a loved one and consented to organ donation. We'd made contact and become friends with a couple who'd tragically lost their teenage son in a terrible accident, but had found some comfort in the knowledge that their son had saved so many lives through donating his organs.

Today we meet this couple for the first time, and their friendship and openness gives us insight into how families deal with such unimaginable loss, yet have the strength and courage to consider helping others through organ donation at the most unbearably difficult time. Hearing them talk so openly makes us feel truly humble and we are genuinely touched that they allow us to share their experiences and memory of their treasured son. It is strange but I feel an instant connection with this special young man, still really only a boy, whom I have never even met.

**

We meet up with other PH and transplant patients at clinic and patient events at Papworth, and make more friends online through transplant support groups. There's a particular supportive Facebook group – Heart Transplant Families UK – where other patients affected by transplant offer each other moral support. It's been set up by a lovely mother, because her daughter had a heart transplant, and a group of people – all touched by transplant – help to run it. We hear many stories of brave young children who've survived transplant or who are still waiting for transplants. Once more we are humbled.

There are many opportunities to promote organ donation that come our way over the months. We engage more and more with members of the transplant community and discover there is a National Transplant Week run by NHSBT. During this week the local media interview us again, and Rob takes part in a concert with a national transplant choir pulled together as a one-off event held in Sheffield alongside the Transplant Games. We've recently discovered that this sporting event is held annually for transplanted patients to compete together and also promote the benefits of organ donation. I'm not fit enough to accompany him, but I'm proud he's taken part in the choir and Sarah looks after me while he's away.

**

I'm sitting on a bench looking out to sea when Rob takes the call. It's shocking and dreadful. The loss of life and the struggles people have within our PH and transplant community are hard. Loss becomes part of the package when you and your friends are very ill. We've lost several friends along the way and it's always heartbreaking to hear. Those of us who keep on surviving the odds know we're blessed. It makes it all real again too; that's what we're doing – surviving the odds.

Whitstable. It's July, the weather has been hot and we're enjoying the cool of the evening, having decided to take a break away for a few days. The air is still, the sun and tide have all but disappeared leaving deep orange ripples and pools in the sand. The clouds look black, but hues of red and gold glow through and stretch across the horizon.

Another friend has passed away. This time it's a close one – my dear friend who accompanied me to the House of Commons. We've been through so much together and supported each other along the way. We'd visited her recently at Papworth as she'd received her heart and double lung transplant. She'd made a wonderful start but then rejection had set in. Rejection by your body of new organs is one of the biggest problems that transplant patients fear.

Heartbreak. We're devastated for her; we're devastated for her family who we'd grown to know. I cannot help but think that the wonderful sunset I'm watching is so very fitting for such a beautiful friend. It helps soothe the night.

In some ways, it doesn't feel quite right to be on holiday in these circumstances, yet in others it feels the best place to be, away from everything – from everyone – a quiet chance to contemplate and absorb this dreadful news. Selfishly, yet poignantly, it brings home the magnitude of what we're waiting for, what we're wishing for. Should we really be wishing and hoping for any of this?

The questions start to rise inside us again. Is it the right thing to do? We know I'll not get better. What we don't know is how long I have left to live. We don't know if I had my transplant today if I would survive, live longer or even if my quality of life would be better. Nobody can tell us the answers. Nobody can tell us what to do. We don't know what to do anymore. From the sorrow and grief of my friend's death, the turmoil and angst inside my tornado rise up again confusing my mind.

Waiting for a transplant is a huge mind game as well as a physical one. The mind game is becoming bigger than the physical one, if that's possible. My mind is spent as well as my body.

I want someone to tell me – no order me – what to do, so I don't have to carry the weight of the decision on me or my family any more, so it's someone else's decision that this is having to happen, and not mine. The doctors can only give you the facts though; ultimately you have to be the one to decide. I know my family will support any decision I make about my future treatment, but I carry guilt around. Guilt at what I'm putting them through – the perpetual crises that are ongoing and the perpetual wait. Waiting, waiting, waiting… all of us are waiting… all my family is waiting… all my friends are waiting…

***

We return to Transplant clinic. I don't go into all the doubts and questions – they will always haunt us whatever anyone says. There isn't really a choice I know – it is something I have to do, to have that chance of a better life and if I want to survive.

I do ask about having a double lung transplant though, instead of having a heart and double lung transplant. It's an option that was mentioned earlier in the process. The waiting period is potentially not as long because the heart and lungs can be split and the heart can go to save someone else in need. I wouldn't have to hold out for three organs and an operation that is rarely carried out more than five or six times a year at the most.

The consultant takes a breath and says, 'It's a possibility, but it would be a very dangerous and risky operation for you. The matching of new lungs and their normal blood vessels to your damaged pulmonary arteries would pose a danger. It isn't something that the team want to do, but if things get much worse it's still an option.'

Having listened to her words, I don't want this to be my option. I really don't.

***

It's summer's end. The end of August. We feel as though we've gone around in many circles this year. We haven't found any new answers though. We resign ourselves back to how we've been – how we were when the year first started – but with renewed determination. We must simply wait. Our decision hasn't changed. It's always the same decision – whatever comes around and goes around – it's always the same decision.

It's been one year and eleven months of waiting – seven hundred days. In seven hundred days, two thousand one hundred people will have died waiting on the transplant list. The toll is rising higher while I wait. However we feel, we know we're still the lucky ones – we know we're still blessed.

We're ready. More ready than ever. There is only one more thing to happen – we have changed as much as we can for the positive – done as much as we can do.

The only changes left are the ones over which we have absolutely no control. My illness. My transplant.

Sixteen

Lamb Tagine

(September 2013)

September. A month of new beginnings. It's always more significant than New Year in my book. I think it's because of school. September marking the end of summer and back to school: new uniforms, books, new teachers, new classrooms. Fresh starts. Repeated with my children and then again during my teaching years.

Even without school, there's the sense of summer's end that is tangible. The white heat and intense yellows and blues of August muting into deeper, darker shades. Nature's colours changing as we adjust and make new changes ourselves. Cooler days quickly narrowing towards longer nights. An unmistakable freshness and scent in the air, tactile on my face. It's as if nature itself is telling us it's time for change.

***

We weave our way through the teeming crowds and into a small gap by the road. It's easy for me. It's a bit like I'm in my own royal box sitting in my chariot. I'm able to take in the view and rest at the same time. The runners are coming through fast and furiously at the eleventh mile to the sound of pulsating music, beating out loud. It feels inspiring to watch these runners in a festival atmosphere with the music and crowds. I hadn't quite believed I'd be able to do this, but here I am. We've come into London once more to watch Rose

156

and her boyfriend, David, take part in the 'Run to the Beat' half marathon.

Rose is tired of waiting too, and feels she wants to do something positive for our situation, so she's raising much-needed funds for the PHAUK charity. I'd been determined to cheer her on, so Rob had made some careful plans to enable me to manage it. Sarah and Oli have joined us, taking the burden off Rob at times with pushing my wheelchair.

The race finishes in Greenwich Park in London, and we've stayed in Canary Wharf the evening before. This enables me to pace myself with the travelling and activities. We've found our way to Greenwich, negotiating the Docklands Light Railway with my wheelchair. Rob has ensured and tested that our route is completely wheelchair friendly. He's picked a spot by the roadside rather than in the heavy crowds of the park, which he thinks may be too over-whelming for me.

Rose and David run past and we cheer out loud, encouraging them on for their last stretch. Sarah and Oli decide to push through the crowds and head up through the park to the finishing line. I'm having one of my better days, so I reassure Rob I'm game to follow as long as he can manage me in my chair. He races up Greenwich Hill, sometimes he breaks into a sprint and I feel the wheelchair might even collapse underneath me, but it's great fun to throw caution to the winds for a moment and we manage to catch further glimpses of Rose and David as they near the finish line.

We are caught up in huge crowds once they finish, but miracu-lously spot them standing just a few yards away before we follow a snake of turquoise green, t-shirted runners walking back exhaust-edly down the hill.

Rose raises over three thousand five hundred pounds for PHAUK, and we are one proud mum and dad. David raises a tidy sum for the Multiple Sclerosis Society, which afflicts his uncle and aunt. It's good to make something positive out of what's now feel-ing like a desperate situation. It's great to be able to give something back to the charity that's helped us so much during these last few years.

A few weeks later, we load the car once more and take Rose back to university. We are half way down the motorway when I realise I've forgotten my second pump for my intravenous drug. I'm totally dependent on it, like an addict. It's basically keeping me alive, to break the flow of drug for too long can cause serious danger.

As I have to change my drug over every twelve hours, I need two pumps. I have to clamp the line running into my chest for a couple of seconds to ensure no air bubbles sneak into my body during the changeover to the syringe of medication on the second pump. Unclamp and then comes the rush of the fresh drug. Its potency makes me nauseous and light headed. My skin flushes to its highest colour, so much so my arms and legs have become permanently inflamed with eczema.

We have to turn around, go home and retrieve the pump and drive back again. It adds hours to our journey. No one says anything. I feel like a burden.

So much hard work and planning has gone into enabling me to make this trip and see Rose ready to move in her new house. It sometimes feels like it'd be easier not to try and join in anymore leaving everyone to it and remain on the sidelines. But I have to. I cannot give up. These are becoming precious moments. Moments I need to hang on and look forward to.

My days feel like they're drawing in, like September itself. I'm not really fit for much in the mornings and I'm not really fit for much in the evenings. In between, I manage what I can, which can vary from day to day.

The truth is I know I'm worsening. I haven't been too good over these last few weeks. I'm having more bad days than good ones. Everything is becoming more of an effort but then, when I manage to achieve something, the rewards feel greater and the memories more special. I just want to see Rose's new house. I want to be able to picture where she lives and where she is should I become much worse, or in case I get my transplant call or the unimaginable happens.

I've been told the average wait for a heart and double lung

transplant is two years. I'm nearly there now. It's like I've been working through these two years and towards this goal forever. It's become another one of those milestones; we're nearly there, but I'm limping towards it. What next, after two years? How will I cope then?

Fortunately, the rest of our trip goes to plan. I see her new house, meet her housemates and we leave her settled and return home. Another family mission accomplished with me, my PAH and chariot in tow.

***

It's Saturday, the twenty-first of September, just another ordinary day. We're getting ready for some friends who are coming to visit. Rob has popped out last minute food shopping and I'm busy preparing a meal, cooking one of my favourite dishes, a lamb tagine.

We've been chatting about plans for next weekend as it's going to be our twenty-third wedding anniversary. We've also been making plans for a couple more short trips in October, one to celebrate Rob's impending birthday, before the clocks go back and the nights become longer and the days shorter and darker. I'm wondering if we've time to fit it all in before the frenetic count down to Christmas starts. I'm so looking forward to everything, so many activities to juggle and keep me busy and my mind occupied. I always get excited about Christmas, I have a romantic picture of Christmas in my mind already: Christmas trees, mulled wine, log fires, present shopping, cosy nights.

As I sit in the kitchen preparing the lamb, it all feels quite content and normal, except for the fact that it isn't any ordinary day. Today I've reached the two-year wait landmark in my transplant journey. Two years since I was listed for my transplant and placed on the active transplant list. I say 'active', though this hardly seems to ring true anymore. No call has come, not even a 'false alarm'.

Mundanely chopping up vegetables, my mind drifts inevitably yet again to transplantation, as I try to imagine what it must be like to inhabit this unique world. Doctors, nurses and whole teams busying about their patients, saving lives. Someone picking up the phone to hear both the exciting and frightening news that an organ donor match has been found. Ambulances bluelighting organs and patients in the dead of night. Intensive care units, full of trauma, in a state of organised chaos. Visiting and waiting relatives. Most of all I can't leave the thought that somewhere, amidst all this activity, is a devastated family, making the biggest decision they have probably ever had to face and granting permission to give the gift of life. Everyday people's lives being changed forever, one way or another, all up and down the country.

Pausing for a moment, I wonder, 'Will this ever be me? When might it happen? Will I feel ready? Will my family cope? Will it *ever* happen? What if it doesn't?' The same old stupid and silly questions that are never answered keep popping in my mind, as they have done persistently for two years. I should really be used to them by now, but I'm not.

I check the tagine and begin to stir in some spices, as my thoughts are lost in flashbacks to those frank conversations with the Transplant team right at the outset, still very much fresh in my mind. They did tell me that an average wait for a heart and double lung transplant was two years; they did lay it on the line that it may be a long wait. I really shouldn't be surprised.

I'm glad we had been prepared. Once you're on the active list, you need to be ready mentally for that call to come out of the blue at every minute of every day, at any time and in any place. We've tried to be prepared from day one, but this in turn has taken its toll and made the wait feel onerous, like an all-consuming ache. There has to be some limit on how far someone can endure the sheer mental anguish of being in a state of constant alert. Still, we have to be prepared. We have to keep on being alert. There is no other option.

Reaching this milestone, I know I've beaten the odds and some of the prognosis statistics thrown at me all those years ago. I've been one of those lucky few that manage to slip quietly through the net and continue softly chancing their good fortune.

My dish is simmering and cooking on the stove, wafts of cinnamon, paprika, ginger and tumeric mingle with aromas of apricots, lamb and honey and, as I soothingly stir the ingredients, my mind meanders to where we are now and just how far we've come.

Two years have passed and we've reached the place that felt a long time coming when I first went on the active transplant list. Two years – the bench mark. So it is definitely no ordinary September morning. It is a watershed, a pivotal moment in an otherwise routine family day. After all the bumps and bruises, ups and downs, sadness and loss, enjoyment and fun, and the challenges of illness and waiting on the list, we've reached the destination, the two year marker that's been in my head all this time.

But I haven't managed to get where I need to be – the boundaries have shifted around me, like sand slipping and changing shape. Where am I going? I still don't know yet. How long will it take me to get there? Another hour, another day, another week, another month, another year – no one knows. No one can tell me. Every time I move further on, the future I so desperately long for moves in parallel with me, staying tantalisingly ahead, the same distance away.

I had no idea where I might be and what I might be doing on this day two years ago when I was handed a future of uncertainty, laid out bare as though on a plate, stark and clear. Here I am though, making plans and cooking for my friends. In fact it's probably one of the finest destinations in life that I could have arrived at after all, following my initial poor prognosis.

When I stop and reflect, it's what I wished for more than anything. Simply to be with my family, making plans, meeting up with friends and doing so many of those ordinary things I once took for granted. Those things that I value now more than anything else. I realise that all the bumps and bruises, ups and downs, sadness and loss, enjoyment and fun, and challenges of illness is called living life and I'm blessed I'm still able to do so.

We will have to carry on doing what we've learned to do best, mixing the very ordinary with the exceptionally extraordinary. Trying hard to live in the moment. Making the most of every minute. Trying hard not to think too much about the future. Transplant is all about prolonging prognosis and improving quality of life. So far I've already achieved the best outcome for now and that's what it's all been about. I've managed to remain stable and strong enough to have a transplant.

The longer I stay stable, the longer I may wait, but at least this will allow me to continue to enjoy life before the next stage arrives. The transplant still hovers on the horizon, quietly offering some comfort and another path. One day I hope it may move nearer towards me while I remain stable, not me towards it should my condition deteriorate. Somehow I know the wind will change course and alter direction, but only when it's good and ready and not a moment before. I just have to be ready when it does.

I return to my cooking, casually adding a few more herbs and spices to the tagine. It's nearly cooked and my thoughts are back in the present where I should be and belong. Rob is unpacking the shopping. It's nearly time for our friends to arrive. Life feels content and good and normal and ordinary. This weekend is going to be a good one.

**

The chest pains punch hard before leaving a residual dull ache. I keep feeling faint and dizzy. Every time we have an ordinary and enjoyable time with friends, it seems as if I have to pay for it later. Two days after our friends have visited, I'm back at Papworth. I'm relieved they've brought me back in – it feels the safest place to be at times like this. It's frightening when things like this start happening suddenly – the big reminders that, although you're pretending to be as normal as possible, you decidedly aren't.

I'm kept in for a few days, wired up to the heart monitor and undergo the all too familiar tests. I'm under the care of both my teams, my PH team and my Transplant team, which gives me double the reassurance. Nothing new is shown from the tests and, although some concern is expressed which might require them to increase my intravenous medication, they decide to hold off for now and I'm allowed home to see how things go. As ever I can phone straight away for help if I need it. It's a stark and tormenting reminder of how fragile my life is.

I take things easy and we try to pull ourselves back once more, knowing it won't be the last incident or crisis – it won't be the last time the tornado will whirl up and then settle back into its surrounding hard shell. It will keep on coming and going as it pleases. It's exhausting. All this uncertainty from one day to the next is totally exhausting. How long will it go on? How long can I keep going? How many more times can I keep on bouncing back? How long can my weary heart and lungs keep it up?

***

Today is another milestone, our twenty-third wedding anniversary. We've come a long way now since our twentieth, the year I found out I was sick. It's nearing the end of September, but it could be August today. There isn't a cloud in the sky and the sun is shining high, with a deeper glow of late summer. We exchange cards and presents. Rob gives me a small gold feather pendant on a delicate chain.

In folklore, a feather can represent many things. It can be a symbol of loved ones guiding and supporting you through; it can represent hope and faith; it can denote travel and the ability to move more freely; in dreams feathers can mean a fresh start and signify flight and freedom, moving beyond normal boundaries and limitations. It is a meaningful gift and I know I will always treasure it.

We spend our day quietly out in the garden. I'm banned from doing anything, as I'm still trying to get over last week's events. There's still much colour: the roses are having a second flush and the Michaelmas daisies are full of buds, but not quite opened yet. I think to myself, 'If this weather continues like this, they'll be out in full bloom in a few days.' I'm looking forward to seeing them do that. The sun and the flowers lift my spirits.

The raspberry bushes are still laden with their fruit and I pick the ripe berries. Sarah and Oli are coming for dinner. Rob tidies the garden and then cooks a Sunday roast. I sit at the kitchen breakfast bar and pull together a raspberry crumble. Later when it's cooked, I photograph it – I don't know why really, it's nothing special. I suppose I'm just proud of my homegrown raspberries! Sarah and Oli appear and they bring two homemade puddings as well. We don't usually have puddings, but on this occasion we've three to choose from.

We enjoy a lovely family dinner, but when it's bedtime Rob cannot sleep as he has awful indigestion. He rarely suffers from this, but he did try all three puddings, so he knows he's only himself to blame. He decides to go downstairs and sit for a while so as not to disturb me. I'm exhausted and fall into a deep sleep.

***

Monday morning six-thirty, and I'm awakened by Rob bringing me a cup of tea and my newly made up syringe of Flolan. Our usual routine. We swap the syringe over. Rob sighs, 'I'm shattered, I've been up all night with that indigestion, but it's eased off so I'm coming back to bed for a few hours kip once we've had this cuppa.'

As he finishes speaking the house phone starts to ring. We look at one another. We carry on looking at one another for a second. Rob grabs the phone handing it to me, but I already know. I knew before he even picked it up. I knew as soon as it rang. I know. It's strange how you just know certain things.

'Hi Kathryn, how are you this morning?' says the friendly voice of one of the Papworth transplant coordinators. 'We have a potential donor. Can you be ready within the hour? We're sending a car.'

Everyone said the call would come when it's least expected and it certainly did. We were thinking of drugs and syringes and Monday morning blues, turning over and going back to sleep. Now we're on full alert – it's 'action stations'.

I get up, shower and dress myself and start gathering my bags – no time to get nervous or excited. I detach myself, check my things. I'm a bit disorganised. I've had all this time, but I used my hospital bag only last week for my unplanned stay in Papworth and it's still strewn open on the spare bed, waiting to be packed again. No time

164

for excitement. I put back in what I think I need. I make a smaller bag for the immediate things I might use while we wait for news. I can't drink my tea. It's tempting, but I'm not allowed anything to eat or drink from this point.

Rob finds the bag he's already prepared – a good job it's there waiting and ready – he's a bundle of panic. I'm detached and more focused as if getting ready for a mission and he, in his own words, is like Corporal Jones from *Dad's Army*. He even keeps saying, 'Don't panic, don't panic.'

I'm not panicking; at least I don't think I am. I'm not allowing myself to, or at least not allowing anyone to see that I am. I have to do this bravely and courageously and in my own way. If I go into panic, everyone else will see and then they will panic. I don't want everyone panicking. I don't need everyone panicking. I cannot let them panic. I need calm. Steely, quiet, determined calm. I won't be able to do it if they all panic. Calm. Calm. Calm.

Rob tries to phone Sarah – no answer. He tries to phone Rose – no answer either. He tries again and again and again. Instead he phones Oli who's just started work on an early morning shift. Oli tries to phone Sarah. Eventually we get through to her. The news startles her and she agrees to join us at the hospital as soon as she can.

We eventually reach Rose. It's the morning of her first full day of her second year at university. A friend had agreed months ago to pick her up when my call came – we'd planned it all meticulously – but as Oli doesn't know what to do with himself, the plans change now it's all become a reality and he sets off to collect Rose from Bournemouth instead. He needs to feel occupied and do something that will help us.

Seven-thirty a.m, and the car's here for me. I'm on the phone to Rose as I climb in and we tell each other, 'I love you.' She wishes me luck and I say, 'I'll see you when I wake up.' We set off towards my new future in the Monday morning rush hour, the extraordinary and ordinary colliding once more.

There's no time for me to phone anyone else, and I leave Rob to call my mum before he sets off. He's decided to follow in our own car, just in case it's a false alarm and we can head back home if it is. He rightly doesn't want to take for granted that my transplant will happen. We've been warned about false alarms and they've happened to some of my friends. We're prepared for this, we think we are, but we honestly don't know. Right now, I don't know anything, other than getting to the hospital and finding out more.

It's so strange as I watch the busy traffic around me hurry by. I imagine overwrought drivers weighed down with the weariness of Monday morning and contrast this with my own emotions, full of eagerness and anticipation, speeding along to a potential new life. I cannot help but cast my mind to other events that will be happening, or have happened, to make this event in my life emerge this Monday morning. One family's tragedy, enabling another family to have hope. My family.

Switching my mind from these difficult thoughts, I focus on what needs to be done. I text my sister. I text my brother. I text some friends. The phone signal comes and goes. Some receive my texts, others don't. I try my best before we reach hospital, as there's little signal once there. It's all I can do.

In the mirror I can see Rob behind us, then I can't, then I can. He's ahead of us now somehow, so stops in a lay-by to allow us to catch up. My car passes him and puts on its blue light as we near the hospital and he follows closely behind. He receives a text from a friend, who happens to work at Papworth, 'Have you had the call? I've just followed your car into work and you're following one of our vehicles.' News is getting out fast.

I'm not sure where I should be going, but the driver thankfully knows and takes me through to a ward. It's a ward I've never been on. The transplant coordinator comes to meet us and takes me to a bed. It's in a small room with two beds. The usual blue hospital curtain, which is supposed to offer privacy but rarely does in practice, sections us off from another lady patient. I can't see who she is. She can't see me either, but she must overhear what's taking place.

Eight-thirty a.m. and Sarah arrives. We're told the donor organs are still being tested and it will be quite a while yet before we receive further news. We're also told that two other patients have been brought in as back up, but if both the heart and lungs are in good enough condition, then I am to be the priority case and will receive my transplant. There is such a shortage of organ donors that other candidates need to be brought in. If the donor lungs are considered unfit for transplant, then the heart could still be used, so a heart transplant patient is here just in case. Similarly, if the heart cannot be used, then the lungs could still be viable, so a lung patient has been brought in as well.

The transplant coordinator is busy trying to prepare all three of us. We are kept apart from one another for confidentiality reasons, but we all know each other is here. It's a tough situation. Any one of us or none of us might receive our transplant today. All three of us must sit and wait for news. My coordinator passes on some lovely sentiments to me from one of the others waiting. He's explained I've been waiting for my transplant for over two years. She says to him, 'I hope the lady gets her transplant today.' I feel so touched that a person who doesn't even know me can be so kind, especially when they obviously are in need of a transplant themselves.

I'd like to think I could be that brave towards someone too. I hope one of us will be lucky. I hope it will be me, but I know if it isn't, then perhaps it will be someone else's lucky day and my day will come another time. Today has answered all those never-ending questions and doubts while I waited though. 'Yes, I definitely *do* want this transplant; there is absolutely no doubt now the process has begun.'

Two hours pass. We have occasional updates. They're still testing the organs and all is good so far.

There is a huge sign over my bed saying, 'Nil by mouth.' Sarah pulls what looks like a brick out of her bag. 'I've brought some Soreen in case we get hungry – that's all I could find when I left in such a hurry…'

'Oli won't be pleased you've nicked his secret fishing snacks,' I giggle. We all laugh, releasing some of our inner tension.

'Soreen? We've had two years to be prepared for this and you lift bloody Soreen out of your bag,' laughs Rob. It makes me smile, the random thoughts and things that you cling on to in moments of crisis. Today's one is Soreen. I think I will always remember Soreen if I'm ever able to look back on this day!

Eleven-thirty a.m. and more news. All is still looking good. A visit by a doctor this time, and we go through the consent form for the operation once more. The last time was two years ago. The doctor reads out all the risks. I know them already. Inside out. I sign the form. Nothing will change my mind. I have a cannula inserted into my arm. Still all good to go.

Twelve-thirty p.m. The coordinator asks me to put on a hospital gown and take my first immunosuppressant. He's ninety-five percent sure it's going ahead and the team is working on the last test. I need to be ready to go when they say, 'Go.' I'm ready. More ready than I'll ever be.

One p.m. It's a go.

I'm wrapped in a warm blanket, helped into a wheelchair and Rob and Sarah gather my things before wheeling me to the operating theatre. The coordinator takes us down one floor in a creaky old lift with metal lattice folding doors. I think I've blanked out every emotion and feeling. I need to be calm for my family. Mind over matter. We hug, kiss and say goodbye. I say firmly, 'See you later.' They need to believe what I believe, that I *will* see them later.

'See you on the other side,' says Sarah tearfully.

I'm pushed through the theatre doors and into a small side room. There the team is ready to welcome me. Their faces, turned towards me, are smiling and reassuring. The anaesthetist greets me, chats away gently and I try and count to ten as instructed when he puts the sedative into my cannula.

I'm serene. Peaceful somehow. Prepared. There's no tornado or its shell anymore. It's disappeared. All gone. Tranquil.

I'm ready to take that leap of faith. With one huge shove, I push the iron door wide open and hurl myself over the mighty cliff with its deep water below, hidden from me behind the door all this time. Surrendering myself to my fate and the rushing air as I fall, I cannot know if I will swim or drown.

PART THREE

Special Handling

'Miracles, in the sense of phenomena we cannot explain, surround us on every hand: life itself is the miracle of miracles.'
George Bernard Shaw

Seventeen

Sleepy Hollow

The clinical lead surgeon is sitting in his scrubs, talking softly. Although I've been desperate for news for hours, I'm exhausted and finding it hard to concentrate and process everything he's saying. He talks at length about the problems we will face over the next forty-eight hours, but my mind is largely mush.

I do, however, gather enough to realise that, although the operation has been successful, he's warning us that the next few hours are critical, as the new organs are extremely tired. In particular Kath's new heart is not functioning as well as he'd like, so it will be necessary for this to be supported by a balloon pump machine. He explains this is an invasive but straightforward procedure, which will give the new heart the extra help it will need until he is satisfied it can work on its own. 'Can we see her?' I ask. That's all that's bothering me right at this moment. I just need to see her. He tells me it'll be another half an hour.

The half hour gives Sarah and me time to step outside to make some calls. Although there's wi-fi in the relatives' room, the phone signal is non-existent. I find a small patch about fifty yards away where I can raise one bar on my phone and call Kath's mum to let her know she's out of surgery.

I'm still on the phone to her when Rose comes rushing out shouting 'Quickly, we can see Mum now!' but as we run back to the building the automatic sliding doors shut in our face and refuse to reopen. We're frantically pressing buttons and banging on the door to no avail when Rose spots a yellow phone. After a few minutes, which seems an age, we are able to raise someone and dash our way back upstairs to the intensive care unit ('ICU').

As we are taken through to see Kath, I am overjoyed that she has made it through the operation but heavily sense that, whilst the surgeon's earlier comments didn't unnerve me, she is obviously extremely poorly. I know deep down we've a long way to go until we can be certain we have the outcome we all crave.

We walk past what seems an endless row of beds and more side rooms. I am staggered at the sheer size of ICU. I had no idea it would be this large. It's a genuine TARDIS moment.

Kath is in a large separate room from the main ward with two other patients. All the lighting is dimmed with the exception of Kath's bed, where a bright angle poise lamp shines down on her immobile body. A medical team of six or seven people is standing hushed near her bed in the shadows, trying to be unobtrusive at this private family moment. Other than the gentle hum of medical machinery, it is quiet and still.

Kath is white. For an awful moment, I think she's dead. She isn't though, she's in an induced coma, but that's how she looks and the whispered tones of the medical team and subdued lighting only serve to conjure up an unhealthy mental image of a funeral parlour.

The sight of Kath lying like this is difficult to take for all of us. There are tubes coming out of her body in all directions, and she is being ventilated. The girls and I weep a little self consciously as we hold her hand and chat lovingly. There is little more we can do and it's obvious to me that the medical team is itching to connect Kath up to the balloon pump machine, which I can see poised in readiness at the end of her bed. We leave and, once outside ICU, we go into a group hug and I start to wail.

I've never made a noise like that before or since. It came from a very dark place.

***

The long hours waiting for news as the operation progressed had been understandably difficult and protracted. After Sarah and I had

left Kath outside the operating theatre at one o'clock in the afternoon, we had walked back to the ward to collect her things, trying
to hold ourselves together, with limited success. We had managed
to pass the first hour or so trying to eat some lunch in the canteen
or, at least, we pushed it round our plates for a while. Sarah made
me smile, 'I know we've been waiting for two years, so I think we
ought to have been better prepared for this moment.'

While we were in the canteen, we'd bumped into the lady who
had texted me earlier, realising the call had come when she'd seen
me driving to Papworth so early in the morning. She had received a
kidney transplant some years ago, so she knew what we were going
through and it was good to speak with her to gain some reassurance.

We passed some time sitting by the hospital's duck pond. Sarah
decided to feed chunks of the Soreen to the assembled throng of
wildlife, but I had to stop her when it appeared one of the ducks was
struggling to eat the dry malt loaf. We allowed ourselves a small
chuckle, 'We don't want a Dead Duck Day,' I said, referring to one
of her favourite films, *About a Boy*.

We made our way to the main relatives' room, but it was packed
and we weren't ready to sit and make small talk with strangers, so
we found a separate tiny adjacent room, which was empty. We
passed more time by chatting until Sarah left at four-thirty to meet
Oli, who had arrived home having picked up Rose from Bournemouth. I tried to grab some sleep in a chair but none came. The
day's events so far just swirled in my head. I started to think about
the donor family, but then quickly and deliberately pushed this out
of my mind. There would be a proper and right time for this. I had
enough emotions to deal with as it was, I reasoned to myself.

By six o'clock and five hours into the operation, I hadn't had
any news from the surgical team so was becoming restless. Sarah,
Rose and Oli arrived shortly after and we settled into the large,
critical care relatives' room, which was now empty. This is actually
quite a comfy room with large settees, soft drinks and a TV, so we
were able to spread ourselves out.

Our transplant coordinator popped in to see us at seven o'clock
and advised that all was proceeding reasonably well. Kath's own

heart and lungs had been removed, the donor organs were in, but there was too much bleeding so one of the joins to the heart was being reconnected. This was all delivered sensitively, yet routinely. It didn't feel routine to us. He estimated it would take another two hours so we should try and grab something to eat, and he recommended a pub in nearby Elsworth village.

We decided to follow his suggestion. I was surprised the pub wanted to serve us. We didn't look great and Sarah had said a little too frankly and loudly, 'You look like shit, Dad.' On reflection, being so close to Papworth, they'd probably seen it all before. We all sat with glazed, zombie-like expressions looking blankly at the menu. Oli was even probably in a worse state than me, having being at work in London at five-thirty in the morning, then driven to Bournemouth and back to fetch Rose and then onto Papworth. He looked like he was close to passing out, but the meal revived him temporarily.

By eight-thirty we were back in the relatives' room. I studied my girls' faces for any sign of worry and stress, and was thankful that they appeared to have dozed off for a little while. I hadn't asked them how they were feeling, and felt a bit ashamed I hadn't done so, but was concentrating on trying to hold myself together. This day was clearly just as stressful for them but they appeared to be bearing up well, at least on the outside.

It wasn't until well after nine that a critical care nurse arrived to say she thought we should be able to see Kath in half an hour. In the meantime she made us some tea. An hour and a half later, with no further news, we had become frantic. Oli managed to discover a red phone outside critical care and rang to see if we could glean what was happening. Profuse apologies followed from one of the team who said, without offering any further explanation, it was all taking longer than expected. At least we had discovered the red phone had a use and it was christened the batphone.

'The surgeon can see you now,' the critical care nurse finally said just before midnight and we quickly followed her from the waiting room into ICU where the girls, Oli and I were ushered into a small side room.

***

As we leave Kath in the hands of the expert medical team, I decide not to wait all night at the hospital, but instead will drive home with Rose, while Sarah and Oli will return to their own flat in Hitchin. I feel some guilt for not staying with Kath, but I reason that it will be sensible to get Rose home after her long day, and that we'd both benefit from having each other's company and sleep in our own beds. This way, hopefully we'll be a little more refreshed than if we crashed on the sofas in the waiting room. I justify to myself that I can be back at Papworth within forty minutes if the team calls me as they promise me they will if Kath worsens.

Heading back down the Ermine Way at one in the morning, I am shocked at the number of juggernauts heading towards us, their lights blazing, along this usually quiet road. I grip the steering wheel and try and stay focused on the left-hand side of the road as lorry after lorry hurtles past shaking our car in their wake. It's relentless. I haven't slept hardly at all in the last twenty-four hours and I'm struggling to keep my exhausted senses coordinated, shouting 'For God's sake, it's like a cruel video game, haven't we been through enough today?'

Thankfully the traffic eases as we pick up the faster road near Royston, and we arrive home just before two o'clock on Tuesday morning. Just as we pull in, Rose's boyfriend, David, is dropped off by his dad, having hotfooted it back from Exeter University to be with and support Rose, who by now is extremely tearful. I'm happy to see him, as we have no immediate family nearby. I'm grateful that both girls have someone close they can lean on right now.

After updating friends and family with a few generic emails and texts, I collapse into bed, happy and scared witless in equal proportions. Sarah was right. You have two years to prepare, but nothing can actually prepare you for this moment.

***

My mind was so wired last night, it took ages to sleep, but looking at the clock I know I must have managed a few hours. It's six-thirty and I call Papworth for an update. I take it as a good sign that they didn't have to ring me in the night. A nurse tells me that there's no change in Kath's condition.

I make it to the hospital for ten o'clock, leaving Rose to catch up on some sleep and, using the batphone, am able to see Kath – there is pretty much unrestricted visiting in ICU. She's in the same room as last night. The sight of the machines, ventilators and chest drains doesn't seem quite as daunting this morning so I'm slightly less teary when I see her lying in the same position I had left her last night. She looks different though. It hits me, a little more colour has returned to her face, which I attribute partly to the effect of the blue balloon pump machine, which is breathing noisily near the foot of her bed. It reminds me of R2D2 from *Star Wars*.

A nurse is coming towards the end of her twelve-hour shift looking after her. I marvel at her dexterity as she juggles medication flows, checks vital signs and enters data into a computer at the foot of the bed, chatting to Kath reassuringly as if she's awake. She is so fast and adept, it reminds me of those acts on TV where artists spin plates, not allowing any of them to crash to the floor. I am witnessing the very best of the NHS.

'Her lungs are doing ok – the oxygen's been reduced down to forty per cent and sats are at ninety per cent. Her heart remains the issue. It's tired and the right side is failing. There's been a very slight improvement from last night, but it's still not where we want it to be, so we're going to keep her on the balloon pump for now. There's no significant bleeding, her chest is reasonably clear and overall she's stable. We're just taking things as they come,' the nurse informs me efficiently. She continues with her work attending to all the equipment as I sit next to Kath, hold her hand, and tell her, I love her.

I'm worried about the right side heart failure but we've been here before when Kath's PH was first diagnosed, so it's not a new issue for me in some ways. One of the lung transplant consultants appears and we have a good chat. He confirms the information the nurse has already told me. He refers to Kath's heart as being sluggish which is an evocative turn of phrase and helps me digest the state of her condition. He says it might take some time to improve, so they plan to keep her asleep for a couple of days.

'How is she doing overall, though?' I ask him.

'We're reasonably positive for a good outcome,' he replies.

He leaves and I start to dissect his words. I play out in my mind, 'Okay, so they're not 'very positive', just 'reasonably positive', which could be better, but then again, he didn't say that things are 'looking bad', so – I'm going to take the positives out of his comment. Yep, I'm happy enough with that.' The girls and their boyfriends arrive a little later and we spend the day playing 'team tag' visiting Kath, as she is only allowed two visitors at a time.

By the evening it's becoming apparent that Kath is not passing enough water and her blood sugar level is giving the medical team concern. I don't pretend to understand all the measurements they are taking, but I glean enough that they're too high for their liking. They're about to give Kath a significant dose of insulin and diuretics to combat the problem but the nurse informs me, if things don't improve, she might need dialysis.

There's no significant change by the time I leave for home at nine o'clock. On the journey home I have some black thoughts about whether we've done the right thing about having the transplant, but these are interrupted by my mobile buzzing. I take the call on my hands free. It's my brother. I give him the latest news and let him into what I am thinking. 'No, stop. Don't even go there. Don't look back, you just have to move forward,' he instructs me firmly. It's just what I need and it snaps me back into positivity. He offers to drive down from Nottingham to be with me but leaves this in my hands, saying he'll let me make that call if, or when, I need to. I'm grateful to know his support is there.

I arrive home at ten o'clock to find Rose and David, who had left the hospital a couple of hours earlier, have prepared me a meal and a cake with a candle on it. I had totally forgotten – it's my birthday.

***

Another night's broken sleep. I reckon I can't have had more than seven or eight hours over the last three nights combined. My head is fuzzy and my chest is sore, as if someone has been hugging me tight all night. I'm sure it's nothing more serious than stress and exhaustion. On the plus side, no call from the hospital. I make the early call to ICU at six-thirty and am delighted to hear that Kath's sugar levels have been improved and the insulin infusion has been stopped. Steady night, improved sugar levels, off insulin.

Kath had given me strict instructions months ago to keep all her PH and transplant cyber friends up to date once she had had the operation. I'm attending to all this when an email from one of my own cyber friends pops up. His own son had had a transplant, so he's been there, done it and got the t-shirt. I call him Doc, for the very specific medical and emotional advice he promises to provide each morning. His words are encouraging, powerful and supportive and enable me to be in the right frame of mind for the day ahead.

Mid-morning at the hospital and I'm delighted to find that Kath's oxygen reliance has reduced from forty, to twenty-two per-cent. Although an X-ray is showing some shadowing on Kath's lungs, the physios are generally happy with her progress. Everyone seems happy that there are some slow signs of improvement. That said, the balloon pump machine is still in full swing.

I take stock of Kath's condition and her medical treatment. She has a nine inch dressed wound scar from just below her throat down to beneath her breasts. Her lungs are being ventilated with the venti-lator held in place by a mechanical arm. Her heart is being sup-ported by a heart pump, running through a catheter from her groin. She has four chest drains running excess fluid from her lungs into containers beneath her bed. Medical ports protrude from the right of her neck to administer the correct dosage of drugs, and a feeding tube is in place through her right nostril to provide fluids and vita-mins. She has urinary and rectal catheters. Her blood pressure, heart rate and sats are being constantly monitored and displayed on the monitor at the top right of her bed. All the data is being fed manu-ally into a computer at the bottom of her bed by one of the specialist nurses providing individual 24/7 care.

I pass time by listing the drugs in the four-foot stack at the top of her bed: Enoximone, Adrenaline, Propopol, Actrapid, Dopamine, Morphine, Furosemide. In a smaller stack on the other side the immunosuppresant drugs are being administered to prevent rejection of the new organs, together with plain old Paracetamol.

Probably seeing that I'm starting to take an unhealthy interest in the medication and the doses, one of the transplant nurses suggests I take a break from being at Kath's bedside, and we go and have a cup of strong tea in a private room in Transplant clinic. She makes it clear that Kath was extremely poorly after the operation, but how the team is quite a bit more positive now. Her comments are meant to give me reassurance, but they also make me realise how touch and go things were on Monday night. She is very kind and supportive but I tell her not to be too nice to me as I'm constantly just one nice comment away from welling up and breaking down.

Mid-afternoon and I'm able to speak with Kath's surgeon, who confirms he is happy with the progress she is making, and that her heart is showing signs of improvement. This is fantastic news and feels like a real turning point. Gradually some of the sedatives are reduced to enable the team to gauge how her senses are reacting, and to ensure there has been no damage to her brain. It's a delicate balance between weaning her off whilst trying to maintain her blood pressure at safe levels. The process of waking tends to spark increased blood pressure and heart rate, potentially at levels unacceptable to the team.

Stretching my legs, I go to see Kath's PH nurses on Baron and Duchess wards. They have already heard that she's had her transplant and are delighted for her. While I'm there, I visit the lovely young girl with Cystic Fibrosis, no older than our own Sarah, who'd featured on the same ITV *From The Heart* news feature with us some time ago. We had by now met her a few times at clinic and struck up a rapport. Today she looks very poorly and is receiving antibiotics for a bug. She's also trying to build herself up in anticipation of her own transplant call, so is pleased with the chocolate bars I bring. She's already heard about Kath's transplant and is delighted for us both. The camaraderie of Papworth can be astounding.

By late evening Kath's eyes start to flicker open for a few seconds as the reduction in sedatives take effect and there are some small movements in her arms, but she remains otherwise unconscious. It's explained to me that they'll keep her sedated overnight and reassess again in the morning.

***

My chest feels doesn't so much feel as if it was squeezed in the night, rather that it was jumped on. Although I've slept better the pain is more uncomfortable, but fortunately eases as I get showered and dressed. I dispense with calling Papworth this morning; instead I head straight up there and arrive at seven o'clock in case they start to wake Kath properly. I need to be there when this happens.

They won't let me in to see her. There's no explanation. I'm worried. Half an hour pacing up and down like an expectant father in the waiting room, I'm allowed through into ICU. The nurse on shift advises me that Kath's heart rate went up to two hundred beats a minute when the sedatives were reduced earlier so her new heart had to be shocked back into a normal rhythm. The sedatives had been increased again to reduce her stress. 'No wonder they didn't let me in,' I thought, 'I'd have totally freaked out.'

She reassures me it's normal. 'To you, maybe,' I reply.

Despite this, I'm overjoyed to see that Kath's face has the most fantastic colour to it, much more so than the first day after her transplant. The difference from the blotchiness caused by the Flolan over the last three years is transformational. I tell her this, but of course she can't yet hear me. I sing a few lines from Elton John's *'I'm Still Standing'* softly in her ear. The nurses probably think I've lost the plot but I'm not bothered – I've become less self-conscious chatting to Kath's immobile body over the last few days. I tell her about what's been happening and admonish her for not getting me a birthday card and that her behaviour is unacceptable. I'm a bit weepy.

On my way to grab some breakfast from the canteen I bump into one of our favourite transplant nurses. She was with us at the beginning of our transplant journey and we also share a common bond as her nephew goes to the same school that Sarah and Rose attended.

'No one is panicking, Kath's lungs are doing okay and the fact that her heart is playing catch up is nothing unusual. Nothing we haven't seen before.'

I'm grateful for her soothing and reassuring words.

I'm able to secure a few minutes with Kath's consultant as he performs his mid-morning rounds. He counsels against waking her until early evening given her reaction this morning, but in the meantime will try to reduce the level of support of the heart drugs and remove the balloon heart pump. The biggest issue will be trying to wake her up without her becoming agitated about still having the ventilator stuck down her throat into her lungs.

After lunch, I decide to head home for a couple of hours for some rest, and when Rose and I arrive back at five-thirty, Sarah and Oli, who are already here with Kath, greet us with the news that the balloon pump has been successfully removed. More importantly, she is stable. Apart from being another significant milestone, its removal has rewarded us with peace. It was a bloody noisy machine, we all realise.

Following some discussion amongst the medical team, it's decided to turn the sedation right down at six-thirty and try and wake Kath. The suspense is killing us. Six-thirty arrives and I go to the relatives' waiting room with Oli so the girls can be at their mum's bedside when she wakes. It's a slow process. Although there are some more exaggerated hand movements and opening of the eyes, it's clear they are struggling to properly rouse her, but at nine o'clock, while I'm next to Kath's bed, I'm rewarded with a small squeeze of my hand. More tears.

All the drugs and sedatives have been majorly reduced, but there's no denying that, although Kath is not yet with us, she's becoming extremely agitated about the ventilator. As it's now getting late it's decided to sedate her again, albeit at much reduced levels, and try again in the morning. We're advised that if she continues to react badly to the ventilator during the waking up process, Kath may need to be given a temporary tracheostomy.

We leave Papworth for the night pleased that there has been some good progress with stabilising the heart, but a little disappointed we will have to wait longer to see her awake.

***

Five o'clock, Friday morning. Please let this be the day we get her awake. I've grabbed a few hours sleep, long enough for someone to stamp on my chest again. I call ICU straightway. The nurse tells me the plan is to give Kath a drug to help wean her off the ventilator and then switch off the Propofol sedative at eight. Here we go again.

The girls and I arrive at eight-thirty but aren't allowed to see Kath until nine. She's extremely groggy and still being ventilated so is unable to talk, but is able to recognise Sarah and me, nodding her head. Sarah and I start blubbing. Quickly I leave to allow Rose to see her mum. Fortunately the relatives' room is empty as I'm bawling for joy as I shakily text family and friends with the good news.

We play team tag for an hour – by nods and shakes of the head in answer to our questions, we determine Kath can't remember why she's here or getting the phone call on Monday morning. We tell her. 'You've had your transplant!' She smiles at her girls whilst squeezing our hands hard. Even with the ventilator in, she manages somehow to blow Rose a kiss. Enough excitement, we are asked to leave for a while.

One of Kath's closest PH friends, our PH daughter as we jokily call her given she's in her early twenties, is at clinic for a pre-transplant check-up and manages to find us. We exchange hugs but Kath is too unwell to receive other visitors, so we accept all the balloons and presents she has brought for her with grateful thanks. She also delivers the most thoughtfully written card, which includes the words, *'Although having PH is rubbish and no one should have to go through half the things we do, I'm pleased that I have PH because it allowed me to meet you.'* This makes me very teary and we exchange more hugs.

By midday, we are allowed back in, and it's clear Kath is becoming more responsive, with her eyes now more focused and able to follow people in the room. We receive more hand squeezes, attempts at kisses and shrugs of her shoulders as we try to communicate. Her ability to tolerate the ventilator as she comes to her senses suggests it's unlikely she'll have to have a tracheostomy after all. She is, however, delusional from the effects of the medication, and we have to repeat much of what we'd told her earlier. It still isn't sinking in.

We have to leave Kath during the enforced quiet time between two and three in the afternoon. I bump into her consultant in this period and he confirms the intention to remove the ventilator later today. This needs to be done under medical supervision so we're not allowed to visit for a while.

By five o'clock we try our luck with the batphone and are excited to be admitted right away. We try not to run through ICU to her bed. The ventilator's out! Kath's still rather dopey and struggling to remember what we've already told her earlier. She starts to mouth softly and hesitantly her first words to us in almost five days.

'Have I had it done?'

Eighteen

Every Breath I Take

I'm just waking up. It must be morning. What day is it? I can't feel or smell the softness and scent of my own bed. I'm confused. There's no pale blind allowing the morning light to shine through. The light looks dim. False. I can see Rob at one side and Sarah at the other. They're leaning over, looking straight into my face, squeezing my hands. I can see a door towards the left corner, not on the right where my bedroom door should be. Rob is smiling tenderly at me. He asks, 'Do you know where you are?' as I look back at him bewildered.

I think I'm in a hospital. It's not a familiar one. I don't know which hospital it is or why I'm here. I'm sure it isn't Papworth. Nothing is familiar. I'm not on Duchess ward. I'm unable to speak. I try, but little sound will come when I move my lips. My mouth feels strange as though it doesn't work in tune with my speech anymore. The words I try to say can't escape my mouth. The noise I make doesn't sound like me.

They keep on squeezing my hands and ask me to squeeze theirs back. It's hard to do. I can't find my squeeze properly, but I awkwardly try and do as they say. I can perceive it's important to them, so I squeeze as hard as I can manage. They smile at me. They wipe tears away. Why are they so sad?

Rob says, 'You're in hospital.'

I respond in confusion – there's some sort of faded memory there, 'Have I had it done?'

He tells me, as he leans towards my face, 'Yes you've had your transplant. You're in Papworth, you're here because you've had your transplant!'

I don't really understand what he's telling me. Everything is blurred. My mind searches deep inside its confusion and hooks onto a fragment of memory that recollects a notion about me having a transplant. I ask him with my new strangled voice, 'Are they getting ready to take me down again?' I think I'm about to go to theatre for a transplant or that I'm going to be taken down again for another one – I don't really know which or what is happening. I'm completely muddled.

'You've had it already. No one is taking you anywhere – you've had it!' says Rob very firmly.

'Have I had it done?' I ask falteringly, still trying to assert my strange voice, 'Have I had it done?' He nods. I grasp at last that I have actually had my transplant.

They keep on squeezing my hands and asking me things. Sarah leaves the room and Rose comes in. She starts squeezing my hands too. She's tearful as well. I don't why they're all tearful. They keep leaning into my face to speak to me. A man arrives dressed in scrubs. I vaguely recognise him from somewhere.

He asks, 'Can you lift your right leg up?' It's difficult, but I raise it up and then down again, 'And then your left leg?' I try hard to carry out all the various commands. It feels important to do it. I don't know why. I know I have to try. He looks important. He seems happy when I do as he asks. I've seen him walk through clinic. Now I remember him. He's a transplant surgeon.

I have no sense of time. What time is it? What time of day is it? What day is it? I don't have the answers.

Rob and Rose are by the door ready to leave. They're happily blowing kisses to me. I attempt to blow one back, but they can't work out what I'm doing. My hands can't remember how to work properly and they don't respond to my mind's commands. Rose comes rushing, frowning, looking worried. Rob isn't far behind her. I can't pronounce my words clearly, but I try to say slowly and forcibly, 'I'm blowing you a kiss!' They hug me gently and start to cry again. Then they hug each other. I don't know why they're so upset just because I'm blowing kisses.

***

Everyone is back. Rob with Sarah. Sarah with Rose. Rose with Rob. There's a commotion and shouting going on not far from my bed. I know it's another patient in the corner wanting to see me. She's being told off for shouting too loud that she wants to see me. She's trying to find a wheelchair so she can come and have a good look. In fact she has flown all the way over from America to see me. She is a PH patient. I think it really would be better if they just let her do what she wants, but they are being difficult and won't let her. I feel a bit sorry for her – she keeps trying to run down the corridor.

One of my consultants is busy doing menial chores by my bed. She keeps smiling back at me as I watch her intently. I think quietly to myself, 'Gosh they really must be short staffed if the consultant is emptying the bins and doing the mopping.'

Rob with Sarah. Sarah with Rose. Rose with Rob. Another consultant is on a computer at the bottom of my bed. I feel cross because he's looking at all my Facebook pictures, especially the one of the raspberry crumble I made for dinner last night. I'm not happy at all. He starts to go away and then even has the cheek to come back to the computer and take another look. What is it with him? It wasn't even a particularly good raspberry crumble.

I catch Rob's attention, 'Take my Facebook page off the computer. Take it down, I don't want everyone seeing those pictures of my raspberry crumble.'

Rob looks confused. 'I thought we agreed we'd keep everyone updated about your transplant on Facebook?' He frowns, but then it disappears, as if in realisation of something I can't comprehend. 'I'll take everything off there, don't worry,' he agrees. I settle down more contentedly knowing my consultant won't be able to see my raspberry crumble.

My bed is manoeuvered painstakingly from the side ward and we pass through a larger ward with flashing lights, bleeps, beeps, machinery, bed after bed, row after row. The lights are dim amongst

186

the flashing. It's busy. I feel busy too. The team around me walks cautiously alongside my own flashing lights and machinery with its beeps and bleeps. We pass through a door into a narrow corridor and I arrive in a single room along with all my paraphernalia. I'm so thirsty. I ask for a drink and a nurse spoons some crushed ice into my mouth. It's orange flavoured. It tastes wonderful.

***

Sarah and Rob are with me. I'm struggling so hard. My mind is saying over and over again, 'You can't go back now. There's no going back. It's final. Done.' I want to go back so desperately, go back to what I'm used to dealing with. I can't cope with this. I don't want these new problems. This new me. These new heart and lungs. I want my old ones back. The ones I'm used to.

I can't see any way back. Gasping, swirling, drowning. I can't keep my head above the water. I'm going to drown. In fact I can hear myself drowning as I take each breath. My chest rattles loud. I can feel and hear every motion within me echoing from the rattles that come deep down from my lungs. Waters are lapping like the sea inside me. I can taste them – but they taste like bleach, not salt. Inhaler after inhaler is administered but I'm still going to drown.

The nurse washes my hair. I don't want my hair washing. Sarah sees my struggle and gently helps, trying to soothe me. But now I'm drowning and have wet hair and I'm cold and drowning. Shivering. I don't want my hair washed while I'm drowning. I'm drowning deep in my lungs. What have I done? Two whole years of deciding what to do and I've made the wrong choice.

Warm tea in a sealed beaker with a spout is given to me. My hands struggle to hold it. The weight of the cup is like holding a solid iron doorstop. I shake badly and am wobbling it everywhere. Sarah holds it and I drink from it as if I'm her child.

'The consultant has explained that some patients have secretions on their new lungs from the operation and that's why you're struggling,' says Rob. 'We need you to try and cough to get it off your lungs and out.' I try and cough, but my nerves have been cut and my body doesn't know how to cough any more. The nurse tries to train me. My cough won't cough though – it starts from my stomach, but disappears into a whisper of air with no strength or push. A weak breath. Nothing that can help me to stop the drowning. But there's a loud beating inside me. I can hear it. Beating in my ears.

***

Inhaler after inhaler. Gasping. Swirling. Drowning. I'm frightened. It's evening. Rob and Rose are reluctant to leave, and wait for the next nurse to come on shift. The doctors are trying to call an emergency physiotherapist to help me clear my lungs. The new nurse comes on shift and once he's settled in, they leave me in his safe care for the night.

Night-time – it's always the hardest. My breathing feels worse. I can't settle. I'm too hot. I'm too cold. The hot, the cold – I think it's the drugs. Which? I don't know – the intravenous drugs I've been addicted to for years that have suddenly been removed? All the sedation and painkillers? My new transplant drugs? The nurse keeps sponging me down to cool me. He places cold flannels across my head. Blankets on. Blankets off. On. Off. On. Off. I must be driving him mad – I'm driving myself mad. I think I might be mad.

I'm agitated and disturbed. My stomach is upset. I have a rectal catheter as well as a urinary catheter. I have four tubes protruding from my abdomen to goodness knows where. There is some funny looking multi-coloured object sprouting out of my neck. The nurse is constantly putting liquids into it.

Inhaler after inhaler, gasping, swirling, drowning. The emergency physiotherapist arrives. She's lovely. She tells me, 'I'm on duty tonight, but I usually work with the PH team, helping PH patients with their breathing.' I don't know her, but I feel more secure. She belongs to my team – the one that used to keep me safe. I want them back. Somehow I feel safer with her there. I need to feel safe. I desperately need to feel safe. I feel so frightened.

I keep complaining about the rectal catheter – amongst everything else my stomach is so bad I don't think the catheter is working properly. As I can't move yet, they help me to roll one way and then another way, so they can clean me. It's arduous. I'm weak, so very weak. I'm still drowning, but they're trying hard to make me more comfortable before they tackle the physiotherapy for my lungs.

The lady teaches me techniques to try and cough more effectively. I'm so weak and fatigued and drowning, I struggle to follow her. We try a machine that helps me to breathe. She calls it 'the Bird' – I think it looks a bit like an ostrich – a random thought that pops up despite my current desperation. This machine is supposed to help when you're too weak to take a deep breath and have an effective cough. I don't really feel like it's helping, but I try and keep calm and focus on her instructions. I manage a few weak coughs. I'm still drowning. Nothing has cleared. Nothing has changed.

She stops. I'm becoming weaker and weaker. I'm in no state to try any more. They try to make me comfortable but I'm still drowning. There's a loud noise in my head – a banging – as if someone is hitting water pipes hidden in the ceiling above me, the noise echoing around my head, over and over.

I'm so, so tired, but I daren't go to sleep. If I do, I genuinely believe that I might actually drown. There's a clock on the wall facing me. It's getting late – ten o'clock I think – I daren't sleep, I just daren't. I can't let myself drown. Something tells me not to sleep. I must stay awake. Stay alert. Stay focused and fight for each breath.

Instead, I establish a routine, my strategy, which develops and grows. I watch the clock on the wall. On each hour it's time for inhalers. There are varying sorts – I can tell because the masks or pipes are different and some taste different. It's a chore and saps my energy, but I can feel a few minutes of relief for my breathing when I've had each one.

The inhalers spur me on as I labour with my breathing. I lie in wait for the clock to reach the top of the hour. I try and conserve my energy during the time while I wait and struggle to breathe. As the hour nears, I pull on every single reserve I have inside me to manage the inhalers and breathe a little once more. I seem to gain an extra minute or two of relief for my breathing each time.

The hours tick by slowly as I examine the clock. I'm gasping to breathe, but know I have to remain calm. A doctor comes to check and reassures me saying, 'All your vital signs are good. Your sats are good.'

I respond weakly, 'But I feel like I'm drowning, there's something blocking my breathing.' I manage to clear something off my lungs after I'm rolled to one side to allow me to be more comfortable. I'm pleased, something has moved at last, but it's only for a second, then I'm disappointed to find I'm still drowning.

The pipes continue to boom. The hours continue to pass slowly. Studying the clock intensely, I urge its hands towards the top of each hour when it will be inhaler time again and I can snatch some small relief. I'm focused on staying awake. I will not sleep; I will not sleep or let myself drop off to sleep and stop breathing. I focus hard on everything that has been good in my life. My life goes before me. People I love; places I love. I think about good times. I won't allow myself to slip gently away. I have to stay entirely focused and take my mind away from what's happening to get through to the next hour.

I conjure up pictures from the past. Rob. Sarah. Rose. The girls as babies, as children, at school, growing up. Family moments. Holidays. I focus on our favourite place, the Lake District. Once again I'm kayaking across Coniston Water, paddling along, having fun. We pause in the middle and I admire the awesome view. I can feel the sunshine warming me. I relive my memories over and over. My mind flits back to the breathing. I can hear its noise. I need to focus again – conjure up more memories, more places. Never-ending beaches in Norfolk. Beautiful sunsets. Concentrate. Concentrate hard on breathing. Breathing through to the next inhaler – the next hour.

It's time to stop trying now. I'm exhausted. I must sleep and rest – losing life should feel dignified, not like this, fighting for each breath. When do I stop? Should I stop trying? Stop breathing? Might I die anyway? Is it worth all this trying? I should let myself go now. Just sleep easily. It shouldn't be this hard to be alive.

Maybe it will feel gentler to sleep. Peaceful even. I just want to be peaceful. Just sleep. It will be easier, less strenuous and more dignified than all this trying.

It's the deep of the night. Pictures on the white wall around the clock have appeared. The whole wall from floor to ceiling is covered in pictures – pictures of all my thoughts. The pictures change as each person and place comes into my thoughts. I must keep looking at my picture memories. I must not sleep. I must watch the pictures. The enticing thoughts of going to sleep have waned. There's too much to live and strive for. Too much to do still. I can't let go. I must stop drowning and start swimming. Breathe, Breathe, Breathe.

Another emergency physiotherapist arrives. I'm still focused on the clock. Dawn is in sight – a new day almost in my grasp. We go over the same procedures and he helps me to practice to cough and then encourages me to try to actually cough. We use the Bird to help me breathe and cough and move the secretions blocking my lungs. I'm so weak, the physiotherapist has to stop, but I manage to clear a little more from my lungs. My breathing still labours. I'm still struggling, but it feels slightly, almost imperceptibly, better. The physiotherapist is delighted. He promises to come back in a few hours allowing me to rest and we'll try again.

The treasured memories from the past. The images of special times with loved ones. They still whirl around in my mind. I need to keep them here close to me. I'll do anything to make more. I need to hold on to them. Feel them. Sense them. Live them again. Breathe again. There isn't really a question of giving up, there's just too much to keep living for.

Daylight. The hospital is waking up. I'm not looking at pictures on the walls any more. I'm not clock watching for each hour any more. I'm exhausted. Daylight comes and with that I allow myself to rest a little. Somehow it feels marginally easier in the safe arms of the day.

I've survived the night. It's an achievement. I'm still floundering, but I'm trying to swim. Drowning, floundering, swimming, exhaustion. I know this part of my fight isn't over yet.

***

I hear the clatter of the breakfast trolley. A friendly lady pops in to check if I need anything. I can't manage much. I have a feeding tube that goes up through my nose and down into my stomach. It's been there for the last six or so days. I can see the bags of protein ready to be replaced in my drip. I can feel the discomfort in the back of my throat. I am cared for and washed, rolled gently from side to side – my catheters are attended to as well as the drains, cuts and scars. I notice my right arm is covered in a deep purple merging into black. What's happened there? I see similar bruising down my thigh as the nurse washes me. I can hear a loud beating inside my weak frame.

The nurse for the next twelve-hour shift arrives and notes are exchanged. My night-time nurse thinks I'm a lost cause, I'm sure of it. I'm convinced he's saying to everyone, 'She's a transplant that's gone wrong. I'll give her till lunch-time.' It makes me so cross. I've worked hard all night. I will show him how wrong he is. The re-solve in me re-emerges, 'I will damn well show him. How dare he give up on me.' I think he wants to kill me. In fact I'm certain he's been trying to finish me off all night.

The physiotherapist arrives again. I'm very weak, but will do anything to try and stop the drowning and feel better. I want to prove to everyone that I'm trying; that I'm worth the effort. I can't manage much, however, and there's no improvement, but he prom-ises to try again later.

After he leaves, using a rolled up towel as I've been shown, I press it against my chest and try to cough once more. The towel helps alleviate the pressure on my sternum, which was cut and then stitched back up during my transplant operation. My chest feels heavy and tight, like it doesn't fit me any more and there's a lead weight pressing down on me.

I'm still struggling. A man arrives to see me. I recognise him from my PH days. It's the hospital's priest. I'm so relieved to see him. If I ever needed a helping hand, it's now. He can see I'm struggling. 'Please can you help me? I need your help, please can you pray for me?'

He says some prayers from the second letter of the last rites. I listen to the prayers, grateful and comforted to hear them. It makes me peaceful, although I'm still rasping and rattling and struggling to breathe. He leaves me calmer, consoled and prepared for whatever may lie ahead.

Discovering it's Sunday morning, I realise I must have been in hospital almost a week. The doctors arrive. 'I'm struggling, I feel like I can't breathe, but I can't shift whatever is stopping me breathing properly.' I look at them pleadingly. The consultant explains once more about some patients being unfortunate enough to have secretions from the operation and I need to start moving around to help shift them. He says I need to get up and sit in a chair, keep coughing and moving and it will get better. I cannot believe he even thinks I can sit in a chair.

He orders more physiotherapy to help. As it's Sunday, the nurse has to phone for an emergency one again. I'm weak. I think to myself, 'This isn't right with my breathing. I won't be able to live like this. What have I done?' I'm feeling woeful, that I've made the biggest mistake, gambled with my life and now I'm paying the price but I know I can't go back. I have to try and do something. I need to be strong. Somehow I'm going to have to live like this and find my way forward.

I'm desperate, but determined to do whatever I can to get out of this situation – to make myself better. I think if I've been told to sit in a chair, then I will sit in a chair. I don't know how I'm going to sit in a chair, but I will sit in a chair somehow. I tell the nurse I want to get up and sit in a chair. I'm very weak and don't have another ounce of energy left. She is dubious, she says, 'I think you're too weak to try that today.' I'm more determined than she is dubious and I insist I want to sit in a chair. She asks me to be patient and compromises saying we'll try later in the day.

As we wait, I persist with my attempts to cough, trying to clear my lungs a little but to no avail. The effort makes me fight for my breath and my chest rattles loudly above the noises of the machines. The energy it absorbs is wearing. Rob arrives. He already knows

I've had a bad night, as he's phoned beforehand. I tell him the nurse tried to kill me during the night. He nods gently and reassures me.

A lady brings a gas and air machine to help relieve the pain while they remove two of the tubes in my abdomen. It's still painful and makes me wince and my eyes water, but it's over quickly – then stitches. It feels like a major step forward to be rid of two of the drains from my chest.

I rest awhile, but it is hard with my breathing. Every time I begin to need to cough and can't clear my chest, I panic – my heart rate rises too high and the nurse has to calm me down – long, deep breaths, long deep breaths – until I calm again. It's a technique I learn to do over and over. I've used it before during my illness, but never needed to do it as much as I do now.

The nurse says, 'Try and move your hands and feet a little, it's important for your circulation.' I nod. I know it's important, I've been trying to do it since I've been conscious. Little bursts of feet twiddling; little attempts to do something to help myself. Rose giggles at my feet twiddling. It seems to be the only thing I can achieve. I'm proud I can manage to feet twiddle and people are pleased with me.

As I lie resting, the booming pipes continue to interrupt my thoughts and there's some sort some of event going on outside in the hospital grounds. There's music playing. I cannot quite understand why they keep playing the beginning of the same song over and over again; it goes on and on. The sound of children's excited voices and families in the background. 'What's going on outside?' I ask Rob and the nurse, 'There's music playing and voices, voices of young children, families...' my voice trickles off as they look at me perplexed.

'We can't hear anything,' says Rob.

The realisation slowly dawns on me that I'm the only one hearing these things. It occurs to me that some of the things I've seen and endured since I became conscious may also be part of my drug fuelled imagination. They feel extremely real nonetheless. It's frightening knowing your mind is out of control. I'm finding it a real struggle to distinguish between what's real and what's not.

I try a small yoghurt for lunch. I manage two spoonfuls with Rob spoon-feeding it to me. It's a major effort. I cannot swallow properly. I cannot eat. I sip some tea instead.

Two extra nurses arrive and help hoist me into a chair as I'd asked. It feels strange being swung through the air, but strange events are part of my life. They just keep on coming and are normal to me. I'm thrilled I've reached the chair. I never thought I would be thrilled to sit in a chair. I've done it. A first. I see Rob and think of the girls and say, 'I have so much to live for.' I challenge myself that I need to start swimming and the drowning needs to stop. I'm inspired and draw a little strength from the simple act of sitting in this chair.

My family visits from Lancashire. My mum, sister, brother and sister in law all come to see me with Rob, who is very protective of me. Sarah and Rose wait with my brother-in-law and nephew. My nephew, who is only ten, is disappointed he can't see me because of the infection risk. I'm disappointed too. They've all travelled a long way just to see me for a few minutes. I'm weak and all the comings and goings feel like a blurred memory, but I'm so pleased they're all here.

After my family leaves, Sarah and Rose come in. I'm so tired, so weak that I can barely speak. They don't stay long as they can see I'm worn out. I'm put back to bed. I can't manage food. The nurse is constantly administering drugs through the set of multi-coloured beads in my neck as I listen to the music from the party outside which is beginning to irritate me, real or not. It mingles with the sound of the soothing, strong beat inside me.

**

Night falls. Night again. I'm scared of the night. Everything is harder in the night. The weight presses down on my chest. They lay me this way, then that way, put pillows under me, around me – I cannot stay in one position for long. I hate the rectal catheter and am frightened it's not working. The nurse rises constantly to my endless demands. I need to move. I'm too hot. I'm too cold. Will you check the catheter? I don't like the catheter. Will you check it again? I'm too hot. I'm too cold. I need to move. Over and over, it goes on.

She relentlessly and happily does everything she can to make me comfortable. In between the coughing, in between the inhalers, in between administering the intravenous drugs through my neck, in between my rasping breaths – she diligently ploughs on.

I don't think I'm going to die tonight. I'm struggling, but my head is just above the water line. I'm not quite drowning any longer, but not yet swimming either. I'm treading water with my head held up above the murky depths below.

Tonight I want to sleep. I desperately want to sleep, but sleep hardly comes. It's as though I'm plugged into the electricity grid. Looking around at all the machinery connected to me, it is not hard to see why. I am, of a fashion.

The nurse reads my every thought on the computer at the foot of my bed. I must not let her read my thoughts. I must think good thoughts if she can see my thoughts. I daren't let her see bad thoughts. I don't like the machines. The party is still carrying on outside. I think it's strange – children being out all night. The same introduction to the same song keeps on playing over and over again. The sound of little children's happy voices rise above it. The pipes in the ceiling start playing up – they're a bloody nuisance. How can I sleep with this entire racket going on? I keep on treading water though, through the deep of the night, staying afloat until dawn.

I can see a glimmer of daylight rising on the horizon. I've made it through another night. I'm exhausted but I'm still alive.

***

Routines. The nurses bathe me, clean my teeth and place me in a new gown. I've been here a week and still haven't needed the bag I so diligently packed in preparation for my transplant. They have a crafty way to change the bed sheets while I'm still in them. I play the rolling game – they roll me this way and that way to do all their morning chores. They wash my hair. It feels nice being all fresh and clean again.

The consultant and doctor arrive. 'I managed to sit up in a chair yesterday,' I inform them, feeling very pleased with myself. I wait ready to be given today's challenge. I'm almost disappointed when the consultant says, 'You should rest today.' He knows I haven't rested much. We discuss the cough, or the non-cough and I say, 'I'm still really struggling, it still isn't much better, I still can't clear my chest. I need someone to do something.' He replies, 'Right we'll take a look down in your lungs today. We'll do a bronchoscopy. We'll give them a clean and see if we can see what the problem is.'

I lie and pray and pray and hope against all hope that they'll be able to clear my chest and do something to ease my breathing. I torment myself about going home and having to breathe and live like this.

The thought of having a bronchoscopy frightens me, though. I've never had one before. I cannot breathe properly anyway, even without having a tube and camera put down my throat, but I need them to do it. I want to feel better. I want them to find what's blocking my breathing. They bring the machinery and I say to my consultant, 'Please if you find something, will you take it away and not leave me like this any longer?' He smiles kindly and says, 'That's why I'm doing it.'

Nineteen

Swimming

I can feel someone gently pushing my arm and saying, 'Kathryn, Kathryn, it's time to wake up, they've found something, they've found something and you're going to feel better!' I stir from my sleep and remember where I am and what's happened. It's my nurse. She's excited. The sedation for the bronchoscopy resulted in my first deep sleep for a few days.

It's immediate. I feel it right away. The drowning has disappeared. I'm no longer treading water. I'm swimming. I'm breathing. There's nothing preventing my breathing. I'm breathing freely. My new lungs are breathing. I'm ecstatic. I want to go outside and run a few laps around the grounds. There's the small matter that I can't sit myself up in bed properly on my own yet, but inside I want to run around and around and shout out loud. I'm actually breathing.

Encouraging hope floods my earlier desperation. My hope had never really gone away. Although it had been pushed to its limits, stretched beyond recognition, disguising itself as despair, it had always been there. Sometimes you have to look in the deepest, darkest corners for the smallest glimmer that it gives but, right now, it's standing stark in front of me in its full glory. Both my hope and I have resurfaced together.

I can continue on my journey, a journey which, in those darker moments, I thought was coming to an end, had nearly stopped. But I'm back with renewed determination. Eager. Enthusiastic. Swimming. I can't wait to embrace this new chance I've been given. A chance for a better life. Another new beginning and with it, the chance to make more dreams come true.

***

My new lungs had been functioning well during this difficult period, but the consultant tells me I'd been struggling because persistent secretions had accumulated following the aftermath of the long operation, despite constant efforts to clear and clean them while I'd been in a coma. One lung in particular was affected with several clots that were removed during the bronchoscopy.

I have a strong sense that the worst is behind me and I'll be going forward from this point. I know there's a long path ahead, but I know now that I've done the right thing. The right thing for my family and me. The right thing for my future. I did make the right decision after all.

I turn to Rob, croaking quietly. 'I think I've turned a corner.'

I'm still on oxygen, but it's wonderful to breathe properly again. The atmosphere in my room feels peaceful and restful. I'm relieved. Rob, the girls and my nurse are relieved. I can still hear the beat of my heart deep inside me. I'm weak, but it sounds strong. It feels peculiar to think it's not my own heart that's beating and not my own lungs that are breathing for me.

I don't know why I can hear my heart beating in my ears so loud and strong, is it because I'm so weak and it's so forceful? I'm unsure of it. It makes me wonder about the person who has lost their life, about the family that must be grieving. It's been a week. It's hard to think of it, but I already owe my life to them, so I'm unable to think of anything else.

Was it someone young or someone like me, or someone even older? I think of it as though the person is with me now. We are joined, an unbreakable bond. Is it another daughter? Is it a son I never had? Is it a friend? A sister? A brother? Whoever they are, they will come with me everywhere I go from now. They'll sleep, eat and live with me – a third presence within me. Who? Who has saved my life?

Amongst the mundane and ordinary trappings of my room –

chairs, beds, windows, doors – the healing wound that runs down my chest to my abdomen tugs and forces me to confront and make sense of the extraordinary situation I find myself in. Once again the ordinary and extraordinary coexist increasing the intensity of this moment of reflection. I am finding it hard to bridge the gulf between the extraordinary event that's happened and the ordinary life I once knew. However much I dwell on it, my mind just cannot reconcile these extremes.

Although I do not sleep much, I enjoy my first peaceful night despite the party still being in full swing outside. I lie against the pillows and smile. I know it's the drugs – there's no party – even though I can still hear it. Rather than wrestle and try to pretend I can't hear, I grin and imagine everyone having fun. Go with the flow. I enjoy listening to the festivities. The pipes above me bang, but again I know it's the drugs, so I just let them carry on with their banging. A faint boom in my head, but it doesn't matter any more – there's no need to fight. They're just the sounds of the night. I'm growing used to them. Accepting them.

A young doctor pops in to check. 'Is everything alright? You're quiet tonight?'

I smile and say, 'Fine, it's a much better night, thank you.' I'm quietly amused, 'Just how bad have I been?'

***

Another day comes around, and it's a busy one. Firstly the doctors arrive. I'm to have the rest of my drains out later, but it's the rectal catheter I make a fuss about instead. I hate it. I want rid of it, but my tummy isn't better so I'm struggling to cope without it. I start demanding medication for my stomach and that it be removed.

Rob smiles and says, 'Well things can't be that bad now, if that's all you are bothering about.'

Glaring at him, I reply, 'It *is* all that's bothering me.'

I think the doctors and nurses expect me to complain about all the other discomforts, but it's the catheter which is troubling me most, as it's making me so sore. I have to be cleaned over and over.

200

I hate the indignity and I don't want to put up with it.

The nurse tells me gently, 'You must focus on getting better now, you shouldn't be worrying about that – focus on the most important things.'

I insist. I insist I will drag myself out of bed and use a commode if they will only take it out. I say I will take it out myself if they don't. I can barely sit up properly let alone get out of bed on my own so it is an idle threat, but I make it sound convincing. I argue that getting myself in and out of bed will be good for me. It will make me move around, be good for my new heart and lungs.

It works. It's agreed to give me medication for the diarrhoea, stop feeding me through the tube and look to remove the rectal catheter later. That's a result. I'm pleased. I don't quite know how I will manage to reach a commode, but in my head it's an achievement, a move forward. If I can sort out my immediate distress, then I reason the rest will fall into place.

The gas and air is brought in and with some huffing and puffing the last two chest drains are removed. I'm given medication to help stop the diarrhoea. I manage to eat a little yoghurt, but I struggle – my throat is swollen from being on the ventilator for so long and my chest hurts from the operation. The dietician visits and removes the feeding tube from my nose to make it easier for me to eat and drink. She offers me some advice on eating. With all my inhalers, drug concoctions and coughing and clearing, I don't yet have much of an appetite.

The physiotherapist arrives and goes through the breathing exercises with me to help me cough and clear my chest. I then have a go at getting out of bed. This is a major operation. This time there's no hoist to lift me to a chair. I'm going to walk to it. I'm shown how to shuffle myself to the edge of the bed, then with a huge effort and some help, swivel my legs round so my feet touch the floor. It's exhausting and my body cannot coordinate itself properly.

After a little rest I'm shown how to rock myself backwards and forwards several times and then, on the count of three, using this rocking method, the nurse and the physiotherapist have me standing. I have to use this approach to stand upright, so as not to press down on my arms and place undue weight onto my injured chest. I'm shocked at how much I need their support just to hold me up. I've no balance. I literally sway from one side to another and then start to fall before I'm steadied. I'm triumphant though. It's another first. Rob is ecstatic and thrilled as he watches me. He and the girls have born the brunt of anxiety and know exactly where I've come from.

With help I take a few tentative steps, and next I'm seated in a chair. I feel amazed. I have risen out of bed and I am sitting in a chair again, with no sign of a hoist. Despite my imbalance, I'm not as weak as yesterday. I'm beaming. I'm confident – determined to recover. I resolve to do absolutely everything I'm told to do. I think to myself, 'This is my second chance. I've got to make the most of it and try my hardest.' The regrets of those first days of consciousness simply dissolve. I've a new mission now – to become well enough to get myself home again and make the best of this new life.

I try having some of my many medications in tablet form, rather than intravenously – I struggle with the larger ones, but manage some. I try and eat lunch – I've been a bit over ambitious in my wanting to get better and ordered shepherd's pie. I cannot manage to swallow much. I'm just not hungry.

The rectal catheter is finally removed, much to my relief. Having had this object inserted for over a week and feeling sore, I cannot quite tell whether I need the loo or not. I feel a nuisance when I have to keep trying the commode and it needs two people to help, as I've still little balance, but I also think all this shuffling and effort, can only be helping my body to start moving again. I'm not despondent, but now I'm properly conscious and feeling a little stronger, it is hard realising that I have to be so dependent on others.

Rob and the nurse tell me stories of when I was deeply sedated. It all unfolds and I piece together what's happened over these lost days. I realise what my family and friends have had to go through – especially Rob and our girls. I hate that they've all had to endure this. I resolve to get better and to show them every minute has been worth it.

I start to tell them my own stories of the last few days, and we laugh as it's evident the majority of my memories are as a result of the drugs. I start to tell another story, only to stop in my tracks and realise that it's another hallucination; another thing my mind made up. I laugh at myself. We all laugh. Now I know for real that there's no party outside; there are no pictures on the walls and the pipes aren't banging, no one has been trying to kill me. I can distinguish properly between what did, and what did not, actually happen.

That said, I can still see weird things at times. Lights hovering in the air – big flowers sparkling like fireworks floating through the room, jumping off people's heads and shoulders. I know it's the drugs, and I have to keep a straight face when people are speaking to me and pretend the bright flowers aren't there – I know they aren't, anyway.

It's been a busy and eventful day. I'm becoming free from the machinery with only a catheter, line in my neck and cannula left, together with the Hickman line from my PH days. It's another peaceful night with neither banging nor parties. I sleep on and off, mostly off, but I'm restful and calm.

Morning comes. This time I have to try and have all of my medication orally which is a struggle, and I nearly cry because I can't manage the big tablets at all. I lie here feeling inadequate, and that I'm letting people down because I can't do it. I've got this far and I committed to this medication for a lifetime as part of the process, and I can't even swallow them. That's not a good start. What am I going to do?

I feel as though I've failed at the first hurdle, that I'm useless. A new nurse takes over. I tell her tearfully, 'I'm struggling to swallow my tablets.'

She brings me a yoghurt. She hides a large tablet in one spoonful, pops it into my mouth and makes me swallow in one gulp. We do it over and over until all my tablets are done. It's worked. I've learned a new trick. It's a good job I like yoghurt – it's a good job I can manage to eat some, as that's all I can eat. The nurses are like magicians and have tricks up their sleeve at every turn.

My doctors are pleased with my progress, and tell me I'll be able to leave intensive care and move to Mallard ward, probably

today. I'm pleased – another big step. At the same time I'm a little
desolate. Do they know I can't do anything? That I can't even get
out of bed on my own. I can't eat properly or hardly hold a spoon to
eat. I can hardly drink tea from a spouted cup without throwing it
all over myself. I fear this is going to be so hard. I'm still so weak.

To put me in a better frame of mind, the nurse decides to give
me a nice pamper. Rob brings the bag I'd hurriedly packed for this
hospital stay, and the nurse and I look excitedly at the clothes as
well as the goodies in my toilet bag. We decide it would be good for
me to wear my own pyjamas and dressing gown, and dispense with
the unflattering hospital attire now that the blasted rectal catheter
has been removed. I feel like I'm in my Sunday best and it's a bit
more like me, the real me, the one who's been trying to come back
for the last few years.

The sister from Mallard ward comes to perform the handover,
and I sit quietly and listen while they exchange paperwork. My ICU
nurse is very positive about me. I want to tell her it's too soon for
me to leave here, that I'm still totally useless and need a lot of help.
It doesn't seem to be concerning anyone that I'm useless. Although
I'm smiling and feeling brand new in my own pyjamas and dressing
gown, my body feels useless. Although I'm much better, I still feel
really terrible. I'm just being brave, but I'm not brave. I'm confused. Terrified. I want to move from intensive care. I want to get
better. I don't want to move from intensive care. I want to stay here
where I know it's safe.

My emotions keep on colliding at every stage. I'm so positive
and determined now, but why am I so scared and frightened? Each
step requires me to muster up more courage to take another one. I
reach deeper within myself for that extra something that will help
me stay the course. Motivation. Courage. Hope. Strength. Determination. I've found the hope and motivation. I just need to find the
rest to see this through.

There's no let up, no slack – one challenge after another, then
another, then another. It's daunting and I fear it hasn't even really
started yet, this new life.

Another nurse arrives to help take me down to Mallard. It's the nurse who helped me through my first night after I woke and was struggling. When I thought I might drown. I thank him for all he did for me. He's kind and pleasant. How could I have thought that he wanted to kill me? I hope he isn't thinking, 'Oh it's that bloody woman again!' We exchange a few pleasantries. I want him to see that I'm not a complete fruitcake, but at that very moment one of my flower fireworks jumps off his shoulder and I have to stifle a giggle. I think better not to mention it, or they might wheel me off somewhere else other than Mallard ward!

Scared and anxious, I'm taken out of my familiar room. It feels like another new adventure. I've had no sense of where I've been all this time and am intrigued by my surroundings as I'm pushed along, Rob following in tandem carrying my bags, oxygen tank and catheter.

I can breathe. I'm deeply conscious of every breath I take as we move along. Where is life taking me now?

Twenty

The Duck Pond

I'm being manoeuvred into my bedside chair. I'm surprised – pleasantly surprised to have my own room.

'You've been in isolation all along,' says Rob, 'I think it's because of your stomach issues. In intensive care they thought it might be an infection or withdrawal from your PH drugs. I don't think they're sure which.'

For whatever reason, it feels very nice. I don't feel like being on a busy ward yet and making polite chitchat to people I don't know. That will come soon but, while I adjust, having my own room will allow me to feel shielded and protected. I even have my own television and the room is quite spacious.

It's another huge stride. Despite my initial anxiety about leaving ICU, Rob and I are delighted. I'm beaming again. The nurses come and check me in and do the necessary paperwork. There's a drug cupboard on the wall and it's swiftly filled to the brim.

They keep trickling through, arriving in the post daily – cards, get well messages, letters and presents. Once I regained consciousness, Rob had been reading them out loud to me, plus all the messages on social media. It's been overwhelming receiving so many kind messages, simply overwhelming. All the good wishes inspire and urge me on to become better and stronger. They help me to find some strength of mind on the occasions it can all feel daunting.

The intensive physiotherapy begins. I still need two people to get me out of bed and to the chair, help me stand up and take a few steps. I still wobble over and have little balance, but each day I do more. I soon learn how to shuffle to the edge of my bed independently, then do a few rocks and shuffles to stand up and take the one or two steps to my chair. Getting out of the chair is another matter, as I cannot use my arms to push my body up owing to my chest wound. They teach me more new tricks – more rocking and shuffling to get myself up and out of the chair without using my arms and hands. It means I can now use the commode independently. Things are getting better and better.

I catch a glimpse of myself in the mirror. I stop – do a double take. I stare long and hard at them. I smooth my fingers over them, checking they're real and it's not something covering them. My lips – my lips are bright pink, beautiful pink and they are mine. I'm not sure I've ever seen myself with such pink lips. I stand and stare. It's a happily shocking moment. Beautiful bright pink lips. I'm astounded. I cannot stop staring and wanting to take another look.

Sleep is hard, even though I'm in my own room. The heavy doses of drugs continue to interrupt my sleep. I'm so tired, but sleep won't come.

I lie and listen to it. My heart. It beats loud. It beats strong. It beats and pounds so strong my body feels unbalanced – like my heart is pulling it – beating and pulling the left side of me away from the right. As though I'm swaying. I lie on my left side and I can actually hear the beat. Hear it in my head as it pulsates; hear it in my ears pressed to the pillows. So many pillows, some cushioning my chest and the heaviness that lingers there from the weight of the wounds inside and out. My heart beats out loud and strong through them, distracting me from sleep – that and the electric current which flows from my drugs.

I'm learning my new drug regime. No more lines and pumps for me this time, though, just tablets and inhalers. I have to learn what they are all for, the individual doses and when I need to take each one. It is mind-boggling, but I know I can do it. After all, I've already mastered complex intravenous drugs and inhalers.

A blue book is given to me to write down all the medication and doses as I learn the routines. I won't be able to go home unless I can confidently self-medicate – here we go again – I know I can do it.

Every day becomes a little easier with them. The transplant nurses come each afternoon to explain more and more about them, help me learn, help me to be independent. My mind is still a fog from all of the traumas, but I'm learning.

I'm tired, very tired. The physiotherapists come every day and I know being active is key to getting better. I want to hide under the sheets when they arrive and pretend I'm asleep, but I know it will do no good. I know by now that I always feel great once I've performed my physio. I learn to take my first few steps on my own, and then I manage to walk round the room. Rob has brought in my old walking stick from home, so I can make my way without toppling over. I'm very wobbly.

I hit a few problems, but everyone knows what to do. I have to undergo sessions of intravenous antibiotics for a few hours a few times each day. The stomach upsets have receded, but I discover I'm in isolation because of suspected MRSA. I'm actually being barrier nursed: everyone coming into contact with me has to be gowned up and gloved, and there's constant hand washing.

I'm desperate for my hair to be washed, so I can look more like me. Sarah and Oli help me to the sink. Oli clips all my bits and pieces of equipment on his belt and they guide me, holding me up to the sink. We laugh, I hurt so much as we laugh, but we can't stop giggling. Sarah leading, Oli, pushing the stand with the IVs, my wee bag clipped on his belt, trailing tentatively behind. What a sight!

They wash and rinse my hair while I hang over the sink. Wash and rinse – it feels lovely. We can't stop laughing, although it's hard going because I'm very weak and I cough constantly – try to cough – I'm still learning how to cough again. My lungs need constant clearing. Sometimes I cough for hours to no avail, and have to sit and wait and then try again. Wash and rinse – we can't stop giggling and laughing. It's another simple but precious moment.

I try to dry my hair, but my hands are too weak to hold the dryer. We see the nurses taking over the night shift. I think they're giggling at us too! I don't think I've ever laughed so much before. I feel great with my hair looking more like mine. I feel even better for having such a good laugh although it hurts me so much.

My urinary catheter is eventually removed after a few days, along with my heart pacing wires. More big steps.

Because of the MRSA, I am the last patient each day to be bathed. It's a tough one, but I know I'll overcome it. I have to be hoisted in and out of the bath, as I'm not strong enough to do it on my own. It feels wonderful to splash and swish in a bath.

The MRSA precautionary measures also mean that I am barred from using the toilets. It's irritating having to call the nurses every five minutes, because I'm on heavy doses of diuretics to remove excess fluids. By the time they've taken the commode away, I have to ring the bell because I need to go again. Added to the ignominy, now that the catheter has been removed I have to wee in a tray each time, so my output can be measured to keep an eye on my fluid retention levels. I have to laugh it off – it's part and parcel of every-thing, and I suppose I'm used to it anyway from when I was ill before. Some days it feels as if there isn't any part of my body or bodily functions that aren't being scrutinised, measured or catalogued.

Weekend again, just under two weeks since my transplant and I'm allowed to go to the canteen with Rob and our girls. I cannot walk well enough on my own, so we use my trusty old chariot, which Rob has brought in from the car. I breathe in the fresh air as we step outside – it feels wonderful. It's a delight to see blue sky and clouds, to feel an autumn pinch in the air. I enjoy an afternoon tea and people-watching with my family. Everything feels different. Sitting in a canteen I've been used to visiting should be mundane, but today it feels such a wonderful and special thing to do.

Afterwards, as the sun is still shining I ask Rob if he'll wheel me to the duck pond. The duck pond at Papworth is a unique place. It's more of a small lake teaming with wildlife, not just a pond. I sit and watch the ducks flurry towards some bread. They're used to being fed, and rush towards anyone in sight in expectation of food. Like so many Papworth patients before me, I enjoy watching their com-ings and goings and laugh as Rob recounts how Sarah nearly choked one poor duck with her Soreen.

Papworth's resident black swan glides towards us, his wings and feathers ruffled aggressively. Unlike the ducks, the swan isn't so keen on humans. He bays and hisses and circles in the water proudly commanding his domain. It's good to see and hear the black swan again in all his glory, although I'm sure he doesn't feel the same way about me as he regards me sternly in my wheelchair.

Nature. I can sense and feel it again. It's uplifting.

Sarah and Rose slowly push me around the pond. I wonder at the turning leaves on the trees and bushes – the russets, reds and golds. It's as if I've never seen autumn trees before – as though I'm having a second chance to see things again and seeing them differently because I thought I might never see them again. I take in deep breaths of fresh air into my brand new lungs. In and out. In and out. I feel free and inspired. Inspired to recover.

The evening settles on me, but I can't sleep. The coughing bothers me, and the drugs just don't let me. I wake with a start: I must have drifted off. I can't breathe. I can't catch my breath. I'm coughing and gasping but my breath won't come. I start to panic and the nurses come – everyone comes running.

I panic. I can't breathe. I panic. I can't breathe. The nurses put me back on the oxygen for the first time in quite a few days. They give me an inhaler and calm me – breathing deep – slow deep breathing – slow deep breathing. The doctor arrives quickly followed by the X-ray machine. Bloods are taken. Slow, deep breathing – slow deep breathing. I'm hooked up to intravenous diuretics as I learn one of my new lungs has filled with fluid. The diuretics soon start to work their magic. I can breathe again and I drift off to sleep exhausted.

Despite this hiccup, I'm gaining more and more strength – beginning to eat and cough more, hold items like cutlery, mugs, my phone, and balance and walk unaided again. The physiotherapist brings me a bike that I can keep in my room. Only two weeks on and I'm using an exercise bike – something I couldn't ever have imagined before. More firsts.

It dawns on me suddenly that the severe eczema I used to have running up and down my arms and legs has disappeared. Gone. I've been struggling so much with everything else since my transplant I'd forgotten about my PAH side effects. No more itching. I recall the jaw pain when I used to take a first bite of food or a first sip of a drink. All gone. These are huge strides. I realise I am leaving PH behind.

My appetite is suppressed. I know I must eat more, but it's so difficult as swallowing is so hard. I'm determined to do it somehow. I think of what I used to teach the small children in school. I picture the healthy diet plate we used to talk about. I focus on this. What does my body need? Protein for the healing, carbohydrates for some energy, fruit and vegetables for the vitamins, dairy for the calcium and bones and some sugars for some fat. I need to practice what I preached.

Managing all this at every mealtime is unrealistic, so I start with having a little of everything over the day. Then I build up to having a little of everything at each meal, trying to give myself a little of all that I need to get better, even if it's only a few bites. The dieticians are on hand to help too, as I've lost so much weight, and they work out a plan. I'm given a large bacon roll for breakfast each morning – well, I say large, they're actually massive. Rob looks on enviously. In between mealtimes, I'm given snacks – packets of crisps and snack bars with my name and room number stuck to them, which Rob finds hilarious. They call it eating for healing.

Gradually my appetite returns and I start to feel much better, more settled, more like me. Eventually I manage to eat the regular hospital meals and can dispense with the bacon butties! Rose bakes me a cake and I tuck into it hungrily. Oli leaves me chocolate bars every time he comes – I think he's bought them for himself for when he goes fishing, but he goes soft on me and wants to help.

Cards and presents continue to keep on trickling in every day. Some are from friends from years ago, and some from people I haven't even met. Every time I feel it's becoming too hard, another one comes and there isn't any way I can feel low. Every message, every card, every present and every kind remark urges and spurs me on to recovery and home. The kindness and good wishes from friends and strangers alike moves me. Their goodwill elevates me, enabling me to feel like I'm just sailing through.

As time goes on, and several tests have been taken to ensure I'm not an infection risk to other patients, the physiotherapists are allowed to take me out of my room for more exercise. Soon I'm pounding the hospital corridors – from a short walk to going round and round again. Then the stairs. I'm determined that if I can climb the stairs, then I'm well on my way towards going home. I manage them! Proudly I return to my room as if I've just won an Olympic medal.

Another bronchoscopy is performed to clean my lungs once more. I'm told if all is looking well and I continue to progress as I am, I will be allowed home on Friday for the weekend. Friday comes and I get the all clear. The MRSA is no longer a concern and my new heart and lungs appear in good shape. I can't quite believe it. Rob and I had been prepared to be in hospital for months, as we were told that it was hard to predict how each transplant operation would turn out. It's not permanently home, just for a couple of days to see how I manage; but it's still very exciting. We clear my room, and Rob undertakes loads of trips to the car with all my gear. I take down the cards that have grown to cover all four walls of my room.

The transplant nurse comes to visit before we leave. We've been bracing ourselves for some news. I've asked for details about my donor. I haven't been able to stop thinking of my donor since waking from my operation. Already I know it's all been worth it – if I don't have another day left it's all been worth it. Worth every single minute of that long wait, worth it to know I no longer have PH inside me; worth it for my pink lips; worth it to feel my legs pedal on an exercise bike; worth it to have that weight of terminal illness and anxieties and fears of the wait lifted.

Donors and recipients are allowed to know only the most basic details about each other through their respective coordinators, but nothing that will reveal each other's identities. Facts such as gender, age range and region of country are the only typical details which they are at liberty to divulge. We sit and quietly anticipate the information, and try and stay composed as we are told these few snippets. It humbles and saddens us. I don't know whether there would ever be a right time to hear what we are being told, but we feel compelled to listen, as we owe this wonderful person our future and our family's future. It feels only right to know something of this person who has saved my life.

The information, although sparse, is enough for us both to appreciate there are certain similarities between my donor and me. I turn to Rob, 'It's as if they've matched the person as well as the organs.'

Once the tears have begun to cease, Rob finally wheels me to the car in the gloom of the early evening, and I strap myself in carefully to avoid hurting the wound on my chest. I close my eyes as we drive from the hospital grounds in silence and I think again of my donor who has saved my life and given me the promise of a future where I can see myself healthy once more. A future of fulfilling dreams and hopes.

All the hope we've had; it's been granted a future.

***

Home. I cannot believe I'm back here so soon – nineteen days post transplant. I climb gingerly out of the car and look up at our house – never have I seen such a welcoming sight – my home. I walk through the door and into the kitchen. Rob takes hold of me and simply says, 'Welcome home, welcome back.'

Then that's it. I cry and cry and cry again. I'm not even sure why I'm crying. For being diagnosed with PAH? For being told I'm in end stages of the disease? For being told I need a transplant? For all that waiting? For nearly losing my life? For my life being saved? For my donor? It all melts together in a big confusion. I think I won't ever stop, as I begin to realise I've stepped out of my awful past and moved into a brand new future. It's the first time I've ever truly allowed myself to let go – to cry and grieve properly about everything. It's time to let go of it all now though and start anew. So I cry.

After I pull myself back together, I set about organising the numerous drugs I've brought home before flopping down on our bed. Nothing beats your own bed. Despite the discomfort in my chest, my coughing and the drugs, not to mention Rob's snoring, I manage to sleep in fits and starts, propped up with about half a dozen pillows. It just feels so great to be in my own bed.

Although it's good to be home, I have a wariness inside me. I feel vulnerable without all the doctors and nurses. For the last nineteen days I've had a whole team around me; surgeons, consultants, doctors, nurses, physiotherapists, dieticians – too many people to mention – all of them looking after me meticulously, checking in on me all day and night long.

Now we're on our own. We're both a little nervous, understandably I reason, as less than a week ago I had a whole team working on me because one of my new lungs had filled with fluid. It'll be Rob bearing the brunt if anything happens. It's just going to be a matter of gaining confidence over time – confidence to know what organ rejection may feel like or what an infection may feel like. I'm just worried I won't be able to distinguish between these risks and the normal symptoms of recovery I'm experiencing.

Morning comes and, fortunately, all is well. We start the day like hospital: six a.m. – first round of tablets; seven a.m. – inhalers; eight a.m. – next round of tablets; ten a.m. – another round of tablets; two p.m. – inhalers; six p.m. – further round of tablets; ten p.m. – last round of tablets and final inhalers of the day. It's a regime that I have to grow used to, that needs to become second nature to me, as it will last for the rest of my life. Some of the medication will reduce in doses and some will finish, but I've been advised that new ones are likely to be added along the way.

It will always be about careful management of drug levels from here; a balance of fighting infection and avoiding rejection, and taking preventative drugs to combat the side effects of drugs such as high blood pressure, kidney failure and osteoporosis. It's a very small price to pay when your life has been saved and you've been given a second chance.

I make up my mind to dye my hair. Rob tells me not to – 'What about your new lungs?' – but when he goes downstairs I sneak and open the bathroom windows wide to ventilate the room and get on with it anyway. He was probably right. I'm exhausted by the time I've just put the dye on. Sarah arrives home and they both go mad at me when they realise what I've done, then Sarah tries to help me as much as she can.

'I need to fix myself back on the outside as well,' I say to them sheepishly.

After that, and with Rob's agreement this time, I decide to have a bath in order to wash all the hospital away. I enjoy a lovely soak, but then realise I can't get myself out of the bath as I'm too weak. The bath is so deep Rob and Sarah can't manhandle me out either.

Rob chuckles. 'Bloody hell, we're going to have to call the fire brigade!' Letting the water out first, they eventually manage to help me to climb out. I decide it's probably better to shower for now.

This is what my weekend at home is all about, finding my feet and seeing what I can and can't manage away from the hospital, gaining confidence to cope without the comfort blanket of having the Transplant team and medical professionals by my side.

I want to go into the garden. I'm desperate to see the Michael-mas daisies – I thought I would miss them this year, but here I am, back home unexpectedly soon and I can just make out from the house that they're in full bloom. Sarah and Rob assist me down the garden – I'm still a bit wobbly and struggle with my balance. It feels wonderfully exciting to be back in my garden and feel the autumn sunshine on my face.

Flowers, messages and cards keep on coming and coming. Eve-ryone's good wishes and messages keep me strong.

Sunday, and Rob cooks me a roast dinner. It feels special, but all too quickly it's time to go back. As anxious as I was about leaving the safety of the hospital on Friday, I'm equally anxious about returning. There will be more procedures – my Hickman line needs to removed, but more frighteningly, a biopsy will be performed on my new lungs to check for that dreaded thing, rejection.

It's dusk, and as we get back in the car, I turn round and look back at my home, like it might be the last time I see it. Just in case. That's what it feels like now, everything is that more special, every little thing and every little detail. I want to savour every moment as though it's the first and last time.

***

I'm back in my old room, back to my solitary confinement and the commode. In some ways I quite like it though – it's like my own little den – except for the commode, which is hardly an en-suite!

Looking positively I reason that, although it's going to be an action-packed few days, there's a chance I may be discharged from hospital permanently mid-week if all my test results go well and there is no sign of my new organs rejecting.

***

It's early morning and I'm being wheeled back into theatre. There's no Rob or Sarah to say goodbye like last time. It feels more than a little peculiar, going back through these doors once more and so soon. It's important to me, though, to get this done before I'm officially discharged. It's a very significant step in my journey.

The Hickman line in my chest is removed at last – the line that delivered the drug that used to keep me alive: alive for three years. It's quite a moment for me – the ending of PAH. I'm taken back to my room and lie there quietly – stitches now, in place of the line – it's gone at last. The whole lot of it is gone. Gone for good. Total closure.

Next and it's time to go for my bronchoscopy and biopsy. This is another big moment. This is my third bronchoscopy. I thought I'd always be frightened to death of these, but as I'm given sedation and fall fast asleep while they're being performed, I am becoming more used to the prospect of these procedures. At the same time the lung biopsy is undertaken.

Later I'm told my bronchoscopy looks fine, but they're a little concerned with the way a certain join in my windpipe – where mine is joined to my donor's – is healing, so they're going to keep a keen eye on it. It's probably this that's agitating the cough, which often keeps me awake at night.

I have to wait until the end of the following day for the biopsy results. This is the big one. I sit and wonder if I will have rejection. I know that if I do, then there will be no chance of going home for some time yet, as I will have to be administered intravenous steroids to help combat it.

Assuming the results are good, and if I have no signs of rejection, I'm advised I will be formally discharged. By this time I'm fully fledged with the ins and outs of medication and learning how to record it all in my transplant diary, and we go through all the signs of rejection and infection with the transplant nurse one more time in readiness to deal with it all at home.

I have to weigh myself as sudden extra weight is a sign of heart failure – it can be fluid retention. I have to record my weight in my blue book, along with my drugs. I need to take my temperature, as a high temperature can be a sign of infection, which could otherwise be masked by the effects of the steroids and immunosuppressants. I'm given a small machine and taught how to take my own lung function readings. A decline in lung function readings can also indicate something is amiss. All these tests and results need to be recorded every day in my diary.

It's all a bit daunting. How will I know what all these things will feel like? I'm not sure I will, but I will have to do as I'm told religiously for the rest of my life, and also trust my instincts. I'm given numbers to phone should I be worried, so I can access support from the team. I'm given all my drug supplies in readiness. We sit and wait – the waiting game again.

Early evening and the Transplant team arrives full of smiles and beams – I have no signs of rejection. We are elated and overjoyed. I cannot quite believe I'm going home tonight – formally discharged from hospital just twenty-three days after my heart and double lung transplant.

A whole new future is waiting.

Twenty One

The Park

(November 2013 – March 2014)

Everyone seems to know exactly what they're doing. Names are being called out, people are chatting and coming and going, and there seems to be a tidy queue for the blood tests. It's my familiar old clinic, but this time I'm at a post-transplant clinic rather than my usual pre-transplant clinic. I'm not sure what I'm supposed to do. It feels like my first day at big school. A nurse soon explains how things work. I'm responsible for making sure my various tests are done, and then I need to wait to see the consultant.

I go about having my tests taken. I'm more involved in my care than at previous clinics, where I'd just sit and wait to be called. I walk a little unconfidently down the corridor, but smile at the radiologist when she says, 'I saw you in intensive care, I can't believe it's you. I'm just looking at the file now to check I haven't got it wrong.'

I realise how far I must have already come in a few short weeks and it feels great.

My tests include an assessment of my lungs' function, X-rays, ECG and blood samples, and then after clinic, I will have a bronchoscopy. This is going to be a regular part of my life from now on, together with biopsies on my lungs at periodic intervals.

Transplant is unlike most routine operations, as a commitment to ongoing care and monitoring is required for life. This is to ensure that the risks of rejection and infection are kept under proper control and the levels of immunosuppressant drugs are kept in balance. It's also to manage the adverse side effects of the drugs.

I've been warned that there will be constant tweaking of the medications. Hopefully the high levels of immunosuppressant drugs and inhaled drugs I'm on at present will reduce. But new drugs may be added to counteract secondary problems as they arise, and preventative drugs may be added in anticipation of known future problems.

The outcome of my clinic overall is a good one, but there is some concern about the join in my windpipe. It's healing, but in the healing process a slight ledge has formed, which they're worried may cause a blockage in one of the airways to my lungs. A cough is quite normal in the early stages of healing, but this is the reason I'm coughing so badly. My Transplant team wants to keep a close eye on it, which in turns means regular bronchoscopies as the healing process progresses.

***

The park. It's Christmas Day.

Standing here in the park, I look back over those first few months, and it's all been about achieving firsts and taking small steps forward, and quite frequently taking one or two backwards as well. Once again, it was a bit like bringing a newborn baby home. Those early months were very exciting and daunting in equal measures, filled with mixed emotions. Even now, they don't seem to stop flowing.

Cards kept on dropping through the letter box – some of them second cards and even third cards, from people who'd already sent them previously. The doorbell kept on ringing. Flowers, more flowers and then even more. We had flowers all over the house for weeks. It was completely overwhelming – even the florist stood at the door giving her congratulations. A sea of flowers consumed the dining table when we ran out of places to put them. They were beautiful. Uplifting. Everyone's good wishes kept spurring me on.

Single-mindedly I concentrated on the route to my recovery –

exercise, diet, rest and firm drug routines. I followed all the advice from hospital religiously. My weight had fallen drastically and some of my clothes wouldn't even stay up – they'd fall from my waist and slip off me. I needed some weight back. I'd learned over the last few years that a little meat on your bones gives you something to fall back on when the going gets tough.

I had to regain my balance and build up my strength, especially in my legs. Initially I was unable to walk far, though I still felt better in myself in recovery than before my transplant. The fact that I wasn't breathless anymore made me sometimes forget, and I'd try and walk more quickly than my body would allow, so I'd wobble and stumble. One day I tumbled down the stairs. Feeling so well, I'd reverted to my old self prior to illness and just marched from the bedroom to the top of the stairs, but my legs couldn't keep up. It was a timely reminder I needed to keep up the exercise and build up my strength.

Rest was also required. I was so tired all the time and needed energy. These issues became my key focus. I'd cough myself to exhaustion attempting to clear my new lungs and then I'd sleep badly, sometimes lying there all night wide awake from the drugs. It was draining, and most days I'd have to sleep again in between the medication rounds.

However bad some days were, I still felt better than before, and I tried to walk more and more. There was no burden of waiting for the transplant call anymore, and no illness closing in on me. There was just a future to recover for. I'd start with walking around the house – round and round the dining table, then rounds of the lounge, through the kitchen and round them all again. I'd stop and admire the flowers – constantly moved by the stream of good wishes that carried on supporting me.

I'd attempt a walk down the garden and through the back gate to look at the park behind us. I'd look out over the park and challenge myself to take a few steps along the path. A walking stick in one hand and Rob on my arm, I'd go a few steps further each day and then amble slowly back again. Each day we tried to keep me walking. Each day, a little further.

Our girls were in their early teens when we moved to our house by the park. The gate at the bottom of our garden opens out directly onto it. They used to enjoy visiting the park with their friends and I always regretted that we hadn't lived somewhere like this earlier when they were younger. We could have all enjoyed the freedom so much more. The future hadn't ever occurred to me – perhaps some hazy thought about grandchildren, or walking a dog in our retirement. Now the park is playing a pivotal role in my new future, suddenly significant to my recovery. I'm walking every day in the park to become stronger.

I used to love walking – going for long country walks, muddy walking boots on – I'd dreamed about doing this. Now I was back walking again, I firmly set a goal in my mind that I would go back to the Lake District and walk all the way around Tarn Hows, a favourite walk we used to do with the girls. I'd missed being able to do this so much over the last few years. While I was sick, I'd accepted I wouldn't ever manage it again. Rob had tried to push me round in my wheelchair once, but the inclines were too much for him, and he had to give up. I could see it would be possible now, and that thought and goal drove me on and on.

Rob protected me from visitors, as we needed quiet family time and just close friends in those early days. He vetted people before he allowed them over the threshold and he wouldn't allow anyone with the slightest hint of a cough or cold anywhere near me. He was overprotective to the point of being rude to people. I had to tell him, 'Of course I need to protect myself from infection, but we need to find a proper balance and learn to live normally again.'

We had an exercise bike delivered, and I used this to supplement my walking to help build up the strength in my legs. I tried to use it every day – even on bad ones. I was driven, however tired I felt and however unfamiliar exercise felt to get better. I knew I would, if I could only build up my strength. I could see myself edging further to my dream of having a proper long walk.

I'd also think that if I could be stronger then I would have more fight in me if my new heart and lungs started rejecting, or if I should catch an infection. The fear of this happening was, and still is, terrifying. To become stronger was a focus for many reasons, good and bad. Raw from fighting for my life, I knew I needed to be strong again to cope should I ever suffer a relapse or setback. I had been warned that the first few months could be especially precarious, and the first year post-transplant could expose me to many challenges. The threat of my body rejecting the new organs or catching infections or viruses, which could threaten my stability, would be ever present. I was already preparing myself for my next fight.

I managed to eat more. I'd been given a long list of things to avoid eating as a result of having little immune system. It all felt daunting. But for everything on the list of 'can't eat', there's another list of alternative foods. There is plenty of choice, but it can be trickier to eat out. There are certain foods, such as unpasteurised and blue cheeses, shellfish and rare meats, which carry risks if my immune system is compromised. To contract food poisoning or infection poses a real threat. It can be lethal potentially, as stomach upsets can thwart the effectiveness of the immunosuppressant drugs leading to rejection of the new organs.

Rob constantly worked hard to prepare nutritious meals and feed me up always with a keen eye on the 'can't eat' list. I struggled with cooking on my own as my arms and chest were still too weak to lift pots and pans, and I'd developed quite noticeable shakes, a side effect from the some of the drugs. I was eating much more, but could only manage very plain food or my stomach would have severe reactions. 'Granny-food', as Rob called it.

I carried on with my quest of walking and walked around the house, down the garden and to the park and along the path. Every day a few steps more into the park and then back again. One day I realised I'd managed to walk half way round the park, and that gave me a new choice. I could either turn and go the same distance back or carry on around. It felt amazing – a momentus achievement – I'd walked around the park! My goals and dreams were getting nearer.

Some of those early days were more difficult. Sometimes it would be late afternoon before I could manage to get dressed, usually because of the constant coughing and lack of sleep, both of which left me exhausted. My body and mind were still recovering from the trauma they'd been through as well. Rob would encourage me by saying, 'Have a go on the bike now and try a short walk, even for five minutes.' I would do it and then pat myself on the back that I'd showered and dressed and been on the bike. Little targets for the day. Little steps. Even on the bad days.

Weeks carried on towards Christmas – drug regimes, exercise regimes, healthy eating regimes, rest regimes, clinic regimes – regimes all in the quest of becoming me again. Finding my old self, but mingled with a new self that was emerging too. It felt challenging, especially with the continuing coughing and lack of sleep, days often paled into a haze, but every week I could look back and see the great strides I'd made.

One of my very first targets had been to stand underneath the shower and sing. It might sound ridiculous, but after having medical equipment attached to my body for nearly three years, the sheer freedom and pleasure of a shower and bath without having to carefully ensure that nothing became wet was indescribable – the most simple, but the most precious of moments. Of course I had to sing while I enjoyed my first shower of freedom!

The elation, just to sink my whole body under the water when I had a bath – I'd do it over and over again and then smile and repeat the process. No catheters and pumps leading from my chest and hanging over the side of the bath. No swishing about trying to keep my chest safely above the water. Just pure unadulterated pleasure, soaking in a bubble bath.

I went to the pub for the first time with Rob and Rose for an early dinner – to do this and feel like I belonged back in the real world once more was intense, even though I needed a walking stick and Rose on standby to help, should I need the loo. I still couldn't get on and off the toilet properly – out of our home I wasn't steady enough to be safe on my own.

Christmas was a great motivator. I wanted the most fantastic family Christmas. Another goal when I arrived home was to survive three months post-transplant, considered the most vulnerable period, and reach my first Christmas. In the early stages it's difficult to think much beyond the short term.

'Mum, now you've had your transplant and you're getting better, where shall we all go for your first transplant anniversary?' Sarah kept on saying. She was trying to encourage me on to get better, give me something long term to look forward to, but I couldn't even begin to think that far ahead.

We'd always said we'd do something significant together as a family and we'd kept dreaming of taking a special holiday together, but my brain wouldn't allow me to jump a year on. It still can't. It's still making sense of all the trauma of the past few years. It's still coming to terms with recovery. Everything is too new. I'm only just processing being able to undertake basic acts of daily living once more, which feel like an overwhelming achievement in themselves.

It had felt marvellous to go out to the shops for the first time – Christmas shopping. We took my chariot just in case, but my walking, balance, energy and stamina were improving all the time, so the wheelchair was used instead for carting all the Christmas shopping around.

Rob and I were constantly pinching ourselves in wonder at what I could manage again, checking that it was real and not just a dream. Over and over again, we couldn't stop having these pinching moments.

The latest Christmas advert for John Lewis had been released – *The Hare and the Bear* – I couldn't resist the urge to have my photo taken with the hare and the bear while we shopped in our store. I had to force myself to resist shouting out, 'Look at me everyone, I shouldn't be here, but someone saved my life. Think about signing the organ donor register – I have a new heart and two new lungs and I can breathe again and hear my heart beating!' I wanted to scream it out loud.

It felt as though I was wrapped in a cocoon of happiness and wonder, so very different from the shroud of the tornado that weighed heavily on me all those years. It still feels this way – no matter how hard this recovery is and how hard it might be in the future, there's a euphoria that won't diminish. It feels like a miracle has happened.

As we'd been involved campaigning for more organ donors, immediately after my transplant we'd been contacted by the media to speak about my experience. We'd deliberately held off, partly because I needed time to adjust and recover, and partly because I wanted to ensure I'd successfully coped through the first few difficult months. Just before Christmas we'd given several press and radio interviews and this time we were able to tell the world what a difference my transplant had made and what a positive impact it had had on our lives and our family and friends' lives.

Rob and Rose had been out Christmas shopping and they saw my face staring back at them from a newsstand. Our story was featured on the front page of the Christmas edition of our local paper. We hoped it had made a huge impact being featured as a Christmas story, but we couldn't ever really adequately describe or put into words the difference that my transplant had made to our lives.

I kept on walking around and around the park. More and more steps. Further and further. In between the constant wind and storms of the autumn, I kept on walking. Watching the autumn turn into winter, I kept on walking. Now standing here on Christmas Day, the red and gold autumnal shades of the park have given way to naked trees standing black and stark against a turquoise sky, the grass still wet from the morning's melting frost.

Avenues of trees are before me, stripped bare of their leaves. Green fields and football pitches even out the landscape, their boundaries marked by pathways heading off in all directions. I shout to the girls and Rob, who are trailing behind me, 'Come on, and keep up!' I'm still practising my walking – startling the girls with how much I've progressed. They're all used to walking very slowly for me, but today I'm leading the way and showing off. The park. It's surprising how something that's been here right in front of me for years, can suddenly become so significant.

We are all excited on this special morning, even more than ever following my transplant. This morning Sarah and Oli announced their engagement. There's so much to celebrate. The future holds so many possibilities and opportunities. I recall briefly my interview with ITV news while I was waiting for my transplant, saying how I hoped I could see my daughters grow up and reach special mile-stones like getting married. Now it truly seems possible.

I look across the park and know I have my best Christmas pre-sent of all – my miracle new heart and lungs, being here with Rob and my girls and simply taking a normal family walk around the park. I pinch myself – yes, again. Is this real? And I weep. I weep for our family's happiness and the future I can see before us. And I weep for my donor and their family – their circumstances so very different to our own. The extremes of this miracle. It's a poignantly moving Christmas Day. I always knew it would be, but I hadn't been prepared for just how deeply emotional it would feel.

***

I'm leaning on the railings of the bridge, looking out over the vast expanse of the river down towards the tall buildings of the city on the horizon. The ripples of the river are sparkling in the late after-noon sunshine and there are echoes all around me of crowds of people. The hustle and bustle of Saturday afternoon revelling. Traf-fic is flowing behind me, the quiet still of the cyclists and the hum of the cars drowned by the drumming of buses and the roar of motorbikes.

In front of me there is more traffic – the river craft. River buses, barges, tugs, pleasure craft – some stationary, some moving, some speeding in exhilaration and fun. It is a feast for my eyes, and I feel life is all around me, encircling me, daring me to join in properly once again.

It's a brand new year – this time with my new heart and lungs. This time I don't want to stop in time and stay in the old year. This time I'm waiting for the whole new year and am ready to embrace it with open arms, excited at what it may bring. All those dreams and hopes – this year they are going to be mine for the taking. It's just over three months since my transplant – it's time to come out of my comfort zone.

I've achieved a good level of health now I've had the chance for some recovery. My pre-transplant problems are gone, and some of my post-transplant problems are resolving themselves. I'm delighted I've managed to come this far, but I know I need to challenge myself further, try new things and start living life to its fullest.

I've decided definitively not to go back to teaching. It has been nearly four years since I taught and my life has changed dramatically. Teaching was my life, but I'd already accepted and come to terms with not being able to teach again and laid that to rest. Even with this second chance, I've decided I don't wish to return to my old world and life that I so suddenly left behind – my world has changed radically and I want to make a brand new future instead. Even if I did wish to return to teaching, I think it may not be sensible, and my consultant agrees. In primary school, there are always so many coughs, colds, infections and viruses going around.

Transplanted lungs have the poorest survival figures for transplanted organs – fifty per cent of lung transplantees do not survive beyond five years. It's because lungs are open to the environment; breathing in the air around us means we are susceptible to any germs, viruses and infections that may be floating around. An infection or virus in transplanted lungs can be very dangerous and damaging – they can cause chronic rejection and the lungs can be progressively damaged culminating in a gradual, yet permanent, loss of lung function.

Instead, I've enrolled on a writing course. After regularly writing my blog, I'm interested in taking my writing a stage further – perhaps writing some magazine articles and even one day writing that book we all think we have inside of us. I'm excited about my new course. I think it will help my recovery mentally and emotionally to have new challenges and do something that I enjoy at the same time.

Gazing down into the waters beneath the bridge, I reflect on the extra freedom I've been given at my most recent clinic. My team had decided that my windpipe is healing sufficiently well, so the risk of any possible corrective surgery has receded. As a consequence, I was told that I no longer needed the inhaled drugs that gave the protection while it healed. I'm totally free of the ties of nebulisers and inhaled drugs. This feels a huge step forward in my recovery.

In addition, the team had confirmed my new heart is working well and no longer requires the help of diuretic drugs. More freedom. After years of taking diuretics and running to the loo every five minutes, I don't have to worry about where the toilets are when we're travelling or just out and about. I'm still euphoric about my transplant, but now I'm finding I have even newer levels of freedom.

I've been pushing myself more, making myself walk up steps without stopping, allowing a little shortness of breath. I never dared to be short of breath before – it spelled fainting and heart failure and more debilitating drugs. I'm learning I can push myself and I'm surprising myself that, yes, I can dash at quite a pace up a few flights of steps. I know that I'm way surpassing the limits I had before my transplant. The exhaustion is disappearing and my energy levels and zest are ever increasing.

We've recently held a few more interviews – this time for magazines. One was for *Hertfordshire Life* about my transplant, following the coverage of my transplant story in the local papers. I'm pleased we may reach a new audience to raise awareness of organ donation. I've also given an interview to the British Heart Foundation about the genetics research in which I've been taking part, and the genetics testing I went through while I was ill. It's to be published as part of an article on genetics research currently being undertaken. I'm delighted as it will feature in the BHF's *Heart Matters* magazine, and should raise awareness about the importance of the research in finding a cure for PH, as well as telling the story of my PAH and transplant journey.

Rob nudges me from my thoughts pointing at a passing cormorant. We're on Westminster Bridge in London. To get here, I simply walked round to the railway station near where we live, raced up the steps and boarded a train, like any other ordinary person. We've spent the weekend meeting up with friends, partying and walking further than I've ever walked for years. We have been pinching ourselves over and over – this pinching thing isn't going away yet, as I'm only beginning to discover the possibilities that lie ahead.

The weak winter sun is starting to set, turning the Thames increasingly pink against the cloudless sky. Rob and I stand and watch the oncoming sunset in silence; amazed at the beauty and that we've come so far. We don't *think* we have a future, we *know* we have one. Rob turns and pulls me close as he whispers, 'I've got you back.'

***

I want to thank my donor's family for this gift of life I've been given, but I'm anxious whether the time is right for them to hear from me, so I seek advice from our friend who donated her son's organs after his tragic accident. She tells me that the family will cry regardless of when they receive a letter, but that I should write as soon as I'm ready, as she welcomes updates on the recipients of her son's organs. It gives her much comfort.

Tentatively, I put pen to paper and, after a while, manage to craft a few lines expressing my gratitude for what they've done for my family and me. How can 'thank you' ever be enough, though, in these circumstances?

I take the letter to my next clinic so it can be passed onto the family through our respective transplant coordinators. I know there will be no obligation on the family's part to reply or even read the letter, but regardless I feel better for having had an opportunity to thank them.

***

Third time lucky and here we are at last. Twice over the last few months we've packed for the Lake District, and then unpacked as weeks of bad weather stopped us in our tracks. In between the wind, rain and gales I'd been practising my walking at home and now I'm standing facing the tarn, looking at the far-reaching views across to the imposing Langdale Pikes. It's a windy, wet, misty day with a seamless blend of mountain ranges, fells and woodland enveloped in murky, dark clouds crowding upon the grey waters of the tarn below.

It's not quite the picture I had in my dream of enjoying a leisurely walk around Tarns Hows – the dream with the blue sky, sunshine and fluffy white clouds hovering above the mountains, casting shadows over a deep blue lake. But we're here now, and I want to do it. This dream of mine represents taking a proper long country walk, admiring nature, breathing in the fresh air and feeling the weather on my face, being able to experience those simple pleasures I'd taken for granted long ago and had so cruelly lost. Living this dream represents having all those pleasures returned to me. I feel a desperate need to walk in honour of my donor – the person who has given all this back to me. Not only has it been one of my challenges, but it feels significant to return here and take this particular favourite walk for my donor.

Wellington boots on, wrapped warm in scarves and gloves, layered up in waterproof trousers and coats, we start our walk. It's quiet today because of the weather – eerie almost – but it feels special, almost spiritual, to have the place to ourselves, as this will be an emotional journey.

We walk the first half of the tarn weaving up and down pathways, minding we don't trip and stumble over any protruding tree roots, rocks and stones and hurdles that may slow us on our way. Uphill, downhill. We make detours to snatch glimpses of the tarn passing fallen trees – signs of the recent heavy gales. Other trees groan in the wind as we make our way gingerly along the path. The threatening clouds begin to close in and try to smother us. We walk on at a pace, determined not to be caught.

Significantly, the terrain and weather of this part of our walk closely reflects the struggles and emotions of my journey with PAH towards transplant. Ups and downs. Hurdles and hazards. Glimpses of hope on the horizon. Danger closing in. But we reach halfway unscathed. We pinch ourselves – yet again. I'm delighted we've done well so far. I paddle in a stream at the head of the tarn like an exuberant small child and then sit on a bench and stare at the view across the water. There's a patch of blue peering from an otherwise overcast sky allowing a little brightness to shine through.

We continue our journey round. The path is uphill at first. I'm not daunted. No breathlessness to impede me, I march up the incline, bright and full of energy. I breathe in the fresh air deep down into my new lungs – deep breaths, fresh air, deep breaths – savouring the moment. Looking down at the tarn from the hillside, I allow myself to shed a small tear, which runs quickly down my cheek and drops on to my coat, already drenched by the wet mist.

It's a very strange and surreal feeling to find yourself doing things you believed you would never do again. It's a feeling I can't get used to or quite believe. I can't help but wonder if this feeling of amazement will ever leave me, I'm not sure I want it to: while I have this feeling I know I can appreciate every minute of the new life I have and every single step I take.

We're on the home stretch now. Nearly there. Nearly complete. Nearly back to the beginning. We reach the end of the walk and I'm elated I've achieved my dream. I hope there's many more walks to come. Favourite walks pop in and out of my head. I'm forming a whole list of where I want to walk next as we head back. The mist enshrouds us and the clouds, now black, are descending but we are already in the warmth of the car.

Twenty Two
Life is for the Living
(April – September 2014)

I throw the balcony doors wide open. I can smell and feel the city air as I stand with an enormous smile on my face looking down at the hustle and bustle in the square below. It's four years since I was last here. Four years. I couldn't ever have imagined or dreamt it. It still feels surreal, as though it hasn't ever happened, but the scars are there. They prove it every time I look in the mirror. They make it real. I cannot wait to go down to the street and just walk, walk to my mended heart's content.

We begin to retrace our steps – each and every one – through the busy streets. I stand outside the old pavilions brimming with flowers once more, catch the fragrance and step inside. Waterfalls of emotions collide and crash, before subsiding and coursing through my veins like a warm gentle stream. I see vivid and colourful flowers, more beautiful than I remembered. I smell their intoxicating scents, much stronger than I recalled. I'm back. It isn't a wistful dream. My feet are firmly on the ground. I'm really here.

Paris. I love it. I've come full circle and it's time to begin again – to lay to rest the dreams I had when I last stood here and go forward with new ones. I'm all brand new, learning to live and learning to be me again. I'm the same, but I'm also very different.

I tread more warily, as I don't take anything for granted anymore. Enjoying the company of my family and my friends; enjoying nature, places and new experiences; being able to dress, walk, shop without anxiety or weakness and pain – becoming independent; having pink lips when I wake in the morning – these are all small wonders for me. Having a heart that beats strong, and lungs that can simply and easily breathe – the most basic of things are the most precious of things. I will never be able to thank my donor, their family and my medical teams enough for what they have done for me, for what they have given me. This gift of a brand new life, the chance to come back and start over, the chance to stand here and deliberately mark the spot where I left off four years ago.

As I meander and breathe in the scents through my beautiful new lungs, I'm drawn towards some trinkets – hearts. I see a simple red one and feel urged to buy it. It is a symbol of my new life – my new heart inside me. It reminds me where I started and how far I've come. It's a symbol to honour my donor, who has given me so much and will never know. I wish they could.

It's calming. Tranquil. I'm at the beginning, with a bright future shimmering ahead. We stride out into the rain. People are grumbling all around us because of the damp and wet, but I love the rain today. It feels vitalising as it splashes my face, reflecting my new energy and peace within. It signifies that I'm alive.

We carry on retracing our steps, turn the corner and there it is – Notre Dame. I feel as strong and tall as this magnificent building, as if I can do anything I care to put my mind to. The dreams I have are no longer distant lights at the end of a dark, dank tunnel. They are within reach. All I have to do is stretch out my arms and grasp them. That's all I need to do.

Paris. Back to where it all began – when my life was changing, but not in the way I was ever expecting. It had been changing physically deep within me and not the superficial way that I believed. I had no idea.

We walk for miles – still a marvel – see all the old sights and new ones too. We return to the Ile de la Cité and have lunch in exactly the same restaurant where we dined last time, those four years ago.

We have come full circle, and it isn't a dream.

***

Home again and I'm more inspired than ever to make the most of life, savour every minute and take every chance. Suddenly there seems to be a flurry of interesting and exciting opportunities coming our way.

I'd completed a few assignments for my writing course, which were articles I'd written for magazines, and I had sent two off with query letters to a couple of magazine editors. My articles were about PH and my transplant, with the purpose of raising awareness to new audiences. I receive emails from both editors informing me that they'd like to publish my work. I'm delighted. I'd been a little wary of sending them at the time, and worried whether my writing would be good enough. It feels like another small achievement in this new life I'm making for myself, to have my writing published.

We travel to Suffolk – a holiday that Rob postponed after I received my transplant call. Rob had a lot of faith in my future when he didn't cancel the holiday we'd had scheduled for October. I'd thought he'd been ambitious rearranging the booking for six months on, but here we are.

This is what I love about Rob. He never accepted that I might lose my life. Although we had questioned the transplant more than a hundred times over when things became shaky or events scared us, he was adamant from the very beginning that I would live and get better. His mind totally refused to accept anything else. His very own iron door would slam shut on anything other than the thought of me surviving and getting better.

Once I asked him to help me write letters to the girls, in case the worst happened. He became upset and refused to discuss it, so I never brought the subject up ever again. I wrote them anyway – just in case. I didn't tell him. I put them with our wills. I knew he'd find them there if they were needed. I had to be prepared, either way. For him there was no either, it was simply one direction of travel towards survival.

I'm noticing the change in me dramatically here on this holiday – walking for miles and miles without a thought; walking into town to the shops; running upstairs – the cottage has two sets of stairs; up and down hills and inclines. It's a miracle – over and over and over again – it's a miracle that's happened to me.

We are by the River Deben. It's beautiful. We listen to the oystercatchers. They wake us at night, but I love to listen to their calls. They should be annoying waking me at three in the morning, and again at five and then seven, but they're not. The sound of nature ringing in my ears reminds me I'm alive.

Pinching ourselves continues to be a regular part of our daily routine – it's replaced the anguish of my illness and the wait, with its anxiety and worry. We wonder, once more, will this pinching ever leave us?

When you have been sick for years and know there's no cure, however optimistic you are, the burden of carrying this weight leaves an indelible emotional mark on you – silently brooding. Physically you wake every day feeling unwell, and go to sleep every night feeling unwell. There is no escape, not even for a minute. Then post-transplant, it's gone – just disappeared, vanished – and it is replaced with a more settled and even living. It's hard not to want to keep pinching myself, or look at the scars to see if it was all real.

At clinic I hear conversations that confirm to me that these pinching, miracle and thankfulness feelings may continue indefinitely.

'When were you transplanted?' asks one patient of another.

'Ten years, three months and two days ago,' comes the reply.

Another voice chips in, 'Three years, six months, and five days.'

It carries on, as other peripheral voices contribute to the conversation, their own 'gift of life' moments vividly etched in their minds and conveyed by the broad smile on their faces. We share a unique bond, not just our physical scars and steroid faces, but the miracle of experiencing a re-birth of our lives.

My clinic visits are scheduled every few months, rather than weekly, now that I'm doing so well. Sometimes I need extra blood tests in between visits, and I've had a few ups and downs with my immunosuppressant drugs. They keep causing my white blood cell count to drop too low, so my medication requires adjusting. I've had a few hospital visits locally for secondary problems too, but nothing that's life threatening or frightening like I've been used to – just smaller issues that can be addressed and nothing that stops me enjoying life. Clinic, hospital and GP visits are routinely embedded in my life.

I furiously continue to write my transplant blog. I thought once I'd received my transplant, I would probably stop, as there wouldn't be much to write about. But there seems to be even more to say, and while there is something to write, I want to continue. I've begun a new blog about my garden, gardens, plants and wildlife. I start this to regain some balance in my life, to write about something other than transplantation and signify that I'm moving on, picking up the pieces of my life again.

Although I've been successful with my writing course so far, I begin to struggle with my next assignments. It isn't because I don't feel confident to write, it's because I only want to write about my transplant experience. The urge to write about this alone prevents me from writing about other topics – it's a necessary urge – a cathartic process that I feel compelled to do. My garden blog is the only other outlet I'm able to manage. I'm confused as to how to take my writing forward.

***

Rob has been able to continue working part-time throughout – we'd fully expected he'd have to give that up during my first year of transplant. I'm glad he manages to go to work and have some engagement in the workplace – something a little more ordinary than the world we have been caught up in. It helps keep us both grounded and gives a structure and routine to our lives amongst the upheaval and trauma.

It's summer again, warmer weather and shorter nights. I see the garden at its fullest and best. This year I actually have the strength and energy to do some gardening – as long as I wear a mask to ensure I don't expose my new lungs to any infections from fungal spores, I can actually garden again. It feels exciting, wonderful, inspiring and motivating all in one rush.

I'm keeping up with my walking and the exercise bike, and I've been using my Wii-fit – the one I bought to try and become fitter all those years ago. There's no stopping me now – no breathlessness, no feeling faint. I'm doing steps, muscle strengthening exercises and simple yoga routines. It is a marked difference from before, when I'd thought I was just unfit. I enjoy the yoga – the stretches, the concentration and above all the deep breathing. I smile as I take those deep breaths in and out, and feel my new lungs working easily within me. I find the meditation and absorption of yoga relaxing and healing after the entire trauma of the last few years, as well as beneficial in strengthening my muscles.

National Transplant Week comes around, and this time I'm able to take part as a post-transplant patient and have the opportunity to undertake radio and local and national press interviews. It feels satisfying to contribute from the other side of the transplant process.

Rob and I both have to learn. I have to learn how far I can push myself and Rob has to learn to step back and let me try. It's been new territory for us both. We skirt around each other tentatively sometimes. I get told off for doing too much and I tell Rob off for fussing too much. I constantly say, 'I'm quite capable you know, I can do things on my own now.' Then I will still cling on to him because I've got used to him caring for me, looking after me – it's become a habit. It's a habit we're both learning to break.

***

I step into the water. It feels cool compared to the heat of this July day. I smile at Rob as though we are conspiring together. This is a very special moment we're about to share, unbeknown to everyone else around us. There are families having picnics, children splashing in the water, boats sailing and people swimming in the lake. An ordinary hot summer's day on Coniston Water. For me this day is going to be extraordinary. It's one I've been waiting for.

Rob passes me the paddles, I clamber on the side of it like I always used to do, rather ungracefully, bottom in first and flop down. Rob, as usual, climbs more sensibly into the back of our two-man kayak. Paddles left. Paddles right. Left. Right. Synchronised to perfection – well almost – making gentle ripples as we glide across. We sail to the middle of the lake. Today it's as still as a deep blue millpond. We look down the lake and admire the gorgeous view. The view that's been in my dreams. The view that always springs into my thoughts when times are tough. It's been years since I've been able to sail along the water in our kayak to see this view. It's stunning.

We stay awhile in the middle of the lake in silence, staring and drinking it all in – the green hills flanking the perfect blue of the lake, the whiteness of the clouds. There is only one person we think of and one thought in our mind at this poignant moment.

My recovery keeps on surprising me. I reach one milestone, manage to achieve another first and then there is always more to discover and achieve. It's a recovery that unfolds gradually each week and month – one that has exceeded my expectations. Every time I think I feel better and stronger, more time passes and I realise I'm even better than before.

**

We walk briskly up the tall and winding stairway. My mind flits to the film *Love Actually*, and I imagine Hugh Grant dancing down past the portraits lining the famous yellow walls. Everyone is trying to take in the historic portraits. I try too, but my mind keeps firmly coming back to one thing – I'm walking up these steps at a steady pace and there are people behind me. I am actually doing this. I don't have to give way and let them go past as I cling to the railings and catch my breath. It stands out prominently in my mind amongst all my other thoughts. It feels satisfyingly shocking.

We are visiting Number Ten, Downing Street, for a reception to launch a new government initiative – the '100,000 Genomes Project'. The project, in which I've taken part, will sequence the DNA of thousands of patients with rare cancers and other rare diseases.

The aim is to transform how rare and devastating diseases are diagnosed and treated by the NHS, while supporting scientists and life science businesses in the discovery of new breakthroughs in the development of drugs and technology.

It's an exciting event with which to be involved, and we are given many opportunities to speak with the executives and staff leading the project, researchers and the Government's Life Minister for Sciences.

The previous day we attended an event at the Sanger Centre in Cambridge, and were filmed for national television in the laboratories, watching a demonstration of DNA being sequenced through specially designed machinery. We were shown a fascinating tour of the centre, and then we gave a televised interview about my PAH and transplant and the importance of genetics research to our family.

The interview features on all the main national news channels, just as we are leaving our hotel to go to Number Ten, which feels very surreal.

We are treated to a tour of Number Ten, which is an unexpected and interesting bonus, and the policemen and security guards patiently allow our party to pose for photos outside on the steps by its famous front door. When we return home, the news article is still running on all the main news channels and local TV, radio and press catch us up in yet another flurry of media attention.

Our life seems to continue being out of the ordinary compared to how things were before. I wonder if it will always be like this. I can't believe sometimes the path that my illness has taken me down – the places it's taken us to, the people we've met.

It's been a productive few days. I feel honoured to have represented PH patients at this event, and delighted that PH has had a moment in the spotlight on the main news. PH doesn't often get represented compared to other major diseases, perhaps understandably when so few people suffer from it. Nonetheless, PH patients have a journey that is no less harrowing or arduous than other patients facing life-threatening illnesses. I'm delighted that PH has been given such national prominence, and that there's been an opportunity to discuss the treatment choices, difficult decisions and struggles that its patients are forced to cope with.

I have hope that there will be answers to this illness, and answers for my friends still suffering with this awful disease. I hope, in finding some answers, that others will be spared from the ordeal of PH and having to face its complex treatments, life threatening surgeries and an uncertain future.

***

Rob and I are standing outside a row of warehouses in Hoxton. I can see the city skyline not too far away. Life with clinic, blood tests and tweaks and alterations with medications has continued, and so have the unique opportunities that seem to keep coming our way. We are about to experience yet another adventure.

We're led through a back entrance, up a concrete stairway and enter a large studio. I'm here because I've won a competition run by *Woman and Home* magazine, and I'm going to take part in a photo shoot as part of my prize.

I've never had a professional photo shoot or makeover before. I don't really know what to expect. There are whitewashed walls, large white paned windows looking through trees towards the City of London, a large bright white area clearly designated for photographs and numerous props – flowers, settees, lamps. It's totally fascinating.

There are at least half a dozen people busy setting up. Tripods and cameras are being assembled; rows of clothes rails, which I keep trying to take a sneaky look at. Blues – I can glimpse many shades of blues. A lady is working away feverishly ironing garments, organising and draping them in readiness. I spot a table with jewellery displayed carefully: bracelets, earrings, necklaces, shoes – neat and orderly rows of blue and white shoes. I'm gathering that blue and white is the theme. That suits me – blue is my favourite colour.

There are mirrors and then another dressing table, this one full of makeup and hair products. One mirror is edged in lights, like you imagine in an actress's dressing room. Music is playing and everyone is making us feel welcome and relaxed. There is a lovely breakfast spread with coffee for us to enjoy while everything is being set up, so Rob is in his element.

They start with my hair and then the makeup. It feels fantastic to have someone pampering me, especially since earlier this week I'd had to have a rather invasive procedure undertaken on my stomach. It was unpleasant, as it involved having a camera placed down in my stomach via a tube for twenty-four hours. It's a routine test required after lung transplantation to ensure that there's no stomach acid that could damage the new lungs. I compare the recent bronchoscopies and the traumas of the stomach test, still firmly etched in my mind, to today and begin to enjoy myself more than ever. There couldn't be a bigger contrast between the start of this week and its end.

We choose clothes from the rails of blue – one formal outfit, one casual. It's hard for me to choose as I love clothes and everything looks great. I allow the stylist to guide me, and we choose a cobalt blue dress for the formal and a similar coloured blouse and white jeans for the casual. I try them on and we add jewellery: everyone comes and has a look and nods in approval. I'm having a fabulous time!

I cast my mind back to my Transplant team – consultants, doctors, nurses – standing around my bed nodding in approval at my recovery. I've always been a reasonably quiet and shy person and never liked fuss or been very touchy-feely but somehow, through all this illness and the constant poking, prodding and testing, I've become a different person. It feels lovely to be pampered and fussed over, after all I've experienced and been through. I allow myself to lose my natural reserve, and thoroughly enjoy myself chatting to everyone around me and picking up hair and makeup tips. I'm totally intrigued with how a fashion shoot is undertaken.

I'd been on Facebook, and a post for *Woman and Home* magazine about a competition to write an article describing why it's important to 'Seize the Day' had popped up. It struck a chord with me automatically, and I sat down and wrote – the words flowed freely because I wanted to tell everyone why it's so important to make the most of every day, as you never know what might happen. I emailed it straight away as the deadline for the competition was that day.

A few days later I received a massive shock when I checked my emails and found out that I'd won the competition. I couldn't quite believe it. I'd never won a competition in my life before. I was thrilled.

We finish the morning of the photo shoot with a lovely lunch. It's been an intriguing and fascinating day. I've had yet another wonderful and unexpected experience. Life feels so fantastic.

Next, I take part in an interview and the piece is to be published later in the September issue of the magazine. This is very poignant and apt to me – September – a very special month – the month I received my gift of a new life, and what a new life it is turning out to be. I'm pleased because although the article is about seizing the day, it will also tell my story, and that means more publicity for PH and organ donation – another audience.

A few weeks later I receive a phone call from the magazine's editor, asking if I'd like to be on the panel at a reader event they would be holding in October. Of course, once again, I say 'yes'. It's another golden opportunity to raise awareness of the issues close to my heart. One positive thing continues to lead to another, and they're new experiences that I hadn't even dreamt of being able to do. Rob returns home from work and says, 'I can't keep up with you and all that goes on happening!'

***

We're checking in for my blood test when I see one of the transplant coordinators coming through to the reception area where we're standing. He gives me a big smile – he always does. I think nothing of it. I smile back and casually say, 'Good morning,' but he carries on coming towards me and I realise it's me he wants to see.

'What can it be?' pops in my head straightaway, my mind searching back to tests and blood tests while I look at him. 'We've had a letter this morning, Kathryn, it's from your donor's family. We've read it through and it's a lovely letter. Would you like to take it now and look? I'm sorry, but clinic is really busy and we haven't got a quiet room for you, but if you'd like to sit and read it and, if you need us, we will be here for you.'

Both Rob and I are totally stunned into silence – the noise of the busy clinic carries on all around. Nurses calling out patients' names; people chatting amongst themselves; phones ringing; doors opening and shutting… I hadn't expected this. I didn't feel I had any right to expect this. My donor's family has done so much for me anyway. I'd hoped for this moment, though, but had put it out of my mind once I'd sent my own thank-you letter to them at the start of the year.

I manage to mumble something about taking the letter. I'm glad in a way that clinic is busy. I know the letter will be emotional to read, and I may become even more upset if the nurses are there when I read it. We hurriedly escape the business of clinic as fast as we can. I can't think where to go – then Rob suggests the hospital chapel, which he'd used a couple of times before for some quiet time during my transplant. A perfect place.

I open the letter and hold it between us, so we can both see and read it together. My eyes start to blur before I finish reading the first sentence. We're both the same – needing to keep stopping, wiping our tears, gasping, trying to breathe properly. We read on through our tears learning more and more about the wonderful and kind person who was my donor. And the family – very similar in certain ways to our own little family. It's both heart warming and heart wrenching.

It's a letter I'll always treasure – a beautiful and most thoughtful letter. I'd told them in my letter previously that they were coura-geous to have made the decision to donate their loved one's organs. They reply that they weren't courageous; they knew that's what their loved one wanted. They explain it helps them to know I'm doing so well, as it means their loved one hasn't died in vain.

It makes our own situation very real to read this. The person who lost their life too early, is now a very real one, with a very real and loving family like our own. It humbles us. We want to reach out to them, but what little consolation can we give as we still have all that they have lost? We are still intact. Their kind and thoughtful words help us, but we know we've been the lucky ones. All we can do to honour all of them, is to live life to its fullest, savour each day and try and do all those things we dream of and more.

There is no reasoning sometimes, no reasoning or sense in what happens to us or others – my donor's family tell me that their loved one had many little sayings, 'Things always happen for a reason' was one. I often wonder about this. Sometimes difficult things happen to us, but then better things may be in store and come out of it. I don't know. Sometimes there isn't much sense to make of a situation; my donor's family says they struggle with this. They tell me, however, they try to carry on – keep on going, because another little saying my donor had was, 'Life is for the living.'

Life is for the living. I read it again through my tears. This will be my ethos from now on – my philosophy. I'll carry it with me every day – my life code, my attitude, my culture. I'll carry my donor's spirit and principle with me forever that life is for the living. It'll give me the comfort in everything I do and will ever do.

***

Beautiful September. My month for new beginnings. Warm. Mellow. Soft fluffy clouds dappling the sea, as we all stroll together along the endless beach. We step in and out of rock pools in our Wellingtons, following the tide's edge. Continuous high skies, sea, sand. Uninterrupted views in all directions. In the distance, flocks of geese. I can hear them as they blare and cackle, rising up and circling together. Like us they are gathering ready for their next journey – the next phase. Today marks one year since my transplant.

September, Norfolk and Holkham once more. Rob, Sarah, Rose, Oli, David and, of course, me. We're all here together, away from everything. A quiet time to stop and reflect. It's three years since I found out I'd been listed for my transplant in this very same place and same month. We're here for a quiet celebration, to celebrate my life, the life of my donor and the gift we've received and cherish.

We enjoy the day walking on the beach, being together and in each other's company. We have lunch in a favourite pub. Before dinner we take another stroll – this time along the salt marshes at Titchwell, near where we're staying in a rented barn conversion. We crowd together on a bench and enjoy the evening light and breeze. The sun is setting as we turn and watch it behind us, throwing its pink hues over the pools on the marsh. The sky is shaded in deep reds and oranges as we watch the sun dipping down.

We turn our heads back towards the sound of the approaching hum. Small black silhouettes flocking in their hundreds – thousands. Swooping. Gathering. Silent. Then the rushed song as they rise – intensifying until they're dancing harmoniously in the sky. Kaleidoscopic pictures and shapes twist and turn above our heads. Stillness falls. Peace. Quiet. Then a sudden finale. Surging and soaring gracefully one last time in unison. A closing party before dusk. A spectacular murmuration of starlings. Nature's own fitting tribute for the day and for my donor.

We walk slowly back towards the comfort and warmth of the barn – a family united. Healed.

Epilogue

We're wandering along the crowded city streets towards Central Park – stop, start, stop, start, as we come to cross each busy avenue. Yellow taxis hooting; limousines, wagons and bicycles screeching to a braking halt; sirens wailing; policemen whistling on every crossing. Fifth Avenue. The pavements are huge and wide – the towering buildings dwarfing the streets, enclosing them, making them appear like deep channels guiding the pedestrians purposefully in the right direction.

New York. Another city. Manhattan. There's a strong sense of knowing exactly where to head here. It can only be in a few directions: it's just like a grid and feels straightforward and easy despite the crowds. It echoes how I feel about my own life – I've had ups and downs, been round roundabouts and become lost in corners, but I'm on a straight path once more.

We're walking by Radio City and the Rockefeller Center with their breathtaking Christmas displays – huge multi-coloured Christmas trees; giant reindeers sparkling in shades of silver and golden angels grandly blowing trumpets. The sound of Christmas bells and Christmas songs ring out on street corners as the Salvation Army lift everyone's spirits into a Christmas frenzy. I can't help but sing along and feel the magic. I think I'm actually walking – no dancing – on air.

These are truly exceptional moments for me and, as I push my way amongst these mighty crowds, I know more than most how blessed and lucky I am. In fact I feel almost special, as if I'm in a dream and really shouldn't be here at all. The reality is I know I shouldn't be here, and I stop and pinch myself to see if it's real. I daren't believe it all – where I am now compared to where I have come from.

I'm standing on the edge of Central Park admiring the view. The sky is watery blue and fluffy clouds are gliding in the crisp December breeze. I look up through the barren trees, which reach for the sky in competition with the skyscrapers. Urban culture and man-made marvels are juxtaposed with nature in all its simplicity and wonder.

There are many twisting paths to follow here in Central Park. Which way do we go? We choose the one leading towards the ice rink. It's a beautiful sight and takes our breath away as it unfolds beneath us. This is what I like about travelling and discovering new places. There's a basin amongst the rocks and greenery with a circle of brilliant white ice, scattered full of colourful figures silhouetted against the dramatic skyline of towering buildings and tall trees. Sometimes you choose an unknown path and are rewarded with the greatest pleasure.

Looking back over the last few years I can see how dramatically our lives have changed. We were forced to walk new paths – paths that were unknown and frightening – ones we didn't want to go down, but they've led to a new and very different life. A life that's full, rich and content, but one still evolving in its own interesting and unknown way, as life often does.

We carry on strolling through the park and reach a Christmas market, almost hidden from sight by the huge rocks that erupt from stretches of grassy parkland. The park is barren at this time of year, but the winter sunshine casts a glowing tint of bronze to the trees and fallen leaves.

There are more trails branching off to an assortment of stalls filled with Christmas goodies and unusual arts and crafts. I brush past the many tourists browsing, looking to find that unusual gift or souvenir to take home.

I stop and buy a pair of New York sketches from a local artist. Then I bump into a stall that dramatically catches my eye. It's full of hearts, beautiful handmade hearts cast in clay, each one individually and delicately decorated.

I browse for a while, looking at each and every one of them. It feels like the stall has been placed there deliberately, just for me. I choose a heart that's been encased in brown paper and tied with string as though it's a special gift to someone. It has *Special Handling* written on it with *First Class* and *Love from New York*. It's an apt and perfect souvenir, which encapsulates, on different levels, all that's happened.

A heart. A gift. A gift that needs to be handled carefully. A gift that's first class. A heart. A souvenir of New York. A memory – a whisper of a dream that we've made come true.

I recall twelve months ago I was only dreaming of taking a long walk. I was still savouring being able to breathe properly, shower and take a bath. Taking a long haul flight to America was way beyond my comprehension, beyond my dreams. I'd thought I'd exceeded all my expectations and dreams immediately after my first transplant anniversary, when I'd been given permission by my Transplant team to take my first flight to Amsterdam. My first flight in more than five years. Amsterdam felt safe – only one hour away. But once in the sky, I knew I could fly anywhere in the world and there's a whole world out there waiting to be enjoyed.

We carry on exploring, leaving the market and wander back through the park. I'm sitting on a bench, watching as Rob takes photographs. I'm inspired and uplifted; the future looks bright and exciting. It's the end of the year nearly and a new year will dawn soon and bring with it yet another new beginning.

I wonder tentatively what the new year will bring. I worry a little too. How can I ever have another year like this one again? How can I ever better this year which has been so amazing crammed full with so many wonderful experiences and opportunities?

I know, somehow, that it is going to be another good one. We will make it so.

We have Rose's twenty-first birthday to look forward to in the spring, Sarah and Oli's wedding in the summer and our own silver wedding in the autumn. There's already so much to look forward to, so much to celebrate, so many more milestones to make and so much to make of life.

Strolling out of the park, we pass colourful horse-drawn carriages, gracefully carrying tourists. They're in sharp contrast to the honking vehicles speeding by. A smartly dressed, tall American man walks past with a big smile and, in a camp drawl, calls out to me, 'I love your hair!'

I smile back, turning to Rob, bemused and a little puzzled as I begin to laugh and touch my hair self consciously, revelling in the compliment. Rob teases me as he is sure the guy is crazy, but I like to think he's just a kind stranger passing on a smile trying to brighten someone's day. An act of kindliness can always make a difference.

We disappear back into the crowds and the noise of Fifth Avenue. People are rushing; people are dawdling; there are lone people; people in groups; people in couples; people in families – all types of people. I wonder what their stories are.

Everyone has a story to tell.

Acknowledgements

I've met a vast number of people on this road who have played a part along the way, some of whom I've written about, but so as not to inundate and confuse the reader with too many names, I deliberately haven't named anyone except my most immediate family. You may, however, recognise yourself – so to those friends, I would like to say 'thank-you' for supporting my family and me and for your true friendship.

I also want to thank all our wonderful and supportive friends – both old and new: from school days; work places; the Templewood community; the Holy Family community; the John Henry Newman community; the PH community; the Papworth PH Matters Support Group; the Transplant community; the Barn Theatre community; staff at Barclays in Canary Wharf and all the other wonderful friends who gave us unstinting support that was significant in helping us through all our ups and downs and the many steps in our journey.

I would like to thank members of the local media for their never ending support in helping me to promote both PH and organ donation and especially the staff from the Hertfordshire Mercury, who have been unstinting in covering each stage of my illness and recovery and also Chris from our local radio station BOB FM, who's become a frequent visitor to our house!

I would also like to thank the BBC and ITV for covering my story with interest and sensitivity at various stages along the way, allowing it to reach a much wider audience. I'd like to single out the work done by ITV when it brought organ donation to the fore with its 'From the Heart' campaign while I was waiting for my transplant, and giving me hope. A huge thank you to Lawrence McGinty, ITV's Science and Health Correspondent at the time, who took the trouble to visit us in our home to produce an excellent piece on the difficulties and uncertainties of waiting for a heart and double lung transplant.

A big thank you to Maxine for her editing, proof reading, advice and encouraging words following so much drafting and redrafting that neither Rob nor I could see the wood for the trees any longer! And Simon, a huge thank you for stepping in at the very end for the last important check through, before we pressed the long awaited 'publish' button. I know that was one long train journey to Durham that day, but we really did appreciate your feedback as one of the first readers of the book.

I want to say a special thank you to my fellow authors Mark and Lauren, whose respective lives have also been affected poignantly by transplant, and have published their own books, for their invaluable advice and tips on the self publishing process which, at the beginning, had felt confusing and daunting. You both put, and kept me, on the straight and narrow.

Then I come to family – especially my mum, my sister Jayne and her husband 'Rob 2' – thank you for your huge support throughout the whole journey and in particular with giving me so much encouragement on my road to recovery. Then Rob's brother, David: you stepped in to help Rob when he reached breaking point the day after my transplant. I will always be grateful to you for that and, as usual, you were right – no point looking back, only forwards! I know, too, that our respective dads will be looking down and most probably be enjoying a pint (or gin?) in celebration and your mum would be so proud of Rob and our girls.

To Sarah and Rose, well, you two kept my feet on the ground... and still do! I'm continually reminded that I'm not a poor long suffering transplant patient and I'm just plain old mum. As you well know, though, I do like to keep pushing my luck, especially when it involves the kettle boiling! In all seriousness though, you have both been so wonderful and courageous. There have been difficult times when you have been forced to be mature beyond your years and points when our roles have had to be reversed. I have hated what I've had to put you through, but I know you both stand stronger for it and you've been an absolute credit to dad and me. Hopefully I'm back to being a proper mum now. Thanks to your boys too, Oli and David, for all their love, encouragement and support to all of us - especially for their endless support to both of you when things were truly tough.

I don't think words can express my thanks and gratitude to Rob - you really have been the 'long suffering husband'. Not only have you put up with me and coped so positively and bravely throughout my illness and transplant, but you've also gone along with all my whims, plans and ideas and always supported and helped me what-ever they were, no matter what you you really thought of them.

You are there constantly; helping me, encouraging me on and, however bad things are, not ever giving up on me. I know I wouldn't have ever managed to come so far if it hadn't been for you and your love. I wasn't sure, however, having survived through my illness and transplant that we would actually make it to our 25th wedding anniversary during those tense moments and clashes when we were relentlessly proofreading and editing this book! Thanks for your enduring patience and putting up with my stubbornness at times, but don't think I don't know where you've tried to sneak in odd changes to your own liking in what is supposed to be 'my' book!

Of course, I wouldn't have survived any of this and even written this book if it hadn't been for the brilliant medical teams at Pap-worth Hospital. Firstly, the PH team, who saved my life – probably more than once – and encouraged me on, keeping me stable until I had my transplant. Secondly to the surgeons and Intensive Care Unit team who performed my transplant and then watched over me like a hawk in those first few delicate and difficult days. Then finally, the Transplant team, who again saved my life, and still continuously care for me and work hard to keep me in optimum health. I really want to name and thank you all personally, but there are so many of you I'd be worried that I'd leave someone out, so one massive 'thank-you' to you all: you are like family and Papworth is my second home.

Finally, words cannot express my gratitude to the family of my donor who, when facing such adversity, gave their consent to organ donation and, of course, I shall be eternally indebted and grateful to my donor, who gave me this gift of life, a miracle, and to whom this book is dedicated.

Thanks to you I can simply enjoy being alive.

Printed in Great Britain
by Amazon.co.uk, Ltd.,
Marston Gate.